The
Winemaker's
Reference Book

The
Winemaker's
Reference Book

Jennifer Curry

David & Charles
Newton Abbot   London   North Pomfret (Vt)

This book is dedicated with love to my uncle, Walter Iley, who first introduced me to the delights and delicacies of good country wines

Illustrations by Evelyn Bartlett

British Library Cataloguing in Publication Data

Curry, Jennifer
    The winemaker's reference book.
    1. Wine and wine making – Dictionaries
    I. Title
    641.8′72′0321   TP546

ISBN 0-7153-8308-6

Typeset by Typesetters (Birmingham) Ltd,
Smethwick, West Midlands
and printed in Great Britain
by Redwood Burn, Trowbridge, Wilts
for David & Charles (Publishers) Limited
Brunel House   Newton Abbot   Devon

Published in the United States of America
by David & Charles Inc
North Pomfret   Vermont 05053   USA

INTRODUCTION

The craft of wine-making has been practised for thousands of years. Back in prehistoric times man was busily fermenting grain or grape to make a drink to enliven and cheer what may well have been a bleak existence. Today, in thousands of homes, the craft still flourishes; wine, and the making of it, still enliven and cheer the daily round.

Contemporary wine-makers tend to fall into two categories. First of all, there are those dedicated to perfecting their skill, entranced by the challenge of creating the finest wine possible from whatever ingredients present themselves. A fine crop of plums, an orchard heavy with apples, a hedgerow smothered in elderflowers, a green corner knee-deep in young nettles, a box of ripe guavas on a market stall – all these are seized upon with enthusiasm and transformed into a fermentation in which to rejoice. For the second category of wine-makers, the end is more important than the means. They want a wine comparable with the one they can buy, and are quite happy to potter about making their own brew in kitchen or winery, provided that the results are palatable and their costs have been reduced.

At one time these two groups of wine-makers were poles apart. The 'country-wine makers' were dubious about chemicals and concentrates and prided themselves on using only natural homespun materials. The 'short-cut wine-makers', interested primarily in quick and easy results, would trudge from shop to shop to find the Best Buy wine kit but would not consider crossing the road to pick a few bunches of luscious elderberries. Now that wine-making has changed from a minority cult into a vastly popular pastime and growth industry, attitudes are changing, and so are wine-makers. Most of the traditionalists are very happy to incorporate grape concentrate with their fruits, flowers and vegetables, and to reap the benefits of the newest yeast cultures to increase the alcohol content of their wines. In the same way the kit wine-makers might well infuse elderflowers, orange blossoms and rose petals into their white wines to enhance the bouquet, or add fruit to the tin of grape juice in their fermenting jar. Both groups can revel in their ability to produce a finished wine fit to grace any occasion, usually at less than a quarter of the price of its commercial equivalent.

The basic method of making wine is very simple, as our ancestors discovered. Active yeast is added to a mixture of sugar and fruit, flower or vegetable pulp or juice, in a fermenting vessel. Water is added. The mixture, or 'must', is kept warm until the yeast has broken down all the sugar and turned it into alcohol, then the yeast dies off, fermentation stops, and the wine is siphoned off its sediment, or 'lees', and is allowed to stand for a while to clear and mature.

But it is a more complicated matter to make *good* wine. First of all home wine-makers have to decide what sort of wine to make, whether it should be a red or white table wine, a dessert wine or a dry wine, a social wine, and so on. Then the ingredients have to be selected and decisions made as to whether to use fruit, grain or vegetables, or grape concentrate, or a combination of the two, and which strain of wine yeast is most appropriate. Equipment has to be provided and thoroughly cleansed and sterilised, and the main ingredients of the must properly prepared according to the wine-making method chosen. For a dry red table wine, for example, you may well ferment the fruit in pulp form for the first few days rather than juicing it, but if you are making a white wine, or a particularly light, delicate one, juice fermentation is better. Then additives may be included – nutrients, acids and tannin. If the ingredients are rich in pectin, a pectin-destroying enzyme will be needed to prevent a haze forming. You may have to 'feed the yeast' in order to increase the level of alcohol produced, by adding sugar solution during fermentation, so you will be measuring the sugar content with a hydrometer from time to time. And, of course, it will be necessary to work out how to keep the temperature of the must at a level conducive to sound and steady fermentation. When sufficient alcohol has been produced, or fermentation is completed, the must has to be stabilised, racked off the lees, left in a cool dark place to mature, racked off again, matured again, until all the deposit has been removed. At the beginning of this clarification process the wine-maker has to decide whether to allow time and temperature to clear the wine naturally, or whether it is necessary to use a filter or fining agent, and this decision may depend upon what is causing a haze. Eventually the wine has to be bottled, corked and labelled for further storage before it is opened, and served at the right temperature and preferably in the best kind of glass.

That is a brief description of how a successful, straightforward wine is made at home. But sometimes, as you will know, the must develops problems, the three major ones being a stuck fermentation, an infection, and an insipid taste. Any of these involves you in remedial work, and activities like aeration, treatment with enzymes or sterilisers, blending, the addition of tannin or acid, and so on. If you choose to make a fortified wine, it requires the addition of spirit; a sparkling wine has to be fermented in the bottle. Today wine-making can be as simple, or as complicated, as you want it to be.

It can be as easy as buying a three-week kit plus some basic equipment, and following about six straightforward instructions which lead you clearly from opening the tin of concentrate to opening the first bottle of finished wine. Or it can be as difficult as making a fine champagne-type wine from fresh fruit, flowers and honey and unravelling the mysteries of sugar-testing, re-fermentation and remuage. Whichever type of wine-making appeals to you there are basic instruction and recipe books to help you master the craft; many of these are listed here under 'Books'. The intention of this handbook is to be a companion to the other volumes on the wine-making shelf. Many of them, of necessity, use technical terms and tell you to use chemicals, additives, equipment and techniques without explaining precisely what they do or how they work. Wine-makers who are not complete beginners, even those with real experience, often want to know more, or to refresh their memories. In these pages you will not find elaborate instructions or complicated explanations but sufficient information, I hope, to answer any queries that may arise, or at least point you in the right direction for finding the answer, and help you to understand what you are doing as you work.

Suppose you are vague about the specific value of the hydrometer, the sacrometer or the vinometer. Imagine you have forgotten which bacteria cause anaerobic infection. Perhaps you have a fine crop of fuchsias or tomatoes in the garden and wonder whether you can use them to make wine. Or you could be confused about the effects of ascorbic, benzoic or acetic acid. Perhaps you are baffled about the relative values of household sugar, demerara sugar or honey, or of Campden tablets compared with crystals of sodium metabisulphite. Or maybe you just want to know how to use the Pearson Square. All of these, and a few hundred other items, have their place in this book, in alphabetical order for easy reference.

As a home wine-maker I have struggled with the complexities of the craft for many years. I have gazed in dismay at what looked like frogspawn floating in the must. I have watched with horror as spilled wine dissolved the kitchen lino. I have wept over a fermentation that had the colour of rubies and the taste of sour vinegar. I have tried to answer the phone with a siphon tube in one hand and a precariously balanced demi-john in the other. I have steeped exquisite elderflower blossoms and filled the whole house with the stink of tom-cat. I've suffered most of the crises that can afflict the amateur. But I've also shared with friends a perfect bottle of my own wine, full of flavour and fragrance, and memories of picking the fruit on a sun-drenched summer afternoon and preparing it in the cool quietness of my kitchen. I can think of few hobbies that can give greater pleasure.

ACETALDEHYDE

A chemical compound of vital importance to the wine-maker – an integral part of the complicated fermentation process. No alcohol can be produced unless acetaldehyde is reduced by zymase, an enzyme. Too much sulphite, too high a fermentation temperature, infection – any of these can prevent the yeast from producing alcohol.

Filtered wines may absorb oxygen during the filtration process and consequently become over-oxidised and contain too much acetaldehyde. This, a condition known as 'bottle sickness', makes them taste dull and lifeless, but it will disappear as excess acetaldehyde is removed through yet another chemical change. Oxidation reaction can be prevented if sulphite is used during the racking process, since it will combine with the acetaldehyde and change the chemical process.

ACETALS

Chemical substances formed during the maturation process of wine-making, through the joining up of aldehydes and alcohol. They are aromatic and pleasantly fragrant and are very important to the creation of the bouquet, which can only develop properly if the wine is correctly matured. *See* Aldehydes; Bouquet.

ACETIC ACID *see* Acid.

ACETIFICATION *see* Infection.

ACETOBACTER ACETI *see* Bacteria.

ACETOMONAS *see* Bacteria.

ACID

Vital to wine-making for several reasons. First, yeast needs an acidic environment in which to flourish. Secondly, acid affects the flavour of wine. Though too much makes it tart, too little makes it insipid. The right amount gives it zest. Acid also affects the keeping qualities of wine; it kills, or inhibits, most bacteria and spoilage organisms. Finally, acid is essential for a balanced fermentation: wine lacking in acid may develop off-flavours caused by undesirable chemical reactions.

Many acids are encountered in the fruits used for wine-making. Those most often found are *malic acid*, eg in apples, grapes, gooseberries, blackberries, peaches, plums, sloes, apricots, cherries;

9

citric acid, eg in oranges, lemons, grapefruit, limes, elderberries, blackcurrants, strawberries, raspberries, pineapples, pears; and *tartaric acid*, eg in grapes, sultanas, raisins and currants. These acids can also be bought (in powder, crystal or liquid form), to be added to the must where the ingredients are deficient in acid in order to bring out the flavour of the matured wine. Flowers, leaves, cereals and many vegetables contain virtually no acid, so this is a matter which will concern the maker of country wines.

Sometimes only one extra acid is needed, and this is usually citric acid, which can be added to the must in the form of orange or lemon juice. Many wine-makers prefer to use ingredients in their natural form instead of buying them from chemists or wine-making supply stores. The various citrus juices are then particularly attractive.

To achieve a satisfactory acid content, the following total amount of citric acid is required to make 1gal (4.5 litres) of dry, medium and sweet wine respectively:

Wine	Citric acid
Dry	½oz (14g)
Medium	⅝oz (18g)
Sweet	¾oz (21g)

Many wine-makers prefer to use a mix of all three fruit acids (malic, citric and tartaric), since citric acid alone can create a hard flavour on the palate. The following quantity is the total requirement for 1gal (4.5 litres) of dry, medium and sweet wine respectively:

Wine	Acid mix
Dry	¾oz (21g)
Medium	⅞oz (25g)
Sweet	1oz (28g)

If wine is being made from very acid fruits, such as blackcurrants, oranges, grapefruit, gooseberries, cooking apples, plums or grapes, no additional acid will be needed. A recipe should make this clear. If grape concentrate is included for added vinosity, it is useful to remember that 1½pt (850ml) contain sufficient acid for 1gal (4.5 litres) of wine. Fruits which contain very little acid (and the riper they are, the lower the acidity) are pears, peaches and bland dessert apples.

To control the acid content of the wine, it is necessary to test and adjust it before bottling. This can be done by titration or by using one of the acid-testing kits now widely available.

Acetic Acid
The chief constituent of vinegar. Frequently formed in wine when vinegar bacteria, called *Acetobacter aceti* or *Mycoderma aceti*, attack the

alcohol, giving the wine a strong vinegary taste and smell. It is impossible to treat the infection unless it is caught at a very early stage. The infected wine can, however, be used in the kitchen as wine vinegar. Film yeasts, usually responsible for the infection known as flowers of wine, can also cause acetification.

Acidity Testing
The acidity of the must should be tested and if necessary corrected to achieve the required acid content in the finished wine. This information can be gained by titration or by using an acid-testing kit bought from a wine-making supply store, but many people prefer the simplicity of using indicator papers, though this is less accurate.

The acidity required for a dry wine is 3.0 to 4.0ppt, for a sweet wine, 3.5 to 4.5ppt, measured on the generally accepted sulphuric acid scale. When the acidity has been checked acid can be added, if necessary, to bring it up to the required level. If the must is too acid, precipitated chalk or potassium carbonate can be used to reduce acidity.

Commercially available acid-testing kits contain simple equipment and straightforward instructions. They usually include: a plastic or glass syringe; a test tube; commercially prepared alkali; indicator solution; indicator paper; and a results chart. Unfortunately, because the equipment tends to be small the results given are not always completely accurate. The keen wine-maker may therefore prefer to gather together a personal choice of equipment for acid testing. If the simplicity of a kit is more attractive than total accuracy, another possibility is to buy a good general wine-testing kit which checks for acid, sugar, starch haze and pectin haze. *See* Titration.

Ascorbic Acid
A powerful anti-oxidant which can be used in the racking process to prevent over-oxidation. It will, however, raise the acidity of the wine, so if the acid content is high at the outset it is better to use a different anti-oxidant. Ascorbic acid can also be used in the form of a salt, sodium ascorbate, which dissolves easily in water.

Benzoic Acid
Usually used in the form of sodium benzoate or potassium benzoate. A chemical which inhibits fermentation by killing yeast. If a sweet wine is required, fermentation can be stopped by the addition of benzoic acid before it becomes dry, instead of using the alternative method of allowing fermentation to stop naturally and then adding sugar to taste. The acid also kills or inhibits bacteria so it can be used as a preservative.

11

Citric Acid

The most common acid used in wine-making. Available as crystals or in the form of lemon juice. The crystals are cheaper, and more convenient to use and are more economically bought from a wine-making supply store than from a chemist.

Citric acid should be used in the following quantities per gallon (4.5 litres): ½oz (14g) for a dry wine; ⅝oz (18g) for a medium wine; ¾oz (21g) for a sweet wine. This is the *total* amount of acid required. If a particularly acidic fruit is being used, the quantity of crystals incorporated should be reduced accordingly. Very acid fruits which need *no* additional acid include citrus fruits, gooseberries, crab apples, cooking apples, plums and damsons, apricots, raspberries, strawberries, sloes, blackberries, elderberries and grapes.

Cereals, vegetables, leaves and flowers, and fruits containing very little acid, such as pears, peaches and eating apples, will need almost the full addition of citric acid.

Citric acid has advantages and disadvantages. On the bonus side, its salts are readily soluble in water so they do not precipitate out; it has a more powerful anti-bacterial action than other fruit acids; and it encourages a healthy and vigorous fermentation. On the debit side, it does not easily form esters, so when the wine matures there is little subtlety of aroma; it has a harder taste than other acids and this can be detected by a sensitive palate; and it is not a grape acid and therefore does not impart that invaluable quality, vinosity. As a consequence, experienced wine-makers tend to use a combination of tartaric, malic and citric acids for a softer flavour and enhanced bouquet. The usual proportions are 50 per cent tartaric, 30 per cent malic and 20 per cent citric acid.

Lactic Acid

A byproduct of fermentation, and therefore naturally present in wine in small amounts. If a wine is infected by lactobacilli, however, it is produced in large amounts. It is not toxic and can be useful in the production of sparkling wines, when lactic-acid bacteria convert malic acid into lactic acid plus carbon dioxide. *See* Fermentation, malolactic.

Malic Acid

Named after *malus* (apple) because it is the principal acid in apples; it is also present in grapes. Ripe grapes usually possess less malic acid than unripe ones, but a wine can absorb more malic acid than either citric or tartaric acid before it is dominated by an acidic flavour. It certainly affects the character of the wine, giving it an attractive fresh fruitiness. It also combines readily with alcohol to form esters, which develop the bouquet of a maturing wine. Other fruits with malic as the principal acid are apricots, blackberries, cherries, damsons, greengages, gooseberries, nectarines, peaches, plums, loganberries, rhubarb and sloes.

Many recipes call for the addition of malic acid, or for a mixture of malic, tartaric and citric acids. All of these can be bought from wine-making supply stores or chemists' shops in crystal or powder form. It is cheaper to buy them in bulk: they will last for years if kept in airtight containers.

Wine containing malic acid can become infected by lactic-acid bacteria which convert malic acid into lactic acid and carbon dioxide. Though this is an infection it does not necessarily count as spoilage: its effect is to reduce the acidity of the wine and give it a sparkling quality. *See* Fermentation, malo-lactic.

Sorbic Acid
A very useful chemical for inhibiting fermentation. Early doubts about its safety have now been officially allayed. One-quarter tsp added to each gallon (4.5 litres), plus a Campden tablet, will stop wine fermenting when it has reached the required sugar and alcohol content.

Succinic Acid
A byproduct of fermentation and largely responsible for the development of esters during maturation and the improvement of vinous quality. It is possible to buy succinic acid and add it to the wine to promote ester formation and enhance bouquet, but it only works if you are prepared to allow time for the important chemical changes to take place. The recommended quantity is up to 1tsp for each gallon (4.5 litres).

Tannic Acid *see* Tannin.

Tartaric Acid
Important in wine-making, especially when the wine is maturing, since it encourages esterification and improves its keeping qualities. However, because of its harsh taste, it should only be present in small quantities, approximately 1–2ppt.

Tartaric acid is the principal acid found in ripe grapes as well as currants, raisins and sultanas, and therefore it is added to the must of wines made from other types of fruit, flowers and vegetables in order to give them a vinous quality. It is common practice to use tartaric acid in combination with citric and malic acid as an additive.

Tartaric acid has a sharp flavour; if there is too much of it in the wine it may precipitate out as cream of tartar or argols. This can be racked off, leaving the wine with a mellower flavour. Precipitation can be encouraged by adding potassium carbonate or calcium carbonate to the must, so that it will combine with the acid to lower the acidity level. The process will be speeded up by refrigeration.

ACTIVATOR

Material mixed with the yeast, eg sugar, nutrients, at the beginning of the fermentation process to ensure that it is vigorously active when added to the must. *See* Yeast starter.

ADDITIVES

Any chemicals or compounds, apart from the basic ingredients, which are added when the must is being prepared and turned into wine. Most of them are nutrients required to feed the yeast and keep it active and healthy, thus ensuring successful fermentation. The most important additives are ammonium phosphate or sulphate, potassium phosphate or sulphate, magnesium sulphate and vitamin B_1. But any comprehensive list must also include acids, enzymes, glycerol, tannin, carbonates and sterilisers.

AERATION

The ensuring of contact, usually by thorough stirring, between air and the must during the aerobic fermentation period. By this means a good supply of oxygen is dissolved in the mixture, enabling the yeast to grow rapidly and become active. During the second stage of fermentation the wine should not normally be aerated because of the danger of aerobic infection. However, aeration is one of the remedies for a stuck fermentation. It is also a good practice to aerate a red wine, or let it 'breathe', for about an hour before it is drunk. This tends to make it mellower and rounder to the palate, removing some of the roughness and allowing the aroma to develop. *See* Fermentation.

AEROBIC FERMENTATION *see* Fermentation.

AEROBIC INFECTION *see* Infection.

AGAR

A polysaccharide produced from seaweed, turned into gelatinous form and used as a culture medium for growing yeast in sterile test tubes. Agar slopes are yeast cultures grown on nutrient agar jelly. They are one of the best ways of buying top-quality yeast which will start fermenting in a matter of hours.

AGEING

The complicated chemical process which wine undergoes after fermentation has ceased. It includes oxidation, the removal of oxygen, the addition of hydrogen, and the production of esters and precipitate tannins, all of which together lead to a general mellowing and improvement of bouquet. However, a wine which is low in acid will not improve through ageing. On the contrary, its flavour may deteriorate.

Various ageing or maturing agents can be bought. The manufacturers claim that they accelerate ageing and give wines the taste, smoothness and bouquet of cask-aged wines in days instead of months, as well as adding vinosity and body. The only way to verify this is to compare two bottles of the same fermentation, one of which has been allowed to age naturally, the other with the help of ageing compound.

Express wine produced in kit form is supposed to be ready to drink as soon as it has stopped fermenting (ie after a period of only two or three weeks), without the necessity of an ageing period. Nevertheless, experience proves that many *do* improve with keeping for up to six months. *See* Maturation.

AGITATION

The novice wine-maker sometimes has difficulty knowing when a wine should be regularly agitated and when it should be left well alone. Basically, during the fermentation period, the must should be agitated daily: two or three times a day during primary fermentation, once a day during secondary fermentation. This will proceed for a few weeks or even months. When the wine has finished fermenting, it should be kept motionless between rackings to allow the lees to settle. Agitation should also be employed for the first few hours after a fining agent, such as bentonite, has been added for clarification.

When agitating a must in a demi-john use a circular movement so that it swirls around the jar, rather than being swished up and down, to avoid the danger of disturbing the air-lock and spilling the sulphite solution into the liquid. This could stop the fermentation or at least inhibit it.

AIR-LOCK

Sometimes known as a fermentation lock and vitally important to the wine-maker. When inserted into the bored corks or bungs of fermentation jars they can keep out bacteria, insects, dust, air and all aerobic infections, at the same time allowing carbon dioxide to escape. They also enable the wine-maker to see, hear and assess the progress of fermentation, and the speed with which gas is being driven off.

Many sizes and types of air-lock, in glass or plastic, are available. They must always be kept scrupulously clean and sterile, and a little stock sulphite solution should be poured into the internal tube while they are in use. (The new corkless air-lock is the exception to the rule and works on a slightly different principle.)

The air-lock should be used as soon as primary fermentation has finished, and is usually left in place for several months after fermentation has ceased, racking has been carried out and the wine is totally clear and stable without a trace of yeast debris. Only at this stage can you be sure that there will be no re-fermentation.

The main types of air-lock commercially available are: straight-sided, large or small, plastic or glass; bubbler (two designs), plastic or glass; and the new corkless air-lock, which converts to a bung.

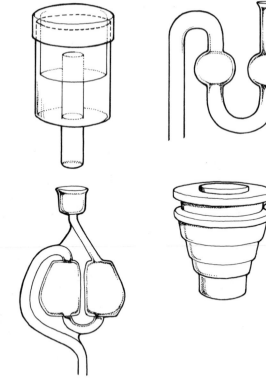

Air-locks

ALBUMIN/ALBUMEN

A protein complex which occurs naturally in grain, blood, milk and eggs. The solution of albumin which occurs as white of egg is known as albumen. It can be used as a fining agent for red wine since it interacts with tannin. One egg-white, beaten stiff, will fine 10gal (45 litres) of wine. This method can be very successful with over-astringent wines since it both reduces the tannin, thereby improving the flavour, and removes any haze. It is unwise to use it with a wine which does not suffer from excess tannin, since it may over-fine it, leaving it lifeless and dull.

Chemically, albumin works by combining with tannin to form a complex which is not soluble in water, and therefore it settles out, taking other suspended matter with it to form a sediment. The wine can then be successfully racked off. Other types of protein fining agents are best bought in proprietary form with detailed instructions for use.

ALCOHOL

Described in the dictionary as 'a class of compounds of the same type as spirit of wine, composed of carbon, hydrogen and oxygen'. Of common, or vinous, alcohols, the best known is ethyl alcohol (C_2H_5OH), produced by the fermentation of sugar by yeast. It is ethyl alcohol that the wine-maker aims to produce, though other types of alcohol may well have a part to play in the fermentation process.

Alcohol Content
The proportion of alcohol in wine. There are two ways of measuring this. One is in *per cent by volume*; the other is as *proof spirit*. The latter is a complicated method of measurement, now largely out of favour, but it needs to be understood.

The 1952 Customs and Excise Act defined 100 per cent pure alcohol as 175 proof spirit. The term has an interesting history; it has been traced back to the time before the strength of spirits could be assessed accurately or scientifically. It is said that in order to test the potency of spirit it was mixed with water and used to dampen gunpowder. The more water that could be added without preventing ignition, the stronger the spirit was, and thus its strength was proved. If only a little water could be added before the gunpowder resisted ignition the strength of the spirit was proved to be low.

The main problem, however, is to work out the relationship between proof spirit and percentage of alcohol by volume so that we can work in either measurement. To convert proof spirit to percentage of alcohol by volume it is necessary to multiply by 4 and divide by 7; so 44 proof spirit would be:

$$\frac{44 \times 4}{7} = \frac{176}{7} = \text{approx 25 per cent alcohol by volume}$$

To convert percentage of alcohol by volume to proof spirit measurement the reverse calculation has to be made, the percentage being multiplied by 7 and divided by 4. So, 16 per cent alcohol by volume would be:

$$\frac{16 \times 7}{4} = \frac{112}{4} = 28 \text{ proof spirit}$$

The following conversion table is useful reference for most of the commonly encountered wines and spirits.

% Alcohol by volume	Proof spirit
10	17.5
12	21.0
14	24.5
16	28.0
18	31.5
20	35.0
25	43.8
30	52.5
35	61.3
40	70.0
45	78.8
50	87.5
60	105.0
70	122.0

In the USA the authorities have defined 100 per cent alcohol by volume as 200 proof spirit, which means that any conversion requires nothing more mathematically taxing than doubling or halving. However, it is still necessary to know whether the alcohol-content measurement is British or American.

Alcohol content is very important, not least because if it is high it inhibits bacteria and stabilises a wine so that it can be kept for years. If there were less than 8 per cent alcohol it would not keep for more than three or four months. Also, of course, it affects the flavour and inebriating quality of a wine. Without alcohol the drink would be no more than fruit juice.

The following table indicates the usual alcohol content of wines and spirits.

	% Alcohol by volume	Proof spirit
Table wines	8–16	14–28
Fortified wines	17–25	29–44
Spirits	40+	70+
Aperitifs	15–20	26–35

The eventual alcohol content of a wine depends upon how much sugar in the must is converted into alcohol by the yeast. A good yeast will not be inhibited until a high alcohol content has been achieved, and its natural tolerance can be extended by adding small quantities of sugar throughout fermentation instead of putting it all in at the beginning. Most yeasts will produce 12–14 per cent alcohol by volume, but with careful control of the fermentation process this can be increased to 18 per cent. Improved yeast cultures may soon produce 20 per cent alcohol. (*See* 'Feeding the yeast' under 'Yeast'.)

A hydrometer is used to work out the initial sugar content of a must, and how much sugar should be added during fermentation to produce a wine of the desired alcoholic strength. It is also used to check the alcoholic strength of the finished wine.

Amyl Alcohol
One of the main constituents of fusel oils, usually derived from the de-animation of amino acids. (However, it has now been discovered that not all fusel oil occurring in wine is derived from amino acids; some is probably created by the breakdown of sugars during the chemical processes of fermentation.)

The addition of nitrogen to the must in the form of yeast nutrients containing ammonium phosphate will help to prevent its formation in large amounts. If it is present in high concentration it makes the wine harsh to taste, unpleasant to smell and possibly toxic; but in low concentration it enhances a wine's bouquet.

Butyl Alcohol
Formed during fermentation in small amounts with a beneficial effect on the flavour and bouquet of a wine. If there is more than a small amount present, however, it will act as a yeast inhibitor and stop fermentation.

Ethyl Alcohol
Common alcohol as we know it in wines, spirits and beers. It is the result of sucrose being converted to glucose and fructose by the enzyme invertase. Another enzyme, zymase, then gets to work and turns the glucose and fructose to ethyl alcohol, with carbon dioxide being the waste product.

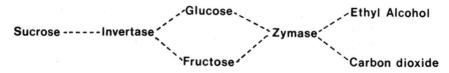

Ethyl alcohol is produced from sucrose by the action of the enzymes invertase and zymase

Methyl Alcohol

Poisonous, but in wine it occurs in such low concentration that it is harmless, and in fact improves the quality of the wine, giving it a mellow roundness. Methyl alcohol combined with ethyl alcohol and pyridine makes methylated spirits, which harms and even kills people addicted to drinking it, but is harmless when used by wine-makers to test for pectin haze.

Potential Alcohol

The alcohol content which should be achieved from a must if it is fermented to dryness without being inhibited, and if all the sugar is acted upon by the yeast. Potential alcohol is estimated from the original specific gravity of the must measured with a hydrometer.

ALDEHYDES

A group of chemical compounds. The one of particular importance in wine-making is acetaldehyde. Aldehydes join with alcohol to form acetals during maturation.

ALMONDS

Almonds can make a very pleasant wine and are a useful standby for the country-wine maker during the winter months when there are no fresh fruits, flowers or leaves available.

Mince together 1lb (450g) raisins and 3tbsp bitter almonds and boil gently in 1gal (4.5 litres) water for about an hour. Strain, and add enough fresh water to make up to the original quantity again. Pour the liquid over 3lb (1.5kg) sugar, stirring until dissolved, then add the juice and rind of two lemons. When the temperature has dropped to 70°F (21°C) add yeast and yeast nutrient and ferment at that temperature, in a covered fermentation vessel, for ten days. Strain into a fermenting jar, fit an air-lock, move to a lower temperature, ferment out in the usual way, then rack off and bottle. Store for at least six months then drink as a dessert wine.

The intriguing flavour of almonds can also be added to other drinks to good effect. For instance, blanched almonds can be put into homemade cherry brandy during the maturation period or floated in flaming punch for a festive cold-weather drink.

ALUMINIUM

This does not have the same disastrous effects on wine-making as iron and tin, for example, but it is inferior to stainless steel and the latter should always be the first choice for a vessel in which to boil ingredients. If aluminium pans are used they should be reserved for ingredients low in acid content, such as bananas or root vegetables. Aluminium vessels must *not* be used for fermentation or maturation.

AMINO ACIDS

Weak acids which occur naturally and join together to form proteins. They contain nitrogen, but not sufficient for the requirements of a must, so more nitrogenous material should be added. If this is not done, autolysis may occur and amino acids will be released into the wine, impairing its flavour and bouquet.

Sherry and champagne actually benefit from the amino acids which are produced through autolysis and released into the wine, but theirs is a different story, depending upon special types of yeast and the conditions under which autolysis takes place.

AMMONIUM PHOSPHATE

A source of nitrogen and phosphate which aids good yeast growth and sound fermentation and helps prevent the formation of too much fusel oil. It is contained in most proprietary brands of yeast nutrient but it is also possible, and more economical, to buy it separately from a chemist or wine-making supply store. Half a teaspoonful of ammonium phosphate is sufficient for each gallon (4.5 litres) of must.

AMMONIUM SULPHATE

A yeast nutrient which can be bought in the form of a proprietary nutrient or separately from a chemist shop or wine-making supply store. If bought separately, half a teaspoonful should be used for each gallon (4.5 litres) of must. Its main function is to provide the nitrogen necessary for yeast growth.

AMYL ALCOHOL *see* Alcohol.

AMYLASE

An enzyme which breaks down starch into sugars. Starch from cereals and root vegetables is not fermented by wine yeasts and can therefore cause a haze in the finished wine. This haze can be removed by adding amylase in a proprietary form, such as Amylozyme. Alternatively, the enzyme can be added to the must to prevent the haze on the assumption that prevention is better than cure.

Amylase is present in human saliva, a fact reflected in the old country practice (one hopes now extinct!) of clearing a cloudy wine by spitting into it. *See* Haze, starch.

ANAEROBIC FERMENTATION *see* Fermentation.

ANAEROBIC INFECTION *see* Infection.

ANEURINE HYDROCHLORIDE *see* Thiamine hydrochloride.

ANTHOCYANINS

Pigments found in plants. In their natural state they are violet-coloured but they become blue when they form alkali salts or red when they form acid salts. They are the chief source of colour in grapes and similar berries and, if released, add colour to a must. They are soluble in alcohol and therefore more colour is extracted from the plant by pulp fermentation, which releases alcohol, than by soaking in water. Care must be taken when their colour is being used for wine since anthocyanins combine with glucose to form glycosides which tend to produce a bitter flavour. Glycoside digitalis, extracted from the foxglove, is toxic, and foxgloves (*Digitalis purpurea*) should *never* be used to make wine.

ANTHOXANTHINS

Yellow plant pigments. They give a golden colour to a must if released by alcoholic extraction and are therefore excellent for sherry-type or Sauternes-type wines.

ANTI-OXIDANT

Any chemical which is added to a must or wine to prevent oxidation and consequent spoilage or discoloration. It is particularly important to add an anti-oxidant during or just after the racking (siphoning) process since racking introduces air. The most commonly used anti-oxidants are sulphite and ascorbic acid.

APERITIF

An alcoholic drink taken before a meal to freshen the palate and sharpen the appetite. It usually has an alcohol content of 15–20 per cent and a dry or medium-dry flavour. Popular aperitifs include champagne, sherry, dry white wine, vermouth and cocktails.

Wines based on citrus fruits are particularly good because of their astringency, as are the country-style favourites, oak-leaf wine and bramble-tip wine. Herbs, either fresh or dried, can add the piquancy required, and can be used as one of the basic ingredients of the must or as an infusion in a wine which has completed fermentation. Aperitif herbs can be bought in the appropriate mixtures from wine-making supply stores.

APICULATE YEAST *see* Yeast.

APPLES

Excellent wine-making fruits because of their versatility. They can make dry white table wine, white dessert wine, dry red wine when mixed with elderberries, sparkling wine, and sherry if oxidised. They are available for a long period of the year, and also come in dried form or as pure apple juice. Crab apples are the first to fruit, from about July, with other varieties ripening a month or two later. Some of them can be stored until the end of the year.

Apples contain malic acid and have a high tannin content. Unfortunately, they also contain a lot of starch and this means that apple wine sometimes suffers from a starch haze which has to be treated with amylase, the starch-reducing enzyme.

Apples should be carefully prepared before use in order to extract as much fruit juice as possible. Cut them into small pieces, then crush, pulp and press for the maximum juice extraction: care should be taken throughout this process to avoid oxidation – drop them as soon as they are cut into sulphited water. This is prepared by dissolving one Campden tablet in a little warm water, then adding the solution to about 2pt (approximately 1.5 litres) of cold water. This stops them from going brown. Juice extraction is to be preferred to pulp fermentation in the making of apple wine: it gives the wine a better flavour, makes it clearer and causes it to mature more rapidly.

APRICOTS

Can be used tinned, dried or fresh to make either a dry white table wine or a sweet dessert wine. They have a high pectin content, however, so it is necessary to use a pectin-destroying enzyme.

Apricot extracts, flavourings and kits are also available for making trouble-free country wines and liqueurs. A little homemade apricot wine can be combined with Polish spirit and T. Noirot apricot brandy extract to make an excellent and economical apricot brandy.

Apricot wine also serves as the basis for apricot punch, a good cooling summer drink. Strain the syrup from a large tin of apricots and leave to one side. Mash or liquidise the fruit, then add the syrup and half a cup of undiluted lemon squash. When ready to serve, add one bottle of apricot wine and three bottles of lemonade. Pour into glasses, with ice cubes and slices of lemon floating on top.

ARGOLS

The crystals which are deposited from a red wine which has matured for many years. They consist of potassium tartrate and are formed by the reaction between a potassium salt (especially if potassium metabisulphite has been used as an anti-oxidant) and tartaric acid, the most common acid of a grape must. Potassium tartrate is less soluble than either the sodium salt or potassium citrate and therefore precipitates as crystals when the wine is cooled.

Formation of argols can be avoided by using citric acid or malic acid instead of tartaric acid, but the crystals do the wine no harm and can easily be decanted off.

ASBESTOS

At one time asbestos pulp was widely used as a filtering agent for homemade wine. However, the medical profession has now established a link between asbestos and cancer: the inhalation of asbestos dust can cause lung cancer and the ingestion of particles of asbestos can lead to stomach cancer. Research into the harmful effects of asbestos has mostly centred on blue asbestos, used for industrial purposes, while wine-makers, both amateur and commercial, have used white asbestos, which does not appear, so far as is known, to have the same harmful properties. Nevertheless, most firms producing filters for home wine-makers have stopped using asbestos in their filter pads and have turned to other material, such as cellulose.

Wine-makers who have been using asbestos pulp for years should not be alarmed. However, it is sensible to change to a different filtering agent, such as cellulose which is non-toxic and readily available in wine-making supply stores.

ASCORBIC ACID *see* Acid.

ASTRINGENCY

The dryness or sharpness of a wine. Some astringency is a desirable quality: without it the wine would be dull and insipid. However, if the wine is too astringent it becomes unpleasantly harsh and rough.

Astringency is imparted by tannin, a chemical found in large amounts in the skins of red fruits, such as elderberries, sloes and damsons. Red wines consequently have approximately four times as much tannin as white wines. If a red wine remains over-astringent, even after a year or two spent maturing, it can be improved by fining. The best fining agent for tannin is egg-white.

White wines are more likely to suffer from a lack of astringency, especially if they have been made primarily from vegetables, grain or flowers. Careful blending of ingredients should prevent tannin deficiency and a resultant lifeless wine. If blending has not overcome the deficiency, tannin should be added in the early stages of fermentation when it will have the additional advantage of assisting clarification.

Tannin can be added in the form of BP tannic acid or grape tannin. Cold tea is a possible source, but is not recommended since it is impossible to obtain a precisely measured infusion and control the balance. *See* Eggs; Tannin.

AUTOLYSIS

The breaking down or self-destruction of yeast when its cells die. It causes the production of off-flavours and fusel oils and for this reason it is important to rack wine off the lees, and to get rid of the decomposing yeast cells, as soon as fermentation has ceased.

BACTERIA

Micro-organisms, each consisting of a single cell slightly smaller than a yeast cell, and an essential part of the natural cycle of decay and regrowth. In humans, bacteria can be valuable as part of the digestive process or they can be 'pathogenic' and cause infection. Alcohol kills pathogenic bacteria so they do not survive in wine. However, other bacteria survive only too effectively and can cause a whole variety of spoilage and infections.

Most fruits gathered for country-wine making are covered with bacteria, but these have a low alcohol tolerance and they are killed off in the fermenting process. Aerobic bacteria, those that breathe air, can be denied access to the wine by the use of an air-lock in the fermenting vessel; any air present at the start of the process is replaced by carbon dioxide which expels the oxygen. Anaerobic bacteria, those that live without air, such as lactobacilli, have to be prevented by immaculate cleanliness and sterilisation, and by the use of sulphite.

Acetobacter Aceti
Also called *Mycoderma aceti*. The vinegar bacteria which attack alcohol and turn it into acetic acid. The best way to defeat them is to follow the strictest rules of cleanliness and sterilisation while making wine, though no system of hygiene is totally foolproof.

Acetomonas
Acetifying bacteria, like acetobacter, which turn wine into acetic acid or wine vinegar.

Bacterial Haze *see* Haze.

Bacterial Spoilage
The infection caused if any harmful bacteria manage to enter the must or finished wine. Care must always be taken with hygiene and with scrupulous sterilisation. The most common bacterial infections are: acetification, malo-lactic fermentation, ropiness, Tourne disease.

Infections normally become self-evident through the appearance of the spoiled wine, its off-flavour, its unpleasant smell or a combination of these factors. Some infections are curable; some turn your wine into wine vinegar which can be used in the kitchen; but some leave it fit for nothing. *See* Infection.

Lactic-acid Bacteria
While some species of lactic-acid bacteria can cause ropiness, mouse and Tourne disease, they can also have a useful effect. They can trigger off a malo-lactic fermentation which breaks down malic acid into lactic acid and carbon dioxide, thus reducing acidity and producing a wine with a slight sparkle. *See* Fermentation, malo-lactic.

Lactobacilli
A species of lactic-acid bacteria. Rod-shaped, they cling together in the wine which they infect to form long oily chains, linked by a sort of slimy jelly. When these are visible in the wine, it is said to be suffering from 'ropiness'. Though they seriously affect its appearance and texture, making it thick and treacly, they do not spoil its flavour. Lactobacilli are also responsible for causing Tourne disease and mouse. *See* Infection.

BALANCE

A wine is described as 'balanced' if the flavour characteristics of astringency, acidity, sweetness and alcohol are matched in such a way that no one predominates. An unbalanced wine is an inferior wine, and balance is one of the factors that judges take into account when they are making their assessments.

Balance is achieved by careful blending of ingredients, additives and nutrients in the must and then, in some cases, by careful blending of the finished wine with one or more others. *See* Blending – ingredients; Blending – wines.

BALLING

An American scale used to measure specific gravity, and necessary for wine-makers using American wine-making books. *See* Brix; Specific gravity; Hydrometer.

BALM

A fragrant garden herb, *Melissa*. Its tips can be infused with the root of ginger to form the main ingredient of a medium white table wine. Alternatively, if other herbs and essences are added, it makes a sharp aperitif.

BANANAS

A vital part of the wine-maker's basic ingredients, with a three-fold value.

1. The flesh of bananas (without their skins) gives body to the must but does not affect its flavour, provided it is used in the correct proportions. Between 1 and 2lb (450–900g) should be added to each gallon (4.5 litres), depending upon whether a light wine or a sweet full-bodied wine is required. The best bananas to use are the spotted, black, overripe ones, which are cheap to buy. At this stage they have reached the peak of flavour, have maximum sugar content and minimum starch. The best way to incorporate bananas into a must is in the form of 'banana gravy'. (Untreated ripe bananas are too soft to be used in pulp fermentation.) To make banana gravy, each 1lb (450g) of fruit should be peeled, cut up and simmered for about 15 minutes in 1pt (575ml) of water in a lidded pan. The fruit juice should then be strained off and the remaining pulp discarded. The juice will probably turn into a jelly-like substance because of its high pectin content. It is therefore imperative to use a pectin-destroying enzyme, like Pecto-

27

lase, in any must to which banana gravy has been added.

2. Banana skins add more flavour than the flesh but this can be overpowering, so they should not be used for a light wine. However, one or two can be incorporated into a full-bodied wine since they add to the glycerine content and give smoothness to the finished wine.

3. The use of very ripe bananas not only speeds up clarification during maturation but can also cure a persistent haze without removing tannin as most proprietary fining agents are liable to do. Boil 1lb (450g) of the peeled fruit in 1pt (575ml) of water, strain and then add a scant ¼pt (120ml) of this mixture to each gallon (4.5 litres) of the hazy wine along with a little pectin-destroying enzyme. Blend together the wine and the banana juice very thoroughly, and leave to stand for a few days to clarify. With luck – though it does not always happen – the wine will lose its haze, gain a little extra body and retain its flavour unimpaired.

The banana therefore has many uses for other wines: adding body, giving smoothness, speeding up clarification and removing haze.

It can also be used to make a true banana wine in which the characteristic aroma and flavour of the banana predominate. There are many recipes for banana wine, and nearly all of them start with banana gravy. If fermentation ends before all the sugar has disappeared, the result will be a heavy, semi-sweet dessert wine which will be improved by fortification with vodka or Polish spirit.

BARLEY

A body-giving ingredient sometimes added to country wines, but not always with success because of its high starch content. Other body-giving ingredients, such as banana gravy, are easier to use. A good white wine can be made using barley as the main ingredient, but this must not be confused with 'Barley Wine', which is a strong ale.

Producing grain wines used to be a popular winter activity for wine-makers before commercial kits, concentrates and frozen and dried fruits became available throughout the year. But they had disadvantages. They needed the addition of spices to give flavour, they suffered from haze, and they took a long time to mature, so it was many months before they were fit to drink.

Now that grape concentrate is available to give vinosity and flavour, and amylase can be incorporated to deal with starch haze, grain wines – and barley is one of the best – taste better, clear more quickly and mature faster. Remember, though, that all grains should be carefully washed before use in case they have been sprayed with toxic chemicals.

Barley

BEANS

French or runner beans can be used to give body to any fruit wine recipe. They should be washed, sliced and added to the fruit in place of sultanas or raisins. Alternatively, bean wine can be made to the same recipe as peapod wine; simply replace the peapods with the same weight of beans. *Old* broad beans also make a good white table wine provided that they are boiled gently in water so that their skins do not split (this would cause bitterness). A starch haze may develop, but this can be cleared with amylase.

BEAUJOLAIS

A light, fruity, dry red wine – in fact, a whole group of wines – that come from the southernmost wine-producing region of Burgundy. Every year, in November, there is a light-hearted race to bring *Beaujolais Nouveau*, the newly made Beaujolais, to England for its first tasting. It is a very popular wine and the easiest of the dry red wines for the home wine-maker to imitate, using deep red fruit, red grape concentrate and a Burgundy yeast. It can be ready for drinking after a year or so of maturation.

BEETROOT

One of the vegetables most commonly used for country-wine making. Small baby beets have the best flavour and make wine good enough to drink within a year. Wine made with large woody beetroots needs several years' maturation if their earthy taste is to be banished.

The beetroots should be boiled to extract as much of their sugar and flavour as possible; the liquid is then strained off. This juice is used in the must, with the addition of yeast, sugar and a little acid, often in the form of lemon juice. Spices such as cloves and ginger enhance the flavour. Unlike most root vegetables, beetroots do not need the addition of pectic enzyme.

BENTONITE

One of the most effective fining agents used to remove hazes from wine. It is a powdered clay which is able to absorb the protein particles in the wine and combine with them to form a sediment, which sinks to the bottom of the jar, allowing the liquid to be racked off. Though time-consuming to use, it does not affect flavour or chemical balance, it is easily obtained and is cheap to buy.

The best way to clarify a gallon (4.5 litres) of wine is to put 1tsp of clay into a small jug, mix it to a smooth creamy paste with a little wine, then add more wine, stirring vigorously or whisking briskly all the time, until there is about ½ pt (285ml) of the bentonite-wine mixture. The jug should then be covered and set to one side for 24 hours, during which time the clay particles will absorb wine and swell. Then, stir the liquid in the jug yet again, add it to the rest of the wine and mix in thoroughly. Agitate the wine every now and then for half a day or so, then leave it undisturbed for a few days for the sediment to settle. After that, rack it off carefully, and make up any wine lost with topping-up wine or water. *See* Fining.

BENZOIC ACID *see* Acid.

BERRIES

The best wine-making berry is, of course, the grape. Others of special value are the elderberry, gooseberry and bilberry. Many fruits called berries, such as the raspberry, blackberry and strawberry, are really 'pseudo-berries'. The true berry is simply one drupelet, a single mass of pulp enveloped by a skin and normally enclosing several seeds. The others are agglomerates or collections of drupelets. Wine-making berries (or pseudo-berries) need not be fresh; tinned, bottled, frozen or dried fruits can be bought, or fruit juice or concentrate.

Berries

BILBERRIES

Known also as blueberries, blaeberries, whortleberries, wineberries, whinberries, huckleberries and hurtleberries and a few other names besides. An excellent wine-making fruit: many would argue that they come second only to the grape, but it is a back-breaking task to gather them! Their superb rich flavour makes them particularly good for making either a port-type wine or a claret-type wine, sweet and full-bodied; they can also produce a dry red table wine or a vin rosé. The fruit can be used fresh, canned, bottled or dried. Dried bilberries are available from wine-making supply stores and give the best results when combined with grape concentrate and elderflowers.

BIRCH SAP

This, taken from the common birch tree, makes the basis of a good refreshing country wine. It rises in late February and March, and that is when the tree must be tapped. The modern method is to drill a hole about 1in (2.5cm) in diameter, sloping slightly upwards into the trunk of the tree, about 2ft (60cm) above the ground. The hole should be just deep enough to penetrate the bark – a deeper incision could harm the tree.

Fit a bored rubber bung into the hole and insert a glass cylinder fitted with plastic tubing. This equipment should be covered with cloth and a waterproof covering to keep out insects and airborne

31

infections. The sap should then run out of the hole, through the tubing, and into a collection vessel placed beneath. It usually takes two days or more to collect about a gallon (4.5 litres) from one tree. Do not take more, for the tree's sake. When the rubber bung is removed, the hole must be sealed with a cork or wooden plug, which is then tarred over to prevent infection or bleeding.

The sap is clear, yellow, sticky and rather sweet. Slightly less than a gallon will make about a gallon (4.5 litres) of wine, since no water is added to the recipe, though it does benefit from the addition of a little grape concentrate. Sap wine can also be made from walnut and sycamore trees, though this is less common.

For birch sap wine you will need:

7pt (4 litres) sap
½pt (285ml) white grape concentrate
2¼lb (1kg) sugar
2tsp citric acid
½tsp tannin
½tsp yeast nutrient
yeast starter

Simmer together the sap, concentrate, sugar and acid for quarter of an hour, making sure all the sugar has dissolved. Allow to cool, then check the gravity and add the tannin, yeast nutrient and starter. Ferment in a covered vessel for a week, then transfer to a demi-john with an air-lock and ferment out in the usual way. The wine should clear naturally without fining agents.

BISULPHITE *see* Sulphite.

BITTERNESS

Caused by a number of factors. In some cases, if slight, it can be regarded as a virtue, especially in an aperitif wine. Some wine-making ingredients, such as the flowers of certain plants, herbs and the pith of citrus fruit, can cause bitterness, but this may be used to offset sweetness if an astringent quality is required. Usually, however, bitterness is regarded as an off-flavour. It can often be the result of an infection caused by lactobacilli, called Tourne disease. Though the infection can be arrested by sulphiting, the bitter taste is very difficult to remove, and if this cannot be done by judicious blending there is no solution but to discard the wine.

BLACKBERRIES

Excellent for combining with other ingredients – especially red grape concentrate or elderberries – to make a good red table or dessert wine. On their own, they have a tendency to produce an unsatisfactory colour and thin flavour. They are ready for picking from late August or early September; the fruit is better for wine-making purposes after a good season. Bad weather, lacking in sunshine and warmth, will increase the acid and tannin content, so pulp fermentation must be brief.

BLACKCURRANTS

Not an easy wine-making fruit because of their high acidity. By the time their juice has been diluted with water to reduce the acid content, much of the body has vanished from the wine, leaving it thin and watery. The solution to the problem lies in blending ingredients. Blackcurrants can be successfully combined with raisins, sultanas, grape concentrate and bananas with good result.

Owing to their pronounced flavour, which could overwhelm the taste of food, blackcurrants are better used as a social or dessert wine than as a dry table wine. They are also useful, provided the proportion is kept low, for adding a fruity flavour to port-style wines made primarily from elderberries, apples or peaches.

BLANDNESS

A vague term used to describe the quality of a wine that lacks 'bite' or 'edge'. It can mean lack of acidity, lack of astringency or over-sweetness. A bland wine is no sooner tasted than forgotten, though if the alcohol content is sufficiently high and you drink enough it will induce the normal state of mild euphoria even while refusing to satisfy the palate.

One of the ways to deal with a bland wine is to blend it with another that has more character. A wine that is over-acid, over-astringent or over-sweet might well become palatable if carefully mixed with one that is too bland.

BLEACH, DOMESTIC

A solution of sodium hypochlorite in water. A powerful disinfectant and excellent cleaning agent which will remove stains and deposits. It can be used to sterilise glass vessels after they have been washed, and if they are left to soak in bleach for 10 minutes all bacteria and yeasts will be killed.

Bleach, though, is toxic, and also has a powerful chlorine smell which could contaminate wine, so vessels must be emptied and rinsed out very thoroughly after contact, and then rinsed again with a solution of sulphite. Bleach is *not* recommended for use in plastic containers, which may absorb the odour and become brittle.

BLENDING – INGREDIENTS

The grape is the perfect fruit for wine-making since in itself it contains all the ingredients necessary to create alcohol: sugar, acid, tannin, yeast and so on. It is for this reason that (with the help of the sun) since time immemorial Mediterranean peasants have been able to make their own very palatable domestic wines without such sophisticated requirements as Campden tablets, assorted chemicals, nutrients and hydrometers. For those of us who do not have a generous supply of juicy grapes ripened in a southern sun, wine-making is a more complicated business. We have to mix several ingredients together to get the balance that nature packages into that one special fruit.

The composition of the must is responsible for the eventual body, bouquet, flavour and vinosity of the wine; also for its alcoholic strength, acidity and astringency. It is therefore the make-up of the must that dictates what kind of wine is produced: whether it is a dry white table wine, a full-bodied dessert wine or whatever. Wine-makers can choose from a huge and bewildering range of ingredients. For the inexperienced, however, the best way to start is by omitting everything that does not seem to have a useful contribution to make, rather than by adding everything that seems possible!

Body is a difficult term to define, but easy for the wine-drinker with a cultivated palate to recognise and assess. It is to do with the fullness of the wine, its roundness and substance when held in the mouth. It is the opposite of thinness. This is not always a virtue, of course, because body does not go hand in hand with delicacy. Some wines, like white Burgundy, Sauternes or port-type wine, must be full-bodied, but too much body in a fine white wine of the Chablis type, or in a dry sherry, would be a flaw.

The main body-giving ingredients that can be added to a recipe are dried fruit in the form of sultanas, raisins or currants, over-ripe bananas and, best of all, grape concentrate. It is also possible to use cereals – barley, wheat and rice – for this purpose, but they can have an adverse effect on bouquet and flavour as well as causing starch haze. A basic guideline is to use 4–8oz (115–225g) of dried fruit or cereals per gallon (4.5 litres) for a light wine, *or* 1lb (450g) of peeled bananas, *or* ¼–½pt (145–285ml) of grape concentrate. These quantities should be doubled for a fuller-bodied wine.

The bouquet, the fragrance a mature wine gives off when it is opened and the pleasure it offers to the nose, should also be

Blending ingredients

considered when selecting ingredients for the must. Dried fruit, grape concentrate and ripe bananas improve bouquet as well as body, so they serve a double purpose. Flowers too are valuable for bouquet, especially elderflowers, roses and honeysuckle, all of which can be used fresh (if possible) or dried. It is a good idea to make a strong infusion from fresh flowers when you can get them at their best and in abundance. The infusion can be strained, sulphited – by adding one crushed Campden tablet, dissolved in a tablespoon of warm water, to each gallon (4.5 litres) of liquor – and then put in the deep-freeze until required. This is generally better than an infusion made from dried flowers.

Do not include too great a proportion of flowers in the must, or they will overpower both the bouquet and the flavour, and the wine will smell and taste like a flower garden. Normally an infusion made from about ⅓–½pt (190–285ml) of flowerheads or petals is sufficient for a gallon (4.5 litres) of must. Often only ¼pt (145ml) of elderflowers is needed but they should come from a bush that grows sparse, smallish heads of pure white. The large creamy blossoms that grow densely packed together on the tree look like a wine-maker's dream but in fact they can impart a strong odour of tom-cats instead of a delicately fragrant bouquet. A combination of equal quantities of elderflowers

35

and rose petals can be very effective, the resulting bouquet being neither catty nor over-perfumed. Only white or yellow rose petals should be used in white wine musts, since pink or red ones affect the colour.

The bouquet is only completely developed when the wine has thoroughly matured, since it depends largely upon esters, which are formed by the slow oxidation of some elements in the wine.

The ingredients required to give the wine its particular *flavour* are legion, and include fresh or dried fruit (blackberries, elderberries, sloes, pears, bilberries, raspberries, strawberries, apples, citrus fruits, gooseberries, rosehips, peaches, apricots, plums, damsons, cherries, bananas, raisins, currants, sultanas, dates, figs); vegetables (parsnips, carrots, beetroot, peapods, beans); herbs (parsley, sage, balm); flowers (elderflowers, honeysuckle, roses, coltsfoot, dandelion, gorse, broom, hawthorn, clover, greater burnet, lime); and cereals (rice, wheat, barley, maize).

Table wines should not have an overwhelming flavour since their function is to complement food rather than to distract from it; strongly flavoured ingredients such as raspberries and blackcurrants should be avoided in favour of milder ones, like apples and pears. For social wines, which tend to be drunk on their own, it is perfectly permissible, perhaps desirable, to allow the flavour to dominate. Similarly, citrus fruits or herbs can add piquancy to an aperitif.

Wine-makers tend to use one flavour ingredient combined with two or more body-giving ingredients, but better wines can be created by using two or more flavour ingredients. Blackberries and apples, for instance, seem to be made for each other in the wine-maker's world as well as the cook's kitchen.

When wine-making ingredients are being blended it is therefore important to take into account, body, bouquet and flavour. It is also vital to consider *vinosity*, the essential vinous quality of wine which gives it its individual identity and sets it apart from any other alcoholic drink. Despite the protestations of those devotees of country wines who claim that superb wine can be made without the grape, true vinosity can only be achieved when grape is added in some form – either by incorporating raisins, sultanas or currants (1–2lb/450–900g to 1gal/4.5 litres of must) or preferably by using grape concentrate (½–1pt/285–575ml to 1gal/4.5 litres). The routine addition of grape concentrate to every recipe can only improve it, since it is a body-giving and bouquet-enhancing ingredient: it adds the acid required for zest and bite, the tannin which imparts astringency, and the sugar on which the yeast works during fermentation, converting it into alcohol.

With experience, and trial and error, the wine-maker learns how to blend those ingredients that give the wine the qualities it needs, and to balance them in a variety of ways, in order to create red, white or rosé wines, aperitifs, dessert wines, fortified wines, social wines and liqueurs, whatever is required. *See* Esters; Oxidation.

BLENDING – WINES

Dull, boring and inadequate wines can be improved by judicious blending, but this is quite a difficult procedure. The beginner should not expect instant success but should be prepared to persevere. As with so many aspects of wine-making, experience is the best teacher.

A composite wine created from several different wines can indeed taste superior to any of the individual components; rash or careless blending, though, can make things worse rather than better. Wines that are being considered for blending should first be carefully assessed with regard to their acidity, tannin content, gravity, alcohol strength, astringency, body, bouquet, flavour, colour and so on. The deficiencies of one should then be recompensed by the qualities of one or more others. For instance, a very thin-bodied wine would benefit from the addition of a full-bodied one, or one with a high tannin content would marry well with one that is over-bland. Do not, though, try to blend wines of a different type. Heavy, sweet social wines are not likely to mix well with dry table wines.

As successful blending is a matter of trial and error, it is sensible to get the mix right by carrying out experiments with only small quantities, working step by step, keeping careful note of proportions used, and tasting at regular intervals. About ¼pt (145ml) is more than sufficient to give the quality of a particular blend, and you can make a few mistakes without wasting much.

After blending, it is quite likely that fermentation will start again. This is a good thing because it ensures a thorough combining of the wines. In fact, blending can also be used as a remedy for stuck fermentation. Almost certainly, blending will also cause a new sediment to be deposited for a few weeks or even months after mixing. The wine should therefore be racked at intervals until it remains clear and then left to mature as if it were a new young wine.

Just as disappointing wines can be made satisfying through careful blending, so very good wines can be made excellent. The experienced and ambitious wine-maker can find this process a great and rewarding challenge. *See* Fermentation, stuck.

BLOOD

Usually ox-blood, and a source of albuminous protein commercially used for fining. It interacts with the tannin in wine to produce a precipitate and therefore, as well as clearing it, it reduces harshness. It may be worth trying with a particularly astringent red wine but is not suitable for white wine. Ox-blood is still available in wine-making supply stores but nowadays most home wine-makers prefer to use a proprietary fining agent or bentonite.

BLOOM

A film of yeasts or other micro-organisms, like mould or bacteria, which sit on the skin of fruit giving it a soft, velvety appearance. It should be washed off very thoroughly, and the fruit sterilised before being made into wine, since it is a prime cause of infection.

BLUEBERRIES/BLAEBERRIES *see* Bilberries.

BODY

The sensation of fullness, heaviness and roundness that some wines leave in the mouth. A full-bodied wine is not any thicker or more viscous than a light wine. Its quality is related to the more concentrated presence of such substances as acids, salts, sugars and tannins than is found in a light wine, as well as – in many cases – a higher concentration of alcohol. The definition cannot be a precise one and must be related to the impression the wine makes on the senses rather than its chemical make-up. *See* Blending – ingredients.

Body-giving Ingredients
These are very important if the wine is not to feel thin or watery to the palate. Those most frequently used by the home wine-maker are dried fruit, over-ripe bananas (in the form of banana gravy) and grape concentrate.

BOILING

Required to prepare some fruits and vegetables used in wine-making. Very hard fruits, root vegetables, most dried fruits and bananas need to be treated this way. Boiling is not recommended for anything else because it gives a cooked flavour to the wine; it also releases large quantities of pectin, and a pectin-destroying enzyme has to be used to prevent haze. Finally, boiling drives off the volatile esters which give wine its flavour and bouquet. Flowers must never, on any account, be boiled or they will lose their vital wine-making ingredient.

Before they are boiled, fresh fruit and vegetables should be chopped, and dried fruit minced or liquidised. They should then be put into a straining bag, immersed in a large pan of cold water and brought to the boil. Fruit can be simmered with the lid on until thoroughly softened, but vegetables need more rigorous treatment to drive off volatile compounds which would affect the taste and aroma of the finished wine. They must be boiled vigorously for up to half an hour in an unlidded pan.

After the boiling stage the pulp can be strained off, slightly pressed and discarded. The remaining liquid is ready for use. Boiling will have sterilised the extracted juices so sulphiting is unnecessary at this stage.

BOOKS

Wine-making books are like cookery and gardening books in that we all have our special favourites. A particular volume that seems helpful or fun to one wine-maker may seem confusing or dull to another, so it is difficult to make recommendations. The list given below includes those which I have found especially useful. They range from the excellent, cheap and easily obtained paperbacks produced by Amateur Winemaker Publications to more specialist, glossy and expensive books; they cover practically every aspect of the craft in the hope that, whatever your particular interest, you will find something to appeal to you.

Many wine-making books are available from lending libraries. It is a good idea to borrow them in the first place, but most wine-makers will want to build up their own personal library over the years and acquire a shelf of tried and trusted friends. Remember, though, that unless you are looking for something quaint and unusual, it is wise to buy a comparatively new or extensively revised book which is up-to-date on methods, equipment and ingredients, as well as giving both metric and imperial measurements. Secondly, a book is more convenient to use if it has a good index.

General Wine-Making Books

Acton, B. and Duncan, P. *Making Wines like those You Buy* (Amateur Winemaker, 1964). This lives up to its clever title and points the way to what most of us are trying to achieve.

Berry, C. J. J. *First Steps in Winemaking* (Amateur Winemaker, 1960). A useful, straightforward and commonsense introduction, with recipes for every month of the year.

Duncan, P. and Acton, B. *Progressive Winemaking* (Amateur Winemaker, 1967). Every wine-maker's 'bible'. It covers the subject thoroughly, interestingly and in depth.

Foster, C. *Home Wine Making, Brewing and other Drinks* (Ward Lock, 1982). A clear, easy to absorb and attractively produced book.

Kurtz, H. and G., *Winemaking at Home* (Batsford, 1982). Basic, fun, with jolly illustrations, and reassuring for the beginner or less-ambitious wine-maker.

Mackay, M. H. *Country Winemaking and Wine Cookery* (David & Charles, 1978). Valuable both for its economy in the use of ingredients and for some unusual and intriguing recipes, as well as for its mouthwatering cookery ideas.

Parrack, A. *Commonsense Winemaking* (Amateur Winemaker, 1978). A good, clear, sensible guide, practical and straightforward.

Sampson, B. *The Art of Making Wine* (Aurum, 1982). This useful volume includes a good section on the growing of vines as well as a lot of good recipes.

Tayleur, W. H. T. *Home Brewing and Wine-Making* (Penguin, 1973). Well-written, informative and usefully comprehensive as well as being studded with fascinating snippets of information. A book one returns to again and again.

Turner, B. *The Compleat Home Winemaker and Brewer* (Emblem, 1976). An attractively produced book, which is clear and concise in its directions.

Turner, P. and Turner, A. *Home Winemaking* (Foulsham, 1982). With step-by-step pictures, this gives a straightforward, easy-to-follow introduction to the mysteries of the craft.

For the Wine-Maker in a Hurry

Bellis, R. *Express Winemaking* (Amateur Winemaker, 1979). How to make good wines in a month or less.

Books of Recipes

Belt, T. E. *Winemaking with Elderberries* (Amateur Winemaker, 1982). Recipes devoted to Britain's answer to the grape, and its flowers too.

Crabtree, B. *The Best Wine Recipes* (Foulsham, 1979). An attractive book which contains something to please every palate.

Ekins, R. *Worldwide Winemaking Recipes* (Amateur Winemaker, 1978). Wines with a difference, using exotic ingredients from all over the world.

Leverett, B. *Winemaking from Kits* (Prism, 1983). An excellent book that shows how, with a little imagination and creative flair, you can add to a basic wine kit to turn it into an extremely attractive wine.

Restall, J. and Hebbs, D. *How to Make Wines with a Sparkle* (Amateur Winemaker, 1972). Simplifies the difficult art of making delicious sparkling wines.

Books for the Liqueur-Lover

Bellis, R. *Making Inexpensive Liqueurs* (Amateur Winemaker, 1976). A useful handbook which covers many types of liqueur-making and brings this luxury drink within everyone's pocket.

Van Doorn, J. *Making your own Liqueurs* (Prism, 1980). One of a range of attractive and mouth-watering wine books from this publisher.

Books for the Vine-Grower

Page-Roberts, J. *Vines in your Garden* (Amateur Winemaker, 1982). Fully illustrated, and useful for keen gardeners with a little space to devote to vines.

Pearkes, G. *Vinegrowing in Britain* (Dent, 1982). Expert advice from a specialist on all aspects of the subject, from growing on a small patio to organising a commercial vineyard. Also details of vineyards in this country, and nurserymen who supply plants.

Books on Special Interests

Andrews, S. W. *Be a Wine and Beer Judge* (Amateur Winemaker, 1977).

National Guild of Judges Official Handbook, *Judging Home-made Wines* (Amateur Winemaker, regularly updated).

These two are required reading for anyone contemplating the challenge of wine-judging. They cover all you should know about rules, qualifications, standards and procedures.

Dart, C. J. and Smith, D. A. *Woodwork for Winemakers* (Amateur Winemaker, 1971). Contains detailed instructions for making a large selection of equipment, ranging from the complete fittings of a winery to a small stirrer for the must.

Watney, B. M. and Babbidge, H. D. *Corkscrews for Collectors* (Sotheby Parke Bernet, 1981). A lovely, fascinating and well-illustrated gift for the wine-maker who has everything!

Magazines

The Amateur Winemaker, Amateur Winemaker Publications Ltd, South Street, Andover, Hants. Monthly.

Practical Winemaking & Brewing, 83 Halstead Road, Mountsorrel, Leicestershire, LE12 7HE. Bi-monthly.

Articles, advertisements from suppliers, news – of great interest to the home wine-maker.

BORDEAUX

Any wine produced within the Bordeaux region of western France, around the mouth of the Gironde, is allowed to bear the name of Bordeaux provided that it reaches certain standards. Bordeaux has five main regions famous for their wines: Graves, Medoc, Pomerol, St Emilion and Sauternes.

Bordeaux is mainly renowned for its claret, produced from Cabernet grapes, which have a very high tannin content. Many of the best clarets consequently need to mature for up to twenty years for their astringency to mellow. Some take as many as fifty years to reach their best. Dry claret-type table wines can be made by country-wine makers from elderberries or sloes.

BOTRYTIS CINEREA *see* Noble rot.

BOTRYTISED GRAPES

Grapes which have been attacked by the mould, *Botrytis cinerea* or noble rot. Because of the special qualities they develop as a result of this infection, they are used in the making of Sauternes wine. *See* Noble rot.

BOTTLES

For the novice wine-maker only two sorts of wine bottles (*wine* bottles, not beer bottles, cider bottles or lemonade bottles) are necessary: clear glass for white or golden wines, coloured glass for red wines, to prevent their discoloration through oxidation. Some starter kits provide six wine bottles as part of the package.

However, there is a whole range of bottle shapes, colours and sizes traditionally associated with certain wines, and it is a good idea to collect them and use them for the appropriate wine whenever possible; the visual pleasure of attractive presentation can enhance the pleasures of taste and smell.

Bottle Brush
Cleanliness is vitally important to successful wine-making, and a bottle brush is necessary to get bottles, jars, demi-johns and air-locks perfectly clean. The brush should have a long, flexible handle and a fan of bristles at the end so that it can reach every part of the inside of the bottle. Most wine-makers will have a range of brushes of different shapes and sizes.

Bottle Drainer
A useful piece of equipment for draining, and possibly storing, washed bottles. There are good models on the market, sturdy and well

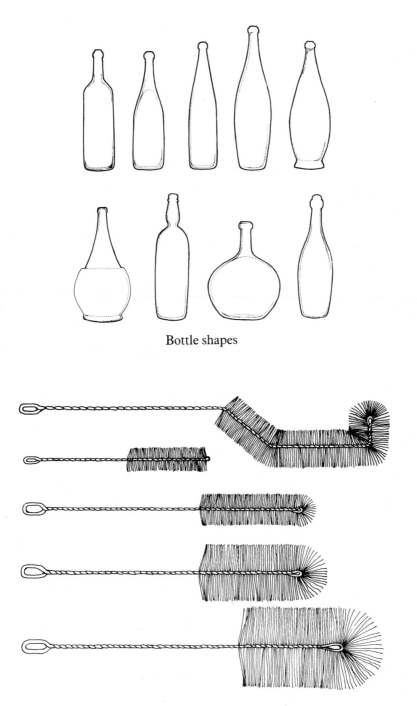

Bottle shapes

Bottle brushes

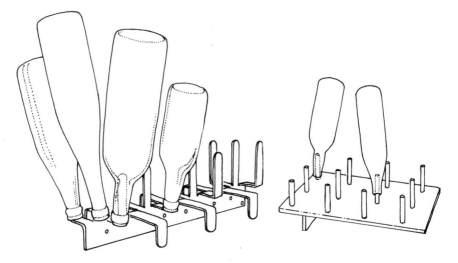

Bottle drainers

made, as illustrated. They do, however, cost a few pounds, but you can make your own. All that is required is a wooden base about 15in (37cm) square, a small batten, a length of dowelling, waterproof glue and screws. Alternatively, an old bread-board or cutting-board would do for the base.

Raise the base at one end by screwing the batten underneath towards one edge: this facilitates drainage. The board should be drilled with 15–20 holes, according to its size, leaving sufficient space for upturned bottles. Into each hole a length of dowelling about 4in (10cm) long should be fitted and glued so that it is tight and secure.

When required, stand the bottle drainer on the draining-board and put the washed, rinsed and sterilised bottles upside-down on the pegs. If they are left at a slight angle the sterilising solution will drain away from their necks and they will dry completely and hygienically.

Bottle Sickness
When a wine is being transferred from jar to bottle it tends to absorb oxygen through aeration, no matter how much care is taken over the process. The action of the oxygen on the wine at this stage will create the chemical acetaldehyde, and the result will be a flatness known as 'bottle sickness'.

The wine should recover from this ailment after a few weeks, but it is better not to drink it until at least three months, and preferably six, have lapsed since bottling. Having a succession of wines in various stages of development lets you give new ones a chance to mature while older ones are being enjoyed.

Bottle sickness is particularly liable to affect wine that has been over-exposed to the air during filtering, which is one of the reasons why it is better to let it clear naturally, if possible.

Bottled Fruit
This can be used for wine-making in exactly the same way as canned fruit, as an alternative to fresh fruit. A useful standby in the winter months.

Bottling
This is normally done when the wine has completely fermented and clarified (and has been tasted and blended if necessary) and needs only to mature further. In fact, some wine-makers prefer to mature their wine in bulk until it is almost ready for drinking, or until they need the fermentation vessel for other purposes.

The wine should be sulphited, and stabilised with ascorbic acid, which also acts as an anti-oxidant, 24 hours before the final racking and bottling. The bottles should be washed thoroughly, sterilised, rinsed and drained. Then the wine should be siphoned in as carefully as possible until it reaches to within about 1in (2.5cm) of the bottom of the cork. Corks should be inserted so that their tops are flush with the top of the neck of the bottle, then covered with capsules. All that remains, for a really professional appearance, is to give each bottle the finishing touch of a neat label.

BOUQUET
The fragrance of a wine or its 'nose'. It is made up of two components: the aroma, which is the scent of the fruit and/or flowers used in the making of the wine; and the esters, which are products formed in the wine by fermentation and maturation. The aroma can be very different from the original smell of the bouquet-giving ingredients. Young wine lacks genuine bouquet since the esters have not had time to form and can only predominate in the fragrance of a mature wine.

There are three main bouquet-giving ingredients which serve a double function as they also improve body. They are bananas, grape concentrate and dried fruit. A fourth prime bouquet-improving ingredient is flowers, especially roses and elderflowers, though wild honeysuckle is also excellent. *See* Blending – ingredients.

BRAMBLE-TIP WINE
Not only the blackberries, but the growing stems of brambles can be used to flavour wine. The stem of the bush pushes outwards rapidly in

May and June and a small cluster of young leaves is formed. This eventually flowers and produces the fruit. The tip of this stem, while it is still young with the leaves just opening, is suitable for making an aperitif wine with a piquant flavour, sharp and cleansing to the palate. The usual practice is to cut a length of 4 or 5in (10cm) from the end of the stem; about half that length, however, just back to the first leaf growing from the stem, gives a softer wine. Once the flowers have set, the tips have too strong a flavour to be acceptable.

To make 1gal (4.5 litres) of wine, gather a gallon of young bramble tips. Pour boiling water over them, leave them to soak overnight, then bring the mixture to the boil and simmer for quarter of an hour. Some wine-makers prefer just to cover the tips with hot water, bring the mix to the boil and simmer for 15 minutes, but this method gives less flavour. The hot liquid should be strained off into a bucket containing sugar, and also raisins if these are to be used instead of grape concentrate. It should then be allowed to cool before the other ingredients are added and the must is fermented out in the usual way. A typical recipe is:

1gal (4.5 litres) bramble tips
1gal (4.5 litres) water
3lb (1.5kg) sugar
8oz (225g) raisins *or*
¼pt (145ml) grape concentrate
juice of 1 lemon
yeast and yeast nutrient

BRANDY

A spirit distilled from wine. It matures only in wooden casks or barrels. Good brandies, the choice cognacs and armagnacs, are allowed to mature for twenty years or more. The brandy most likely to be used by the home wine-maker, to make fortified wines or liqueurs, is the cheaper fortifying brandy or eau-de-vie. *See* Fortification; Eau-de-vie.

BREATHING

The process by which bottled red wine absorbs oxygen from the atmosphere after the cork has been removed. Red wine should be opened and allowed to stand without a stopper for at least an hour before drinking, whether it remains in the bottle or is decanted. This allows it to become mellower and rounder to the palate.

BRIX

A specific gravity (SG) scale used on the Continent. The approximate SG is obtained by multiplying degrees Brix by 4. *See* Specific gravity.

BROAD BEANS

When picked towards the end of the growing season, they make a pleasant dry white wine with a distinctive flavour. They should be shelled, then simmered *very* gently: if the skins are allowed to split, the flavour will be ruined.

BROOM

The delicate lemon-yellow flowers of broom, which bloom in May and June, can be used, like the more common gorse, to make a scented flower wine. There are no prickly spines, as with gorse, but the blossoms may be rather sparse and there is some labour involved in gathering enough even for a gallon of wine. Approximately 3½pt (2 litres) of flowers are needed for 1gal (4.5 litres) of water.

A note of caution. A few people seem to be allergic to both broom and gorse wine and can be quite ill after drinking it. This should not happen if the proportions recommended above are followed, with the volume of petals only half, or less than half, that of the water used.

Broom flowers

BROWN SUGAR *see* Sugar.

BUCHNER FLASK AND FUNNEL

Equipment used for vacuum filtration. The special flat-based filter funnel holds a filter pad, and sits on a rubber gasket in the mouth of the extra-strong flask. The flask has an open side arm which is connected to a vacuum pump by tubing. The wine to be cleared is then poured into the funnel and quickly sucked through the filter agent and down into the flask by the vacuum process. *See* Filtration, vacuum.

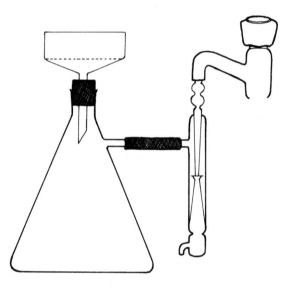

Buchner flask and funnel

BUCKET

A simple but invaluable piece of wine-making equipment, provided that it is not made of metal. Plastic is the best material, pliable plastic being better than the rigid sort which can impart a plastic flavour. White plastic is better than coloured as the colour can be leached out by the acid content of the wine. It is particularly important to avoid yellow plastic in wine-making because of the controversial toxic potential of yellow pigment.

Buy buckets of 2gal (9 litres), or 3gal (13.5 litres) capacity with well-fitting but not completely airtight lids. Use them for: pulp fermentation of fruit, vegetables or flowers; the initial preparation of the must; and as storage containers for small pieces of equipment in between wine-making sessions. For all these purposes buckets must be kept scrupulously clean and sterile.

BUNGS

Tapered cork or rubber stoppers used to seal standard gallon fermentation vessels. Some are bored with a hole in which an air-lock can be fitted.

Rubber stoppers have several advantages over cork stoppers. Rubber is comparatively impervious to air and will therefore prevent oxidation; it is flexible, and consequently gives a very tight fit; it will last for years without disintegrating; it can be easily sterilised by boiling or by soaking in sulphite solution; and it is cheaper in the long run than cork, since it can be used again and again.

It also has disadvantages, however. It may impart a rubbery flavour to the wine, if left in contact for long; it is difficult to bore to the right size to fit a fermentation lock, so it is necessary to buy pre-bored bungs; it will eventually perish and become tacky, and must be discarded – if it sticks to the neck of the vessel while the wine is fermenting an explosion could occur; it is expensive to buy in the first place; and it is not as pleasant to look at or to handle as cork.

BURETTE

A useful measuring tube for use when titrating for acid. It is calibrated, and usually fitted with a tap so that the flow can be carefully controlled. During titration, the burette is filled to the zero mark with an alkali. This is added, very gradually, to a sample of wine until the end point is reached. At this stage the amount of alkali used can be read from the scale, so you can calculate the acidity of the must. *See* Titration.

BURGUNDY

The top wines of this French province near the Alps are among the best – and consequently the most expensive – in the world. Burgundy can be red or white, but the red is the more popular and sought after. It is generally soft and full-bodied.

Burette

49

BUTYL ALCOHOL *see* Alcohol.

CALCIUM CARBONATE *see* Precipitated chalk.

CALCIUM SALTS

A precipitate formed by the reaction of chalk, or calcium carbonate, with the acids in a must. Chalk is therefore useful for reducing acidity when it is preferable to avoid dilution by water, provided that only a small proportion is used. If more than ½oz (15g) is added to a gallon (4.5 litres) a slight chalky flavour might permeate the wine. The white precipitate is very fine but it will settle out, along with the lees, and can be racked off without difficulty.

CALCIUM SULPHATE *see* Gypsum.

CAMPDEN TABLETS

A form of sodium metabisulphite, the prime sterilising agent used by wine-makers. One Campden tablet, which is composed of 450mg of sodium metabisulphite, is the equivalent of 1tsp (5ml) of strong sulphite solution made up from the crystalline form of the chemical.

Campden tablets, which are used crushed, are universally available in chemist shops and wine-making supply stores. They are more convenient to handle, but also more expensive, than sulphite crystals. The tablets are normally used for sterilising equipment, sterilising musts and preserving maturing wines.

CANDIDA

An attractive name for an unattractive genus of micro-organisms which can cause infections in man and in the wine he drinks. The species of candida of particular interest to the wine-maker is *Candida mycoderma*, a film yeast which causes spoilage of wine. It is recognisable first as small whitish patches, then as a grey–green scum which settles on the surface of the liquid or on the lees in the bottom of unwashed containers. Again, this is an ugly condition with a pretty name: 'flowers of wine'. Proper hygiene and sterilisation help to prevent the infection, as does the fermenting of wine in anaerobic conditions, since this is an aerobic organism and needs air to survive. If it escapes your care and vigilance and manages to gain a hold, the wine is recoverable, though the flavour may be damaged. The treatment is to sulphite the wine thoroughly and to break up the skin. After a few days the disturbed film will sink to the bottom of the jar and the wine can then be racked off.

CANDY SUGAR *see* Sugar.

CANE SUGAR *see* Sugar.

CANNED FRUIT

Canned or bottled fruit is a perfectly good ingredient for making wine. For busy or lazy wine-makers it has the advantages of being easy to obtain and quick to prepare for the must. It has the disadvantages, though, of being expensive (though bargain offers of tinned fruits are sometimes available at supermarkets or cash-and-carry centres) and of being unsuitable for making dry wines if it contains artificial sweetener, which could well be non-fermentable.

Suitable canned fruits include apricots, gooseberries, pineapples, bilberries, cherries, guavas, peaches, cranberries, blackcurrants and many more.

CAP

When wine is fermented on the pulp, solids from the pulp are carried to the surface by the rising bubbles of carbon dioxide and collect there

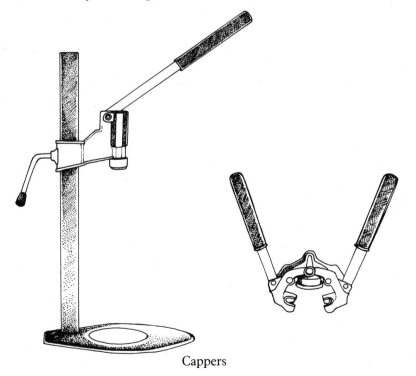

Cappers

to form a crust or 'cap'. The cap is an even better breeding ground for infection than the must itself. When fermenting on the pulp, therefore, you should cover the container to keep out bugs, and break up the cap twice a day, then stir it in vigorously. This stirring process is also a useful aid to extraction, so it is well worth the daily routine.

CAPPERS

Tools designed to seal bottles with metal crown caps. Now widely used for sparkling wines, and much easier to deal with than wired corks. Either one-handled bench cappers or two-handled hand cappers are available from wine-making supply stores at a moderate price.

CAPSULES

These are foil or plastic and can be applied over the cork of a wine bottle to give a smart finishing touch. A foil capsule is mainly a decorative feature, but since a range of colours is available it can also serve as a form of colour coding, making it easy to select at a glance the type of wine required, whether a table wine, an aperitif, a sweet dessert wine or a social wine. For a neat appearance, a foil capsule should be given a tight fit with a tool called a capsuler.

Plastic capsules are more useful than foil because they do not need to be applied with a capsuler; they add an extra seal to the bottle; and they help to prevent corks from spoilage. There are several sorts, both soft and rigid. The soft capsules can be bought stored in liquid which keeps them pliable until they are exposed to the air. When placed in position on the necks of the bottles they dry out, shrinking to the required shape and size. Alternatively, they may be bought dry and steamed into shape with a kettle. Rigid capsules are bought as firm cylinders. They need to be softened to fit into place, but once they are on the bottle necks they become rigid again.

Capsuler
Available from wine-making supply stores. Used to fit foil capsules over the necks of wine bottles, which cannot be achieved as effectively by hand.

CARAMELISATION

The burning of sugar to change its colour, flavour and texture. Caramel is not of great significance to the wine-maker except that some people use tiny quantities of it to give a rich mature flavour to sweet red dessert wines. Madeira and Madeira-type wines owe their colour and flavour to their heating, and the consequent caramelisation of the residual sugar, after fermentation and before maturation.

CARBOHYDRATES

Compounds which contain carbon, hydrogen and oxygen, and no other elements. Sugar, starch and cellulose are the main carbohydrates used by wine-makers, and alcohol is the main carbohydrate produced by wine-makers.

CARBONATION

The forcing of carbon dioxide into a liquid such as cider or sparkling wine to make it fizzy. This is done by using a pressurised cylinder and is normally undertaken by commercial wine-makers only. Other methods of carbonation are through bottle fermentation or malo-lactic fermentation. *See* Fermentation, malo-lactic; Sparkling wine.

CARBON DIOXIDE

A waste product of wine-making, a gas produced by yeast in the fermentation of sugar to alcohol. The gas is liberated as bubbles which can be seen rising through the must and forcing their way out through the air-lock.

If fermenting wine is contained in a sealed vessel so that the carbon dioxide cannot escape, the gas dissolves in the wine and builds up pressure; this may become so great that it breaks the seal or the bottle. However, if only a little unfermented sugar is left, the wine will become sparkling through this form of bottle fermentation. When the bottle is opened, the gas will be released out of solution and will form bubbles in the wine. Sometimes this happens by happy accident; at other times the wine-maker has taken certain steps to guarantee the sparkle.

Carbon dioxide has a greater density than air. As it is formed it therefore displaces the air from the top of the fermenting vessel and forms an anaerobic shield which prevents the must from infection and spoilage by aerobic bacteria. Secondary fermentation should always take place in anaerobic conditions. *See* Fermentation, anaerobic; Sparkling wine.

CARBOY

A rotund glass vessel which is ideal for the storage of wine that has been produced in large quantities; carboys usually hold 5, 10 or 12gal. Because of the weight of the liquid contained, larger carboys have their bases protected and strengthened by wickerwork cradles.

Attractive though they are, they can be dangerous if used for the wrong purpose. Designed to hold chemicals rather than wine, they are not strong enough to withstand the pressure of fermenting liquid or rapid temperature changes. And when full, the 10 and 12gal sizes are too heavy for many people to handle.

CARROTS

One of the best of the wine-making vegetables since their flavour is not overpowering. Whereas parsnip or beetroot wine can take years of maturation to get rid of the vegetable taste, carrot wine is ready in about a year. The best carrots to use are those in their prime, neither young and tasteless, nor old and woody. Carrots are high in pectin and free of acid, so it is advisable to incorporate into any carrot-wine recipe both a pectin-destroying enzyme and some citrus fruit. So-called Carrot Whisky is made by adding wheat or hops and crushed black peppercorns to the must.

CASEIN

The principal protein in cow's milk. Pure casein is a good fining agent since it combines with suspended solids to remove haze without removing or altering flavour. Casein is difficult to dissolve in water so it is best used dissolved in sodium bicarbonate. Alternatively, it can be dissolved in strong ammonia, then boiled until the ammonia is driven off. It is a good idea to make a fining agent from equal quantities of casein and tannin, since the tannin will combine with any extra protein and aid the clarification process.

Casein can be bought from wine-making supply stores and instructions for use will normally be found on the packet. Milk is in some ways easier to use than casein, and only a few drops are necessary to fine a gallon (4.5 litres) of wine. Unfortunately, it can turn the wine white.

CASKS

Casks or barrels, usually made of oak, used to be the only containers available for the storage of large quantities of wine. They have the advantage over plastic or glass of being porous, so that air can gradually permeate the contents, assisting the process of maturation while excluding bacteria. However, their cost, the difficulty of ensuring their absolute cleanliness and the complications of maintaining them have much reduced their popularity for home wine-makers.

The problems of maintaining a wooden cask are threefold: if left empty it will shrink, and the hoops and staves will no longer fit tightly; if it is not cleaned meticulously after use it may pollute any subsequent contents; it must be kept on its side, bung-hole uppermost, and unless effectively supported off the floor it will warp. Despite this, many home wine-makers have at least one oak cask in which to mature the best fermentations. As an investment a cask will pay dividends, as well as being a joy to look at, and it will produce excellently matured wine.

The names of casks are as picturesque as their appearance: a 4½gal is a pin; a 6gal a six; a 9gal a firkin; an 18gal a kilderkin; a 36gal a barrel; and a 54gal a hogshead. At home, the most useful cask sizes are 4½ and 6gal. Those above 9gal are too heavy and cumbersome.

To prepare a new cask for use, stand it full of water for two or three days to let the wood swell. Then wash it thoroughly with hot water and soda, and rinse it through, again and again, with tap water. It should next be sterilised with 5 per cent stock sulphite solution. Use it first of all for fermentation rather than storage, because this will give the wood the opportunity to adapt itself. Afterwards it will be less likely to absorb tannin from a finished wine. A secondhand cask is perfectly acceptable provided that it is in good condition and looks clean: it is still necessary to go through the soaking, cleansing, rinsing and sterilisation process to condition it before use.

To prevent a cask from drying out, it should be kept in constant use; never empty it unless there is another wine ready to refill it, after it has been rinsed out with cold water. One final word of warning. In smaller casks the surface to volume ratio is high, and too much oxygen may be absorbed to suit delicate white wines; they should not be stored for more than a few months. Red wines are normally quite safe.

CASSE

Metallic Casse

A discoloration and haziness in wine which results from contamination by metal. In some cases it can be treated by adding a little citric acid and then filtering or fining. Casein may remove copper contamination and bentonite will reduce the level of iron. If, however, lead is suspected as the source of the casse, the wine must not be drunk as it will be toxic.

Metallic casse is a problem which is almost impossible for the home wine-maker to solve. So take pains to prevent all possibility of metal contamination when wine-making.

Oxidative or Oxidassic Casse

A brownish discoloration of wine caused by the reaction with air of an enzyme found in over-ripe fruit. This enzyme, which rejoices in the name of o-polyphenoloxidase, oxidises tannins to brown pigments. As usual, prevention is better than cure, and the casse can be avoided if fruit is sulphited the minute it is prepared. If a cure is necessary, the wine must be sulphited with 50–100ppt of sulphite every two or three months until the discoloration is rectified.

CELERY

Celery which is too old and tough for eating, or has gone limp, can be used to make an aperitif wine by the method normally used for vegetables. The blanched white stalk, the green end and even the leaves can be boiled to make an extract in which the sugar is dissolved. If white sugar is used, some wheat should be incorporated and allowed to ferment with the must for about four days during primary fermentation to add colour; most wine-makers, however, prefer to use brown sugar and omit the cereal. Very little nutrient is provided by the celery so more than usual – perhaps ⅓–½oz (10–15g) – should be included. As celery also provides very little acid, two or three citrus fruits should be included in the recipe, and a trace of ginger to add flavour. Some people say that celery wine is a remedy for rheumatism if drunk regularly and there may be a grain of truth in the rumour.

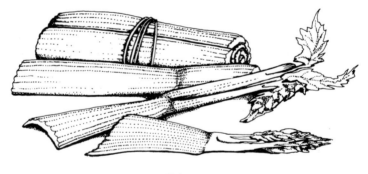

Celery

CELLAR

Few home wine-makers own the luxury of a true underground cellar lined with bottle racks. For most people the cellar is the place where their wine is stored, and may even be the cupboard under the stairs. A good cellar should be dry, so that labels do not become mildewed, nor corks attacked by mould; free from vibration; dark; fairly cool, reaching no more than about 59°F (15°C), and fairly stable in temperature; roomy enough for bottles to be stacked on their sides; and of course readily accessible.

While an underground cellar is an excellent place for the storage of wine, it forms a refuge for moulds and is almost impossible to sterilise, so it should never be used for the making of wine. *See* Winery.

CELLARCRAFT

The care of the wine from the end of fermentation, through the processes of maturation, bottling and storage, until serving.

CELLULOSE

The chief component of the fibrous parts of plants; it forms a long chain of glucose. Until recently, it has been difficult to break it down but now an enzyme preparation is available which can do this, and release the plant's yield of juices.

Cellulose has largely replaced asbestos as a valuable filtering agent since the medical profession established a link between asbestos and lung and stomach cancer. Cellulose is non-toxic and is available in the form of pads and powders from wine-making supply stores. To avoid 'filter-pad flavour', the first washings should not be used a second time.

CEREALS

Barley, wheat, rice and maize can be used as body-giving ingredients in wine, although they have some disadvantages. Some wine-makers feel that they impair bouquet and flavour; and if they are included in a recipe the finished wine does take longer to mature. They can also cause the formation of a starch haze which has to be either prevented or cured by the starch-reducing enzyme, amylase.

CHABLIS

A region within Burgundy which produces many fine French wines, but a name also applied to a particular wine which is crisp, white, dry and delicate. It can be drunk as an aperitif or served with shellfish, salmon or bland white meat such as poultry or veal. It should be chilled in the fridge for no longer than two hours or it will lose its distinctive bouquet. The home wine-maker can make a Chablis-type wine from green gooseberries, apricots or oranges, with the addition of white grape concentrate and a good Chablis yeast.

CHALK *see* Precipitated chalk.

CHAMBRÉ

Red wines should be served 'chambré', that is, brought up to room temperature while they are 'breathing'. If the environment is cold their temperature can be raised by immersing the bottles in warm (not hot) water. They should not be put near a fire or radiator, since strong heat will drive off the volatile esters and ruin the wine.

CHAMPAGNE

Revered as the best of the white sparkling wines, and often classified as a fortified wine. The sparkle, or bubble, is due to the presence of carbon dioxide, caused by the fact that the wine is bottled before the fermentation has ended.

Champagne makes an excellent aperitif, but being expensive (and quickly euphoria-inducing) it is more often used as a celebratory, special-occasion drink. Wine can only be called 'Champagne' if it is made in the Champagne region of France, but the amateur can make some good champagne-type sparkling wines with a little care. *See* Sparkling wine.

CHAMPAGNE BOTTLES

Made of thicker, heavier glass than ordinary wine bottles in order to withstand the pressures of continuing fermentation. Other wines have normally completed the fermentation process by the time they are bottled (though accidents do happen!).

Champagne-type wines should not be put into ordinary wine bottles, or into any bottle with a flaw, otherwise an explosion is likely. Also care should be taken when opening a sparkling wine, since the pressure that has built up can transform the cork into a dangerous missile.

CHAPTALISATION

The addition of sugar to a commercial grape must in a poor year in order to increase the alcoholic strength, as regulated by French law. The law on chaptalisation is of some interest to makers of country wines since it illustrates how much sugar is considered permissible before the quality of the wine is judged to deteriorate.

Most 'country wines' are really sugar wines: the added sugar is the principal or only source of alcohol, and the fruit or vegetable is merely flavouring or bouquet-enhancement. It is rare to find a fruit other than the grape with a high enough sugar content to make a good wine, and this is one of the reasons for the increasing practice of adding grape concentrate to country-wine recipes to improve the finished product.

The term 'chaptalisation' comes from Jean Antoine Claude Chaptal, Compte de Chanteloup, who was Napoleon's Minister of Commerce. Under pressure from the sugar producers of the West Indies, he legalised the previously illicit practice of sugaring the must, but only within regulated and limited amounts.

CHARCOAL

One of the purest forms of carbon. It can be used for fining, especially in the making of Madeira-type wines as it will remove the estufa flavour which may have developed if the wine has been warmed at a fairly high temperature. Vegetable charcoal is best, used in a fairly fine powder form, in the proportion of about ½–1oz (15–30g) per gallon (4.5 litres). If it does not settle out in a few days the Madeira should be filtered, or fined with a reliable proprietary fining agent.

CHEMPRO SDP

A bleaching agent and steriliser which is used in solution with hot water to remove stains from bottles and glassware. It is caustic and therefore all equipment which has been treated with it must be thoroughly washed afterwards in copious quantities of cold water. *See* Cleanliness.

CHERRIES

Cherries are ripe for eating from June, but it is better to wait until July before using English-grown cherries for wine. Imported cherries are available from May. If they become over-ripe they may be sold off cheaply enough to be used for wine but in this condition strong sulphiting is advisable, so wash them in 1gal (4.5 litres) of water containing 1tbsp of sulphite.

There are various types of cherry, all of which make wine. Wild cherries tend to be astringent and are best blended with a blandly flavoured fruit like the banana. Red and white cooking cherries can be high in acid and are perhaps best made into a sweet wine, though there are many people who prefer their sharpness in a refreshing dry wine. Red and black dessert cherries are fairly low in acid and make a simple red table wine. Morello cherries are high in acid and make a noble dessert wine, or they can be steeped in brandy for a liqueur.

In practice, there is wide variation in the amount of fruit used and

Cherries

in the methods of extraction, so that the resulting wine can vary from a soft, cherry-coloured accompaniment to a meal to a strongly cherry-flavoured social wine. The minimum quantity of fruit used is about 3lb (1.5kg) per gallon (4.5 litres) of water, but recipes using up to three times that amount of fruit to the same quantity of water are followed and praised by some wine-makers. As an alternative, it is possible to use half cherries and half prunes to make a different but equally delicious wine.

For a cherry brandy-type liqueur *see* Liqueurs.

CHILLING

For wine-drinking, this means cooling rather than making very cold. A wine can be chilled to a temperature of between 42° and 48°F (5° and 9°C) by being kept in the refrigerator for up to 2 hours. It will take three hours to become really cold, that is between 36° and 40°F (3° and 5°C). Crisp, dry white wines are normally served chilled, sweeter ones are served cold. Though red wines are usually served at room temperature (*see* Chambré), sparkling rosé wines are at their best when chilled. Pale dry Fino sherry, drunk as an aperitif, is best chilled, and nowadays it is often served 'on the rocks', ie poured over ice cubes. *See* Temperature.

CITRIC ACID *see* Acid.

CITRUS FRUITS

These include oranges, tangerines, satsumas, clementines, mandarins, lemons, limes and grapefruit and are very useful to the craft of wine-making for a number of reasons. They are an invaluable source of citric acid, and many country-wine makers prefer to use it in this 'natural' form rather than as bought crystals; they make a good white dessert wine of the Sauternes type; they make a good sparkling wine or 'citrus champagne'; and they are excellent for the production of aperitif wines because of their zest and piquancy. When the juice, combined with the liquor strained from an infusion of finely grated peel, is fermented together with grape concentrate it gives a sharp, clear flavour that is excellent for freshening the palate.

Citrus fruits

CLARET

A group of dry red wines produced in the Bordeaux region of France. The best clarets contain too much tannin at the outset and are consequently left to mature for two or three years in the cask and then up to twenty more in the bottle. Claret is probably the best of all the dry red wines, and these are most likely the hardest for a home wine-maker to reproduce. Nevertheless, it can be done if the must is right and the maturation sufficient. A quality claret-type wine depends primarily upon good deep-red fruit (elderberries are especially suitable but so are bilberries, sloes, cherries, damsons and red plums); red grape concentrate, sultanas or raisins, for vinosity; a good red wine yeast such as Bordeaux or Burgundy; and, of course, time.

CLARIFICATION

The removal of the small particles of solids which make wine cloudy and are found suspended in a wine that has just finished fermenting. The best clarifying agent is *time*. Most wines will clear of their own accord within two to four weeks after the end of fermentation; some may take six months, and some, if not properly formulated, may never clarify on their own. (Proper formulation includes the use of enzymes to break down pectin or starch, careful treatment of the fruit to avoid extracting unwanted solids and the avoidance of spoilage bacteria.) Self-clarification is promoted by storing the wine at just above freezing point. This throws solids out of solution so that they coagulate and settle, and when the wine is brought back to normal temperature it appears quite clear.

For wine-makers in a hurry, or with a difficult wine, there are three methods of clarification. The first, *centrifuging*, is not for the amateur, though anyone with access to a centrifuge will probably know how to use it. The second, *fining*, is the addition of a reagent which combines with the suspended matter to form a precipitate. This settles at the bottom of the vessel so that the clear wine can be siphoned or decanted off. The trouble with fining is that it can also remove valuable flavour components from the wine. There is a saying that no fined wine is a fine wine! It may also be difficult to select the fining agent appropriate to the cloudiness: sometimes a series of haze tests has to be carried out first. Thirdly, *filtration* through a fine-mesh sieve will remove the worst of the suspended matter, but for real clarification proper filtration equipment is necessary. Filtration is a more laborious process than fining but can be less damaging to the wine; some people nevertheless claim that they can always detect a 'filter-pad flavour', though this will usually disappear after maturation. The rate of filtration is very important: if it is slow it will encourage oxidation through prolonged exposure of the wine to air.

The recognised stages in clarification are as follows. Cloudy: one cannot see through it; hazy: the suspended particles are obvious to the naked eye; clear: suspended particles can hardly be seen; bright: the wine is completely translucent. *See* Filtration; Fining; Hazes.

CLEANLINESS

Amateur wine-makers often think that the 'experts' are over-fussy in their insistence on cleanliness and the sterilisation of all equipment used in the wine-making process at every stage. But cleanliness is even more vital in wine-making than in the normal daily kitchen activities of preparing food; if it is even slightly neglected the result can be a chain reaction which will render the wine undrinkable. Dirty equipment is the most frequent cause of infection. It allows harmful organisms, bacteria and fungi, to thrive and multiply, and attracts the dreaded fruit fly. The wine can be affected and sometimes ruined by acetification, flowers of wine, ropiness, Tourne disease and so on.

It is therefore vital to cover fermenting musts, to remove lees from uncovered bottles and jars, to wipe up splashes of wine on surfaces, and to wash equipment, without delay, in hot water and detergent, using a bottle brush. Though a boring occupation, cleaning-up should never be neglected or postponed.

Bad staining tends to occur when glassware has contained wine for a long time, and this is particularly true of red wine. The product most useful for stain removal is Chempro SDP, available from wine-making supply stores or chemists. Two teaspoonfuls of Chempro should be dissolved in 1gal (4.5 litres) of warm water and the glassware soaked in this for about half an hour, and then rinsed very thoroughly in cold water. Cleaning and stain-removal, vital as they are, are not sufficient in themselves; they must always be combined with effective sterilisation. *See* Sterilisation.

CLEMENTINES *see* Tangerines.

CLOVER

White or pink clover makes a good table wine; the white variety has a particularly attractive bouquet. One word of warning: a great many flowers have to be picked since they need to match the volume of water; 1gal (4.5 litres) of wine requires 1gal of blossoms. Alternatively, the flowerheads can be bought dried from wine-making supply

Clover

stores. A 2oz (60g) packet is usually enough for a gallon (4.5 litres) of wine. Lemons, oranges and ginger added to the basic recipe give extra zest, acidity and flavour.

CLOVES

Their dry distinctive taste can be used by the home wine-maker, either as 'cloves' – the dried flower-buds – or as oil of cloves. It is possible to make clove wine, but its striking flavour is something of an acquired taste. Cloves are more usually used as a flavouring for vegetable wines, especially beetroot, and cereal wines. Some people like to combine them with root ginger, black peppercorns and caraway seeds to make a spicy additive mix. This is tied in a little muslin bag and suspended in the must until the first racking off. Cloves can also make a fine liqueur.

COFFEE

A perfect partner to alcohol. Coffee can be drunk with alcohol in separate glasses; it can provide the basis of superb liqueurs; it can be incorporated into rum punches; and it can be mixed with spirits, topped with cream and drunk hot or cold. It can even make coffee wine.

To make 1gal (4.5 litres) of *Coffee Wine*, simmer about 6oz (175g) of ground coffee and the grated rind of two lemons in 1gal (4.5 litres) of water for about 30 minutes, then dissolve just over 3lb (1.5kg) of sugar in the coffee while hot, stirring well. When the mixture is cool add a tablespoonful of citric acid and the juice of the two lemons, along with yeast and yeast nutrient, and ferment out in the usual way. It will be ready for drinking in about three months. It can be drunk cold as an amber-coloured medium sweet wine or warmed *gently*, so as not to drive off the alcohol, and taken with added sugar.

For *Coffee Rum Punch*, put 8 sugar lumps into a saucepan, add the grated rind of two oranges, cover with 1½ cups of red wine, and leave to stand until the sugar has absorbed as much wine as it can. Add a liqueur glass of rum and a stick of cinnamon and heat gently, stirring all the while. Add 8 cups of hot strong black coffee and serve immediately.

COLD EXTRACTION

The best method of recovering the required ingredients from fruit in order to make the clearest wine. Hot-water extraction, or infusion, as well as boiling, have a better recovery rate but are liable to leave haze-forming pectin, starch or cellulose in the wine.

Cold extraction is particularly recommended for flowers, because the essential oils which give them their fragrance, and which are wanted in the wine, may be made volatile by hot water. Though it produces less colour and flavour than other methods, it avoids giving the wine a cooked flavour. The fruits for which cold extraction is particularly suitable are apples, pears, peaches, oranges, lemons and rhubarb.

The method is quite simple. In a sterilised bucket put about half the volume of water that will be required for the wine, sulphite it lightly, and put the chopped-up fruit into the bucket as it is prepared. Do not prepare the fruit first and then add the water since this will allow oxidation and discoloration to take place. To boost extraction, it is a good idea to add pectin-destroying and cellulose-destroying enzymes. Leave the fruit (or flowers) in the water for 24 hours and then strain off the liquid for incorporation in the must, or follow up with pulp fermentation. *See* Fermentation, pulp.

COLOUR

In wine the colour is given by the extraction of pigment from the materials used in the recipe. White wine can be produced from white grapes or from red grapes, provided that the pulp and skin are removed before fermentation, since the juice is not normally red. For red wines fermentation is carried out on the pulp for up to a week until sufficient colour has been extracted. Rosé wines need less pulp fermentation and should achieve the required colour in up to two days.

Colour Extraction
The proper method is to begin fermentation on the fruit pulp. As alcohol is gradually produced by the ferment it will leach out the pigments in the skins of the fruit, these being soluble in alcohol but not in water. When the desired depth of colour has been achieved (bearing in mind that if the wine is to be diluted by water the colour will be diluted too), the fruit pulp is strained off the must.

COLTSFOOT

Coltsfoot flowers make a pleasant light wine and have the advantage of being available as early as February or March, when few other wine-making flowers are in bloom. Only the yellow petals must be used; the greenery makes the wine impossibly bitter.

A teaspoonful of tannin should be added to every gallon (4.5 litres) to counteract flatness, and a race of crushed ginger to add piquancy. Herbalists reckon that coltsfoot flowers are a remedy for coughs and chesty conditions, and if honey is used in the recipe instead of sugar the finished wine will be all the more soothing.

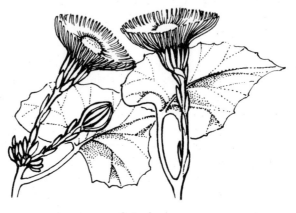

Coltsfoot

COMPETITIONS

One of the great pleasures of the home wine-making world is the chance of entering competitions and of having your product evaluated, assessed and commented upon. Competitions provide the stimulus to keep standards high, and the opportunity to discuss wine-making techniques, problems and pleasures, both with the experts who preside as judges and with other competitors. Usually they are enjoyable social occasions where new friendships are formed in the process of swapping recipes and exchanging tips.

Many competitions are held throughout the country, especially during the summer, ranging from local events – perhaps a small club competition, or part of the village fête or horticultural show – to the great 'National', the annual show of the National Association of Wine and Beermakers. *Amateur Winemaker* magazine lists 'Diary Dates' in which details of many competitions are given, as well as having a monthly round-up of 'News From The Circles' which often includes information about competitions still in the planning stages. *See* Judging wine.

CONCENTRATE

Fruit juices are concentrated by evaporating water from them, usually under sub-atmospheric pressure so that the water boils at quite a low temperature and less of the volatile oils are driven off. Some of the aroma of the juice is evaporated with the water, but this is usually trapped and restored so that the concentrated juice is, according to the manufacturers, exactly the same as the original juice but without the water. When the correct amount of water is added to the concentrate the result is, in principle, identical to the original juice.

Grape juice is, of course, the concentrate of most interest to wine-makers. If nothing is added to it except preservative, it can be sold legally as 'concentrated grape juice'. If anything else is added to it, perhaps acid, as in most wine-making kits, it must be sold as grape juice 'compound' not 'concentrate'. Compounds attract VAT; concentrates, being foodstuffs, do not.

When grape-juice concentrate is prepared for use by the wine industry, juice from the great wine-growing areas is often extended with juice of a similar grape from an inferior area. For this process, it is cheaper to transport the cheaper juice in the form of concentrate. The marketing of concentrates for home wine-making was originally an offshoot of this business, but it has now grown to such an extent that some concentrates are prepared purely for this purpose.

The grape juices that make the really great vintage wines are not concentrated, so it is unwise to expect a superb fermentation from concentrate alone. The aim of many makers of country wines is to improve on the potential of a grape concentrate by a hint of another ingredient, and particularly good results can be achieved by adding elderberries to red wine and elderflowers to white wine. Concentrate is also an invaluable addition to many country-wine recipes. Most of these call for the use of raisins to give vinosity, but grape-juice concentrate can always be used in their place, to advantage: the procedure is simpler and the flavour clearer and fresher.

CONTAINERS

The traditional and picturesque vessel in which country wines were made was a crock: an earthenware bowl, usually covered with a cloth. However, it would be romantic to imagine that wine made in a crock was any better than that made in a modern glass demi-john. On the contrary, a wine crock is more difficult to clean properly and considerably more difficult to seal against bacteria. If the crock is glazed, the glaze may crack and provide a harbour for bacteria, or even liberate toxic lead. As a fermenting vessel, a glass demi-john is best.

For the preparation of fruit and for pulp fermentation, a white plastic vessel is acceptable. But plastic should not be used for the main fermentation because plasticisers can be leached out by the alcohol as it forms, and even the polymer can be attacked by alcohol. Stainless steel is a sound alternative to glass or plastic. Other metals should not be used because they can so easily contaminate the wine. Enamel will do only if it is not chipped, exposing the underlying metal to contact with the wine.

For the storage of wine, the larger the bulk the better. If a gallon (4.5 litres) is made in a demi-john, it is better, and less trouble, to store and mature that quantity, after racking, in a demi-john until it is ready to drink. Wooden casks can be used for storing wine; in fact, a wooden container is preferable for the maturing of claret-type wines, but a large scale of production is required to fill the cask, and much determination to prepare and maintain it properly. *See* Demi-john; Bucket; Cask.

COOKING WITH WINE

Wine is not only a delight to drink: it can make a simple meal miraculous. The cheapest cuts of meat can be persuaded to taste like Cordon Bleu, and the most convenient of convenience foods can assume the flavour of French cuisine. Whether it is a salad or a stew, a cake or a casserole, a drop of wine can transform it.

Penny-pinching packs of meat or fish, scrag-end of lamb, shin of beef, chicken portions or anything on special offer at the freezer centre can be transformed beyond recognition with a marinade. Mix together ½ bottle of wine; 1 cup of oil; 2tbsp of vinegar; 1 onion and 1 carrot, roughly chopped; seasoning and a generous sprinkling of mixed herbs. Into this, dunk the meat or fish, and leave it overnight until it is oozing juicy goodness and the house smells like a five-star restaurant. The marinade can then be used in the cooking or kept separate and thickened into a rich sauce.

Almost any everyday dish becomes special if part of the liquid recommended in the list of ingredients (probably water or stock) is replaced with wine. It does not matter whether red or white wine is used: experiment until you find out which you prefer. Try using a glass of red wine in your steak and kidney pudding, beef cobbler, hot-pot or pot-roast, braised kidneys or meat balls in savoury sauce. Pour some white wine into your chicken casserole, rabbit stew or fish pie. Bake lamb chops in a buttered dish, sprinkled with lashings of rosemary and the juice of half a lemon, and generously sluiced down with white wine.

Alcohol is marvellous for pepping up convenience foods, and the most convenient of all is probably tinned soup. To serve soup as a stylish starter, use tinned consommé with 1tbsp of sherry-type wine stirred into it; try it well chilled, but for a winter party it is more welcome warmed, with a sprig of parsley and a twist of lemon floating

68

on the surface. Or combine 1 can of condensed mushroom soup with 1 can of milk, stir in 3tbsp of sherry-type wine, season and bring to the boil. Add 1½oz (45g) dressed crab and garnish with chopped chives. It could not be easier – or more exotic.

Convenience foods can be dressed up to make delicious desserts too. One of the simplest is made from thick rich custard, over-ripe bananas, sherry-type wine and ice-cream, all beaten up together and served elegantly decorated with chocolate chips and flaked almonds. Or try an Austrian Coffee Cake. Bake a sponge cake in a ring baking tin. When it is cool pierce the cake all over with a skewer or knitting needle, then slowly trickle through it 1 cup of cold, sweet, strong coffee laced with 2tsp of your own cherry brandy. Put it on a pretty dish, decorate it lavishly with whipped cream, and top it with cherries and chocolate drops.

The most convenient food, of course, does not have to be cooked at all, and again wine can work wonders. For instance, salads are superb with white wine dressing. Mix together: ½ cup of olive oil; ¼ cup of white wine; 2tsp of lemon juice; seasoning; a pinch of sugar; ½tsp of dry mustard; 1tsp of minced onion. Chill and pour over a salad – perhaps one concocted from a lettuce, a green pepper, a cucumber, four tomatoes and four hard-boiled eggs, all sliced up and decoratively arranged on a big dish with a centrepiece of cold meats and slivers of cheese.

Many fruits – fresh, frozen or tinned – become exotic when given the 'tipsy treatment'. Dribble port over slices of pineapple, mash strawberries with your own peach brandy and spoon over peaches, or simply steep raspberries in red wine and sugar. Then serve them up with sweet biscuits and custard or cream.

COPPER

Copper contaminates wine, discolours it and affects its flavour, causing a reddish haze or sediment. Since it is mildly toxic, it is safer to discard affected wine and make quite sure that future fermentations never make contact with copper equipment or containers.

CORDIAL

A cordial, in common with a wine, is a combination of the extracted juice of fruits, flowers or vegetables mixed with sugar and water. The vital difference is that no yeast is added, therefore it is not fermented and not alcoholic. Some high-quality commercially produced cordials, syrups and squashes make good wine-making ingredients. They include lime-juice cordial; tropical fruit cordial (which combines well with figs); pineapple and grapefruit cordial; raspberry cordial; strawberry cordial.

CORK

The bark of the cork-oak tree, grown largely in the south of Europe and North America, is a naturally porous material and is excellent for stoppering wine containers. It seals them sufficiently to prevent the attack of infection but at the same time allows the entry of enough air to aid maturation.

When the whole of the wine-making process, fermentation and maturation, is carried out in one sort of vessel – probably a demi-john – two different types of cork are needed: a bored cork fitted with an air-lock for the fermentation period and an unbored cork when the wine has cleared.

Standard, straight-sided corks are the best if wine is to be stored for a long time. Drive them deep down into the neck of the bottle so that the tops are flush. This can be done with a hard push using the heel of the hand, or more easily with a 'corker', either a simple wooden or plastic hand-plunger or a more ambitious two-handled or bench model. Straight-sided corks, inserted properly and adequately sterilised, are the least likely to allow wine to seep out or to admit infection. A good corkscrew is required to remove them and obviously they cannot be used a second time.

Flanged corks, sometimes topped with plastic, or all-plastic wine stoppers are usually shorter than the straight-sided ones, have a little cap on the top and are tapered. They are easy to insert and remove without equipment, but are no good for long-term storage because they are not leak-proof. Their main uses are for wines which are to be drunk soon or which are to be exhibited.

Sparkling wines need to be bottled in champagne bottles, and either sealed with champagne corks, which are then wired to guard against the possibility of being blown out by the build up of carbon dioxide, or – more usually nowadays – fitted with crown caps pushed into place with a crown capper.

Corks need careful storage, preparation and sterilisation. New corks, for instance, are hard, and those of inferior quality can be too porous. Before use they should be soaked in a mild sulphite solution until they are soft; about 2 hours should be long enough. Then roll them in a towel and stand on them to squeeze out the excess moisture. Finally, smear them with glycerine so that they are easy to insert (or add a few drops of glycerine to the sulphite solution). Corks should not be boiled as this will make them dry and brittle and they will eventually disintegrate. Nor should they be allowed to dry out, since this causes shrinkage. It is for this reason that wine bottles are stored on their sides with the bottom of the cork in contact with the wine; if plastic 'corks' are used wine can be stored upright.

Corked
Wine is said to be 'corked' if the cork becomes infected and imparts an unpleasant smell and flavour to the contents of the bottle. The infection can be caused by the cork having shrunk or by inadequate sterilisation of the cork before use. Corked wine is normally discarded.

Corker
A corker or corking gun is a piece of equipment designed to push a

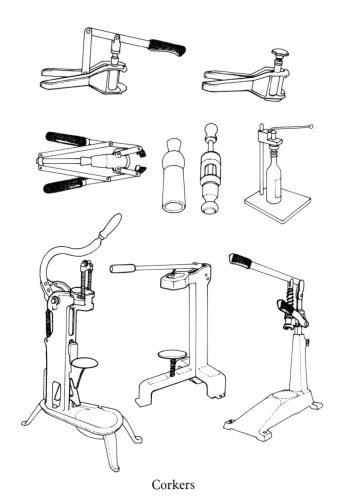

Corkers

cork snugly down into the neck of a bottle so that it fits flush and gives a tight seal. There are many designs available and a wide price range. Choose from small, plastic hand models, larger two-handled tools sturdily made from metal or metal and wood, and big bench models, according to your wine output and what you wish to spend. Simple corkers work on the system of plunging the cork into the bottle. More elaborate ones provide adjustable lateral compression and automatic corking, and can be adapted for use with different sizes and shapes of bottles.

Corkscrews
Corkscrews range from the simple twist of metal with a grip handle to complicated tools. The most effective is probably the tool with a cork grip and double lever action. This makes cork removal a more precise process, requiring less wrist strength.

Lovely antique corkscrews can be found, made of ivory, wood, tortoiseshell and so on, often incorporating a brush to remove cork crumbs. Many wine-lovers find that these make fascinating collectors' items, being both useful and decorative. A good book on the subject is *Corkscrews for Collectors* by B. M. Watney and H. D. Babbidge (Sotheby Parke Bernet, 1981).

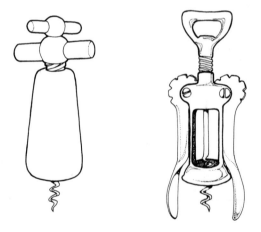

Corkscrews

COUNTRY WINES

Traditional wines made from fruit other than the grape, or from flowers, vegetables, grains, herbs, bark, sap or leaves, with the addition of sugar, nutrients and – in the past – baker's yeast. Nowadays most country-wine makers add grape concentrate to their ingredients and use proprietary yeast, since the two most significant

Country wines

advances in the area of home wine-making are the availability of reasonably priced concentrates and of true wine yeasts. Concentrate adds vinosity, body and bouquet without greatly affecting flavour, and also aids faster maturation. The only valid reason for omitting it from a recipe must be as an economy measure.

Similarly the quality of yeasts available to the wine-maker has improved enormously, due to research into strains of *Saccharomyces ellipsoideus*, the yeast indigenous to the great wine-growing regions of the world and far more suited to the fermentation of the grape than *Saccharomyces cerevisiae*, commonly known as baker's yeast. Complementary wine yeasts bring out the inherent qualities of a must, promoting its natural bouquet and flavour. They produce a sound fermentation which can create up to 18 per cent alcohol by volume. They help to form a firm deposit that makes racking off easier and minimises the danger of the development of off-flavours. Few if any experienced wine-makers would argue that baker's yeast can yield results as good or as reliably.

COWSLIPS

A famous and favourite country-wine ingredient. Cowslip wine is not only delicious, it is also a wonderful potion for inducing sleep. Unfortunately, large quantities of cowslips are required (a volume equal to the water) and since this glorious flower is vanishing from its natural habitat and in urgent need of conservation, it is not to be

73

picked for wine-making, even if you can find it in sufficient numbers. However, dried cowslips can be bought in wine-making supply stores and may be a happy compromise, provided that you can be sure the countryside is not being denuded to please your palate.

CRAB APPLES

Of particular value to the home wine-maker since they are one of the earliest wild fruits to ripen and are found growing naturally along roadsides and hedgerows. They can be used on their own to make a refreshing wine, provided that their high acidity is reduced, or a few crab apples can be added to a sweet apple wine. Better results are gained by using pure extracted juice rather than relying on pulp fermentation.

CRANBERRIES

To be treated like bilberries as far as the wine-maker is concerned: they ripen at the same time, make a similar excellent wine and can be used in the same quantities, in the same way, in the same recipes.

CREAM OF TARTAR

The common name for monopotassium tartrate, the salt of tartaric acid. It is formed in wine by the reaction between potassium, which may have been added in the form of the sterilising agent, potassium metabisulphite, and the tartaric acid of the grapes. It precipitates out in small crystals known as argols. *See* Argols.

CROWN CAPS

The flattish metal tops with edges which are crimped tightly around the neck of the bottle by a tool called a crown capper. At one time used

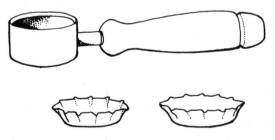

Crown cap and capper

only for beer, they are now used also for sparkling wines, largely replacing the traditional wired champagne corks which are more difficult to fit and more dangerous to remove.

CRUSHING *see* Pulping.

CRUST

The precipitate formed as port matures. It is composed of large amounts of tannin. It is important not to disturb the crust, so when the wine is stored on its side the upper side should be marked; it should be carried in that position. Crusted ports are of very high quality, second only to vintage ports. They are shipped and bottled before maturation and the crust is created during maturation and storage. Great care must be taken when opening the bottle so as not to disturb the contents, and then the port must be decanted, in order to separate off the crust and leave it behind in the bottle.

CRYSTALLISATION

When materials which have been dissolved in water come out of solution they often form fine crystals. The crystallisation most often encountered by the wine-maker is the formation of argols, which occur as potassium tartrate precipitates out. The rate of crystallisation speeds up once a few crystals are present as these act as seeds on which more crystals can grow. Consequently, if a wine is being cleared by cooling, it is a good idea to shake it first. This distributes the seeds which form several crystallisation nuclei as growth points.

CUBE SUGAR *see* Sugar.

CURRANTS

Dried seedless grapes which can be used as an alternative to raisins in wine-making, and are of particular value for deepening the colour of sherry-type wines. They are also used to add a vinous quality to country wines, but it is probably preferable to use grape concentrate which, now that it is easily available at reasonable prices, is largely taking the place of dried fruit in many homemade wine recipes. *See also*: Blackcurrants; Redcurrants; Whitecurrants.

CUVÉ CLOS

'Closed vat' is a method of making sparkling wines. The second fermentation of the wine is done in bulk rather than in the bottle, in large stainless steel vats. *See* Sparkling wine.

CUVÉE

A blend of new still wines from different vineyards which will be fermented in the bottle to produce sparkling wine. *See* Sparkling wine.

DAMSONS

At their best in August, they can be used in wine-making in the same way as plums; they are better for a sweet dessert wine or a port-type wine, though, than for a dry table wine. Since damsons yield more pectin than plums, the use of a pectin-destroying enzyme is advisable. Damson gin can be made, as a good liqueur, following the method used for sloe gin.

DANDELION

Makes a good, traditional country wine. Only the yellow flowers should be used; the green parts give a bitter flavour. The blossoms should be picked with the sun on them; the amount needed is half that of the volume of the finished wine. They should be washed free of insects and infused. There may be an unpleasant smell in the early stages of infusion but this will disappear. Beware of drinking too much of this wine because it is an effective diuretic!

DATES

A useful wine-making ingredient since they can be bought at any time of the year, to be used either as the basis of an interesting sweet social wine or, more commonly, incorporated into the must of an oloroso-type 'sherry'. The compressed de-stoned 'cooking' dates are just as good for wine-making as the expensive boxed brands. For date wine it is a good idea to add a mixture of rose petals and elderflowers for bouquet.

DECANTING

Most of us pour our wine straight from bottle to glass. But wines with a sediment in the bottle should be transferred to decanters for the purpose of separation; this applies mainly to ports and red wines that have been maturing for a long time.

Decanters

Decanting must be done very carefully to disturb the sediment as little as possible. Remove the bottle from the storage rack, keeping it on its side. Draw the cork gently, then tilt the bottle slowly and trickle the wine into the decanter. At the same time you should be looking through it at a light (traditionally candlelight!) beyond it, so that the liquid is illuminated. Then you have a clear view of the sediment and can stop pouring the moment it reaches the neck.

DELPHINIUM

Some wine-makers are tempted to use the delphinium as a wine ingredient hoping for a novelty, blue-tinged country wine. But the blue pigment is unstable in acid conditions and delphinium seeds contain a poison which may find its way into the must.

DEMERARA SUGAR *see* Sugar.

DEMI-JOHN

A glass vessel suitable for the domestic fermentation of wine. It has straight sides and a narrow neck able to take a bung, which may be of cork, plastic or rubber, either solid or bored to hold an air-lock. It normally has ears or lugs below the neck for ease of carrying.

The capacity of a demi-john, when full to the underside of the bung, is slightly more than a gallon, so it is the ideal vessel for the fermenting of 1gal (4.5 litres) of must. When the initial frothing has subsided the liquid is topped up to fill it completely.

The glass of a demi-john may be clear or it may be coloured to

Demi-johns

protect red wine from exposure to light and subsequent loss of colour. A clear glass demi-john allows the wine-maker to watch what is going on and to make sure that the vessel is thoroughly clean before it is used. Red wine can be protected in a clear glass demi-john by a simple wrapping of cardboard or brown paper or a more sophisticated demi-john jacket.

Demi-john Jackets
When a must is fermenting in a demi-john, it can be kept at a stable temperature and protected from the light if the demi-john is wrapped in an insulating jacket. These can now be bought in various styles and materials, by mail order or from some wine-making supply stores. There are white, fleecy jackets which are tied around the vessel, or quilted ones. There are also washable acrylic furry covers with elasticated necks that allow them to slip over a demi-john even when fitted with an air-lock. They are particularly useful to insulate vessels standing on an electric heating tray. Small-scale wine-makers can achieve the same results, however, by wrapping the fermenting jars in towels or blankets.

DENATURING

The irreversible altering of the structure of protein by heat or by alcohol. For example, cooking denatures the white of egg, changing it from a substance that is clear and runny to one that is white and solid by the application of heat. Similarly, the protein in wine can be turned into a solid when alcohol is added for the purposes of fortification, and this will show itself in the form of a haze. The haze can be removed by an inorganic fining agent such as bentonite, but an organic fining agent, such as albumen, could make the problem worse.

DESSERT WINE

A wine intended for drinking at the end of a meal, preferably with fruit. It has a higher alcohol content than table wine, and is rich, sweet and full-bodied. It is likely to be richly coloured and strongly flavoured, with a luscious bouquet. Many fruit-based country wines make excellent dessert wines, especially those too strongly flavoured for table wines, such as blackcurrant. Traditional dessert wines include Madeira, Sauternes and port. White dessert wines are best served slightly chilled, red at room temperature.

DEXTRINS

Unfermentable sugars, chains of glucose, which are formed through the breaking down of starch or the partial destruction of pectin. If they are present in wine they will cause a haze which may be difficult to clear. *See* Hazes.

DEXTROSE

The old name for glucose or grape sugar.

DILUTION

Normally required in home-produced wines in order to reduce over-acidity or to achieve the required bouquet or flavour. If dilution is necessary it affects the level of sugar and the proportion of additives, and these must then be adjusted.

All wines from kits have to be diluted, but since this has been taken into account in advance there is no need to tinker with the other ingredient proportions. It may be necessary to dilute fruit juices with water in order to lower acidity to an acceptable level. However, dilution can also result in too low an acidity, and it is then necessary to add acid.

If a wine is over-flavoured, diluting with water will correct it effectively, but if the flavour is right it is better to dilute with a bland topping-up wine. Similarly, water will weaken the colour of a red wine so dilution with another red wine is better.

DINNER WINE

Wine to be drunk with a meal rather than before or after; now usually called 'table wine'.

DISACCHARIDES

Sugars made up of the joining together of two monosaccharides. The most significant disaccharide for the wine-maker is sucrose (from cane sugar or beet sugar), which is made up of one molecule of glucose and one of fructose.

DISCOLORATION

If a white wine becomes brownish, it is probably due to oxidation of the fruit during the preparation of the must. This may be rectified by repeated sulphiting. If red wine is too dark, it has either been fermented too long on the pulp or too high a proportion of fruit has been used. If it is too pale, the reverse is true. Alternatively, the wrong sort of fruit may have been used: blackberries, for instance, rarely give a good colour and should always be used in conjunction with another fruit. The depth of colour may be altered and improved by judicious blending of dark and pale wines.

Red wines also become discoloured by exposure to light. If they are fermented and matured in clear glass vessels they should be protected by paper or cardboard or by demi-john covers, and they should finally be racked off into coloured bottles. *See* Casse, oxidative.

DISTILLATION

The process of heating a mixture of two liquids with different boiling points to a temperature above the boiling point of one of them, so that the lower-boiling liquid evaporates; the vapour which has become separated is then condensed and collected. The most familiar mixture for distillation is water and alcohol, in order to recover a distillate rich in alcohol which is called 'spirit'. Preparation of spirit by distillation has long been part of country-wine making, but it has been illegal for almost as long. The law relating to distillation is set out in the current Alcoholic Liquor Duties Act. Amateur distillation is dangerous – it is liable to cause a concentration of fusel oils, often toxic, in the distillate (and a concentration of excise officers!).

A mixture of water and alcohol can also be separated into an alcohol-rich portion and an alcohol-lean portion by freezing. The water freezes first, the alcohol later. It used to be a moot point whether this was 'distillation' within the meaning of the Act, but now the law has been tightened up and the preparation of spirit by any method is illegal, except under licence. Fortification is the only way in which home wine-makers can increase the alcohol content of their wines.

DOM PERIGNON

A name important to wine-makers, not only because he has been immortalised in a good champagne. He was the Benedictine monk who, in the seventeenth century, first used cork to stopper bottles. Only then, when wine could be effectively protected from infection, did it become possible to create well-matured and vintage wines.

DRIED FLOWERS AND HERBS

Though not quite as good as their fresh equivalents for giving a floral fragrance to wine, they have the great advantage of being available all year round. They can be bought loose or in sealed packets from wine-making supply stores. The sealed packets are comparatively expensive, but the flowers' fragrance will have been well preserved.

Dried flowers can be substituted in any recipe that requires fresh flowers, provided that the quantities are adjusted accordingly. Roughly speaking, ½oz (15g) of dried flowers equals 1¾pt (1 litre) of fresh flowers, except in the case of elderflowers, where ¼oz (8g) of dried flowers will substitute for 1¾pt (1 litre) of fresh. Incorporate them into the must exactly as with fresh flowers. (It is customary to measure dried flowers and herbs in ounces and grammes, while fresh flowers are measured in fluid measurements, pints and litres.)

DRIED FRUIT

Can be rehydrated and made into wine, with the same pulp fermentation techniques used for fresh fruit. Dried apricots, peaches and apples are all valuable wine ingredients. In general, one-third of the weight of fresh fruit is required if you use dried fruit. One of the problems of dried fruit is that it may have been treated with steriliser to suppress bacterial action. Wine yeast is usually able to cope with the amount of steriliser which enters the must from this source, but play safe by using a strongly fermenting starter culture.

Dried fruits from the grape – raisins, sultanas, currants or muscatels – are the basic ingredients for giving both body and vinosity to the wine in many old recipes, but these have now been largely replaced by grape concentrate, which tends to give better results, is simpler to use and has a less dominant flavour.

DRIED BERRIES

Dried bilberries, elderberries, rosehips and juniper berries can be bought in wine-making supply stores and this is a convenient way of using them if there are no fresh berries to hand. They seem to be more concentrated in flavour and tannin than other dried fruits, so use one-quarter of the amount recommended for wines using fresh berries. One of the joys of using dried or frozen wine ingredients is that it is possible to cheat the seasons. For instance, it is pleasant to be able to make elderberry wine scented with elderflowers.

DROSOPHILA MELANOGASTER

The vinegar fly or fruit fly, dreaded by wine-makers because it carries the bacteria acetomonas which turn alcohol into acetic acid, or wine into vinegar. The fly is attracted by the sweetness of fermenting wine: even though the concentration of acetifying bacteria in the air may be so small that you can safely leave a batch of wine open for a few minutes, if there are fruit flies about it is unsafe to leave the wine open even for a few seconds. *See* Acetomonas.

DRY WINE

Normally defined as a wine which has a low sugar content and therefore tastes dry to the palate. The sensation of dryness is the result of the dehydration of the mouth by alcohol, but this can be masked by sugar. The absence of sugar is more noticeable in a wine with a high alcohol content. But one drinker with a sweet tooth may find a wine too dry, while another may consider it on the sweet side. For instance, a truly dry sherry as sold and enjoyed in Spain is considered over-dry for most British tastes and impossibly dry for American palates. Broadly speaking, a wine fermented down to a specific gravity of .993 or .994 will be considered dry to the average taste. Above an SG of 1.000 the sweetness will be noticeable, and anything in between can be considered as ranging from medium-dry to medium-sweet.

Excess tannin can make a wine taste dry, but the astringency caused by tannin is rather different from the dryness caused by alcohol without sugar. Balance is very important in the making of a dry wine. If alcohol, acid and tannin are well balanced the wine can acceptably be drier than if the various components have not been balanced properly. *See* Blending.

DUSTBINS

Heavyweight polythene dustbins (garbage cans) are useful fermentation vessels for the home wine-maker wanting to make wine in 5 or 10gal (22.5 or 45 litre) quantities. The bin should have a tight-fitting lid. Read any attached label carefully before buying a bin as some state categorically that the bin is not suitable for brewing.

EAU-DE-VIE

The name commonly given to grape spirit to differentiate brandies such as cognacs and armagnacs from fortifying brandy. Eau-de-vie-de-vin is fortifying brandy distilled from wine. Eau-de-vie-de-lie is fortifying brandy distilled from the lees remaining after the wine has been fermented and racked off. Eau-de-vie-de-marc or marc brandy is fortifying brandy distilled from the used pulp left over from the pressing of the grapes for wine.

EDELFAULE

The German name for *Botrytis cinerea* or noble rot.

EFFERVESCENCE

The liberation of bubbles from a wine containing carbon dioxide: either a sparkling wine or one that has just finished fermenting and still contains some of the gas formed during fermentation.

The bubbling or fizz can be caused either by release of the pressure which has kept the gas in solution (as, for instance, when a bottle of champagne is opened) or by agitation, which causes dissolved particles to coalesce into larger ones and then to escape as bubbles. If a drink is made sparkling by secondary fermentation in the bottle, rather than by carbonation, more of the gas combines with the alcohol, and the resultant bubbles are smaller and can survive for about 20 minutes. *See* Carbonation; Sparkling wine.

EGGS

Eggs can be used in a variety of alcoholic drinks, such as egg-nogs and egg liqueurs. (*See* Liqueurs for a recipe for egg flip.)

Eggs have other uses for the wine-maker. Egg-white, or albumen, is a useful, though old-fashioned, fining agent, particularly for red wine. It reacts with tannin to form an insoluble complex which will precipitate out, taking with it other suspended particles, and making it possible to rack off the clarified wine. It has the extra advantage of reducing astringency, but this is a disadvantage if the wine is already lacking in astringency and will result in a dull wine. Only a very small amount of egg-white is needed to treat a large volume of wine: one egg is enough for 10gal (45 litres). Use dried albumen if possible, as there will be much less risk of using too much.

If egg-shell is cleaned, baked and powdered and then added to wine, it will remove discoloration and aid clarification.

ELDERBERRIES

Probably the favourite wine-making fruit in the United Kingdom, where they are frequently referred to as 'the poor man's grape'. In the nineteenth century elder trees, *Sambucus nigra*, were planted where they are still to be found today, in hedges and copses, to form windbreaks and shelter for livestock, and it was then that their berries began to be particularly valued for wine. They were popular among country people as a substitute for port wine, though elderberry port made according to a nineteenth-century recipe would taste too much like elderberry syrup to please today's more sophisticated palate.

A rather different elder, *Sambucus pubens*, the common elder tree of Scotland, looks like its cousin but produces white berries. These can be used for making a pale golden wine but, like the purple berries, they have a high tannin content and therefore give a result which is unexpectedly astringent for a white wine. The white elder's berries ripen very early, sometimes as soon as July, when the more common elder has only just finished flowering.

The purple-black berries grow to their full size by the end of August and begin to ripen. By the time the last berries in the bunch are beginning to lose their green colour, most of the rest are suitable for making wine, but if more than two or three berries in the bunch are still green leave the clump alone. September and early October are normally the prime elderberry-picking times, but this obviously varies according to geography, climate and the summer weather. If the berries are left on the tree for a few weeks after they have turned black they become softer, less acidic, sweeter and have a lower tannin content.

Tannin is the most prominent component of the elderberry, though this is slightly lower after a good summer. In fact the elderberry is the only fruit, with the exception of the sloe, which yields as much tannin as the grape. Much of this, especially if extracted with hot water, will be precipitated during fermentation.

Most recipes for elderberry wine call for the addition of acid but this needs to be treated with caution; newly ripened elderberries already have a high acid content. However, as the ripening process continues the acidity falls, so berries picked at the end of their season may well need a little extra acid in the must to create a balanced wine.

Elderberries also contain a good supply of vitamins to keep the yeast working happily, and this may be another reason for the popularity of the elderberry before the days when you could buy convenient packets of yeast nutrient.

Stripping the berries from the bunch to prepare them for the must can be a tedious business; the usual method is to pull the stems through the prongs of a fork so that the fruit drops into the bowl, leaving the greenery in the hand. Alternatively, the must can be prepared by pulp fermentation without meticulously separating the berries from the stalks, but this involves the danger of extracting unwanted materials from the woody parts of the stem. The juice can be drawn from the berries by cold water extraction, by hot water infusion, or by pulp fermentation. Simmering is not recommended.

A wine made from elderberries alone tends to be strongly coloured, attractively scented, richly flavoured and astringent. This is not to everyone's taste and elderberry wines are often used for blending purposes. Alternatively, elderberries can be used with another fruit, such as apples or greengages, to make a good table wine. As little as 10 per cent of elderberries is sufficient to give a predominantly elderberry flavour to almost any wine. One combination which does seem to produce more than the sum of its parts is elderberry and rosehip wine. There is only a short period when you can gather both fresh rosehips and fresh elderberries, since the former are at their best after the first frost, but this problem can be surmounted by freezing the elderberries once gathered, or by using dried fruits, or by combining fresh elderberries with dried rosehips or rosehip syrup.

Pure elderberry wine can make the basis of an excellent hot winter punch. Put 2½ cups of wine into a saucepan with 1 cup of cold water, the juice and thinly peeled rind of 1 lemon, ½ cup of brown sugar, and cloves, cinnamon and ginger to taste. Bring the mixture slowly to boiling point, but do not allow it to boil, then let it infuse for 5 minutes before serving.

The elderberry and its flower are so important to home wine-makers that they now have their own book: *Winemaking with Elderberries* by T. E. Belt (Amateur Winemaker Publications, 1982).

ELDERFLOWERS

Blossoming from May into July, they make the queen of the flower wines, just as elderberries make the king of the country fruit wines. Every head of elderflowers cut is a bunch of berries lost, but so few flowers are needed for the wine that one can afford to take a few blossoms in the spring without fear of robbing the purple fruit of the autumn. Besides being a basic recipe ingredient for a delicate white wine, elderflowers are used to add bouquet to white wines, and many red ones too; to enhance a homemade Sauternes; to make a simple cordial; to create a sparkling wine which is one of the more successful country 'champagnes'; and to perfume a liqueur.

A noted drawback of the elderflower is that it sometimes has a smell which competes with the flowery fragrance: an odour of tom-cats! Various attempts have been made to identify which particular flowers or what conditions create this objectionable smell and it now seems probable that it is produced by the blossom of a sub-species growing in a specific soil condition. Certainly the small white flowerheads, growing sparsely, are much safer to use than the huge creamy blossoms which grow in abundance and look so perfect. In the event, only experience can be trusted: find out for yourself which trees to use in the locality. It is a wise precaution anyway to keep the quantity of flowers down; a volume of blossoms equal to one-tenth of the volume of wine to be made would be suitable.

The only part of the flowerhead that is needed for wine-making is the floret. The sprigs connecting them contribute nothing, but it is a tedious task removing them. However, the larger green stalks can introduce a bitterness to the wine so they must be cut away. The best way to collect elderflowers is to approach the bunches with a pair of scissors and to cut them so that the sprigs fall directly into a bucket, the flowerheads being left on the tree. In this way the time spent actually gathering the blossoms is greater but the total preparation time is reduced. Ten to twelve elderflower heads yield about 3½pt (2 litres) of florets. About a quarter of this will create 1gal (4.5 litres) of wine in which elderflower predominates clearly. Use pulp fermentation to prepare the flowers, as boiling may evaporate their delicate fragrance. Do not add them to the must too soon, or their fragrance will be lost in the carbon dioxide given off in the first vigorous fermentation. Only after the first few days, when the initial ferment has subsided and there is sufficient alcohol present to extract their scent, should they be immersed in the liquid, in a muslin bag weighted down with a marble to prevent them floating to the surface.

Just as elderberries are often improved by being combined in the recipe with other fruits, so elderflowers make excellent blends, especially with rose petals. Again, the sum adds up to more than the total of the two parts. The combination of elderflower and rose petal is unbeatable as a bouquet-enhancing ingredient.

ENAMELWARE

It is safe to boil wine-making ingredients in enamel pans if they are thoroughly sound and the underlying iron is completely sealed off.

Not the slightest chip, crack or other damage is permissible.

ENZYMES

Organic catalysts which cause chemical transformations of materials in plants or animals. For instance, fermentation is the result of the action of enzymes in yeast upon sugar, turning it into alcohol and carbon dioxide.

Enzymes are affected by heat. They are destroyed by boiling and put out of action by freezing, and each one has a temperature at which it works most effectively. Yeast ferments most satisfactorily at 70°F (21°C) and this is the reason why a fermenting liquid should never be allowed to become too warm (in which case the yeast might be killed off) or too cold (in which case it might stop working and produce a stuck fermentation). Apart from yeast enzymes, those which are of particular interest to the wine-maker are oxidative enzymes, pectin-destroying enzymes and starch-destroying enzymes.

EPSOM SALTS

The common name for magnesium sulphate crystals or magnesium salts.

EQUIPMENT

Equipment for wine-making can be costly, complicated and space-consuming and this often deters beginners from taking the skill very seriously. They take fright almost before they have made a proper start, baffled by talk of hydrometers, burettes, fermentation cabinets, steam extractors and so forth. The fact is that a starter kit can be put together, or bought already assembled, for a very small financial outlay. After using that, home wine-makers can decide whether they wish to limit their output, and equipment, to a basic level or whether they want to add more expensive items gradually as they become more experienced and ambitious, and wine-making becomes both a hobby and a joy. To begin, all that is needed is: a 1gal (4.5 litres) glass demi-john; a small funnel; a siphon and U-tube; sterilising agent; a bung and air-lock; wine bottles; corks or stoppers; grape concentrate, sugar, yeast and any additives listed in the recipe being used.

ESSENCES

Various essences are commercially available to incorporate into vodka or Polish spirit to create liqueurs which are comparable to those one

Basic starter kit

can buy. A good range of essences is produced by T. Noirot. These include extracts of cherry brandy, apricot or peach brandy, curaçao, mint and so on. Amateur Winemaker Publications produces a useful book called *Making Inexpensive Liqueurs* by R. Bellis (1976), which includes details about the use of essences in liqueur-making.

ESTERS

Formed by a combination of an alcohol with an acid. They are extremely important in the wine-making process since their sweet aroma is responsible for most of the flavour of a wine. Esters obtained from the ingredients used in wine are volatile and therefore can be lost through boiling. Consequently, it is important to avoid boiling flavour ingredients whenever possible. Flowers, in particular, must never be boiled since their most important constituent, their fragrance, will be driven off.

Other esters in wine are produced by the chemical changes that occur during fermentation, and especially during maturation. Time is essential for the development of fine flavour and bouquet, and wine should be kept for at least a year, if possible, before drinking unless it has been made from a special express kit or recipe.

Succinic acid aids ester formation during maturation. It is available commercially, and it is a good idea to add a small amount to each gallon after the last racking and before maturation, provided that you are prepared to leave the new wine long enough for chemical changes

88

to take place. Otherwise it is a waste of time and money, since the acid itself cannot create any improvement: it results from acid *plus* time.

ESTUFA

The room used to heat Madeira, at a temperature between 90° and 140°F (32° and 60°C), for several months of maturation after fermentation. The estufa's temperature is carefully controlled so that the wine becomes warmer very gradually until it reaches the required heat, and then cools down again at the same slow rate. The better-quality Madeiras are heated for a long time, up to a year, at a lowish temperature. The cheaper ones may only be heated for about three months, at a higher temperature. It is the period spent in the estufa which gives Madeira its characteristic flavour and bouquet by caramelising some of its residual sugar.

ETHYL ALCOHOL *see* Alcohol.

EXOTIC FRUITS

Country-wine makers have long been accustomed to making wine from elderberries, gooseberries, apples, damsons and so on, but now there are many exotic fruits to add to the list of possible ingredients. They are available in many forms – fresh, tinned, bottled or dried, as juice, or even as jam or jelly which can be turned into wine. Exotic fruits are expensive to buy fresh and often have a short season. However, if there is a large supermarket near you, or a good street market, it is sometimes possible to pick up bargains at the end of the day's trading. The produce must not be bruised or over-ripe, or the quality of the wine will suffer.

Unusual fruits which make good wine include members of the citrus family, such as citrons, pomelos, and especially the excellent ugli fruit; guavas and kumquats, probably in jars; tinned lychees; mangoes; maple (syrup) and coconut (milk); juiced passion fruit or granadilla; tinned pawpaws; persimmons and pomegranates; and tamarind pulp. The acknowledged expert on making wine from exotic fruits is National Guild judge Roy Ekins, and his entertaining and informative book, *Worldwide Winemaking Recipes* (Amateur Wine-maker, 1978), should be consulted by anyone particularly interested in this type of wine-making.

EXPRESS WINE

It is now possible to make palatable wine very quickly as a result of advances in the scientific culture of strains of yeast, the availability of grape concentrates and improved types of finings – and the growth of demand for home wine-making kits – so that money has been poured into scientific research into ways of improving them. Express wine kits include two-to-three-week table wines and five-week aperitifs and dessert wines. The kits use carefully calculated blends of juices and a special yeast strain which ensures rapid fermentation, then settles rapidly when fermentation has ceased. Selected fining agents clear the wine brilliantly within two days, sometimes overnight.

Express wines are supposed to be drinkable as soon as they have fermented and cleared and they should not need maturing: but many of them, if not most, improve with some keeping. No improvement is likely, however, after a six-month wait. If the home wine-maker is prepared to store his or her wine for this length of time, however, there is nothing to be gained from using an express kit.

Many wine-making books also contain special recipes for 'instant wine' that is not created from a kit. If speed is important, see *Express Winemaking* by R. Bellis (Amateur Winemaker Publications, 1979).

EXTRACTION

The removal of the components required for the must from the fruits, flowers, vegetables, leaves, sap or whatever you are using as the starting material or raw ingredients of the wine. There are many forms of extraction. Crushing or pressing expresses the juice from fruit or vegetables. Boiling, infusion or soaking (cold extraction) leaches out the required ingredients into water. Pulp fermentation leaches them out into alcohol. Steaming uses the power of steam to break down fruit in order to extract juice. *See* Colour extraction.

FEEDING THE YEAST *see* Yeast.

FEHLING'S SOLUTION

A mixture of two chemicals or reagents. It has a blue colouring, but when it reacts with certain sugars it turns red. The amount of solution needed to produce the colour change gives an estimate of the sugar content of a wine. Fehling's Solution is 'reduced' by the sugar, reduction being used here in its chemical sense of the removal of oxygen; consequently sugars that react to the solution are called 'reducing sugars'. Glucose, fructose and maltose are all reducing sugars, but sucrose is not. Therefore, if a wine has been sweetened with sucrose, several weeks have to pass, during which time the sucrose is converted to fructose and glucose, before its sugar concentration can be measured. Fehling's Solution has now been largely superseded by proprietary products, available in wine-making supply stores.

FENNEL

A fragrant herb, the leaves of which are used both for cooking and wine-making. When making wine they should be infused, and the infusion can then be added to liquidised sultanas or grape concentrate to make the basis of a must for a medium social wine.

FERMENTATION

The breaking down of sugar by yeast to form alcohol and carbon dioxide: the essential central activity of the wine-making process, upon which all else depends. In chemical terms, $C_6H_{12}O_6$ (sugar) is fermented to become $2C_2H_5OH$ (ethyl alcohol) plus $2CO_2$ (carbon dioxide).

Aerobic (or Primary) Fermentation

When yeast ferments in the presence of air – ie in aerobic conditions – it produces large quantities of carbon dioxide and practically no alcohol. When the air supply is cut off and all the oxygen is dissolved in the must, the yeast ferments more slowly. In this anaerobic condition, it produces equal amounts of carbon dioxide and alcohol. These two stages of fermentation are called aerobic, or primary, fermentation, and anaerobic, or secondary, fermentation.

Aerobic fermentation is only desirable for as long as it takes to establish an active yeast colony. This will be clearly visible by the large crop of bubbles produced. During this period of aeration of the must the fermenting vessel, whether plastic bucket or glass jar, should be loosely covered with cloth, polythene or cotton wool, and left in a warm place – about 70°F (21°C) – for a few days. Take care not to overdo the heat for the yeast cells will be destroyed if the temperature exceeds 80°F (26.7°C).

Aerobic fermentation should last for about five days. If it is allowed to continue too long there will be a danger of infection infiltrating the liquid. During this process a cap of fruit pulp, or pulp of other vegetable matter, may form on the surface of the must. This should be broken up and stirred into the must about twice a day so that the maximum flavour and colour can be extracted from it, and so that the surface is prevented from becoming an active breeding ground for bacteria.

After aerobic fermentation, when the yeast activity has begun to slow down, the pulp should be strained off and the liquid transferred to a sterile fermenting vessel for anaerobic fermentation to commence. If juice is being fermented rather than pulp, no straining is necessary. The covering should be removed from the fermenting vessel, a cork and air-lock fitted and the temperature reduced to about 60°F (15.5°C).

Anaerobic (or Secondary) Fermentation

When aerobic (or primary) fermentation has finished and a healthy colony of active yeast cells has been established through the contact of the yeast with oxygen, the secondary stage of fermentation is carried out in the absence of air, and is therefore called 'anaerobic'. When it is deprived of air, yeast continues to flourish, though at a slower rate, and produces alcohol. Gradually, as the alcohol content increases, the yeast cells are killed off since they have only a limited tolerance of alcohol. When the yeast cells die fermentation ceases, and the fermented liquid has become wine.

Anaerobic fermentation lasts much longer than aerobic fermentation; it may go on for weeks or even months. Air is kept out of the fermenting vessel by the layer of carbon dioxide which forms above the must as a result of the chemical reaction which has taken place between the yeast and the oxygen. At this stage it is important (a) to allow excess carbon dioxide to escape, and (b) to keep out bacteria and insects which could cause spoilage. The fermenting jar should be fitted with an air-lock containing sulphite solution.

The best temperature for anaerobic fermentation is lower than that for aerobic fermentation: a *stable* level of about 60°F (15.5°C) is ideal. If the temperature is higher, fermentation will be too fast and the quality of the wine poor. If it is lower, the fermentation might 'stick' before the yeast has fermented out, with the result that the wine will be high in sugar and low in alcohol. Agitate the jar once a day so that the whole of the must is affected by the action of the yeast, which is not allowed to immerse itself in a layer of pulp sediment which would prevent it from being fully active. (*See* Stuck Fermentation, below).

The continuance of fermentation can be seen by the occasional bubbles of gas that rise through the air-lock. When fermentation has ceased, the wine should be left to settle for about 24 hours and then racked off, ready for the maturation process. Racking off is important not only to clarify the wine but also to make sure there are no yeast cells left which might cause re-fermentation.

Juice Fermentation

The fermentation of an extract after the pulp has been removed. It is particularly suitable for very soft fruits, for very hard fruits such as apples and pears, for citrus fruits and for the production of delicate wines, particularly white table wine and sparkling wine.

Juice can be extracted from fruit by hand pressing, but this is a very laborious process. If you make a lot of wine, an electrical juice extractor can be a good investment. A wine-making circle might buy one as a piece of communal equipment. Many extractors are advertised in wine-making magazines, but the way to find the one best suited to your needs is to study the full range available in a large wine-making supply store and get professional advice from a member of staff. Wine-making shops are largely staffed by wine-making enthusiasts whose advice is generally helpful and well-informed.

Freshly extracted juice should be treated immediately with sulphite to prevent discoloration and to inhibit the growth of bacteria. It should then be transferred to a sealed container and left undisturbed for 24 hours in a cool place. This serves a double function. First it gives the sulphite time to lose its inhibiting effect on the action of the yeast; secondly, it allows most of the pulp particles to form a sediment, allowing the cleared juice to be racked off before it is added to the must.

Malo-lactic Fermentation
The result of an infection, but often there are happy consequences. It is caused by lactic-acid bacteria and occurs most frequently in wines based on fruit with a high malic-acid content, such as gooseberries, apples and peaches. However, it can also develop in wines to which malic acid has been added, either on its own or as part of the acid mixture.

The bacteria act upon the malic acid to convert it into lactic acid and carbon dioxide; the wine becomes less acidic but also develops a sparkle. In a dry wine this usually improves the quality, and it is the easiest way of creating sparkling wine. In a sweet wine, however, the results are not so fortunate, since the bacteria work on the sugar in such a way that byproducts and attendant off-flavours develop. This can be cured if the wine is sulphited at an early stage with 100ppm of sulphite.

Sparkling dry wine with malo-lactic fermentation should be racked into clean, unsulphited bottles and sealed with wired corks or crown caps to avoid explosions. Do not store it for too long or the acidity will be reduced to such a level that the wine will lose its flavour.

Primary Fermentation see Fermentation, aerobic (above).

Pulp Fermentation
Pulp fermentation is a good method of extracting colour and flavour

from dried fruit, dark red fruit, berries, fruits with stones, and for the production of a full-bodied red wine. It works so effectively because the red colouring in the skins of fruit is soluble in alcohol, but rarely in water. In the initial stages of fermentation, as the yeast is beginning to create alcohol, the colour is leached out of the fruit pulp; when a satisfactory depth of colour has been reached the pulp can be strained off, pressed and then discarded.

The technique of pulp fermentation requires some care but is not difficult. The fruit should first be stoned and crushed; the skins must be broken, otherwise juice will be extracted very slowly. Next, put the fruit into a wide-necked container, cover it with water, sulphite to prevent infection, cover it and leave to stand in a cool place for 24 hours. The preparation of the must can then continue as usual with the addition of sugar, yeast, nutrients and so on. When active fermentation has begun, the carbon dioxide will force the fruit pulp to the surface, where it will form a cap. This cap must be broken up and dispersed throughout the must at least twice a day if possible.

When the must has taken on sufficient colour (bear in mind that if water is to be added later the colour will become paler), the pulp can be disposed of. The colouring process cannot be timed precisely: it has to be seen. Some fruits will produce sufficient colour in 12–24 hours; others will need up to a week. It is important, however, never to leave the pulp fermenting longer than necessary or too much tannin will be absorbed from the skins and the wine will become harsh and over-astringent, and will require a long period of maturation and perhaps blending as well before it is acceptable. *See* Colour extraction.

Secondary Fermentation *see* Fermentation, anaerobic (above).

Stuck Fermentation
Practically every wine-maker knows the frustration of seeing a must stop fermenting prematurely, that is before sufficient of its sugar has been transformed into alcohol to produce a good wine. Technically, a wine which maintains a specific gravity of more than 1.025 for a fortnight or longer can be said to be a stuck fermentation.

Several factors can cause this irritating problem.

1. Inadequate temperature control. If the temperature of the fermenting area is higher than 80°F (26.7°C) the heat may kill off the yeast cells. If the temperature drops to below 50°F (10°C) the yeast may cease being active, though this may be only a temporary phase and fermentation could restart once the warmth becomes more conducive to yeast-cell activity. In other words, it is less dangerous for the fermentation to get too cold than too hot, though either should be avoided.

2. Inadequate yeast starter. If the yeast is of poor quality or has not been properly stored, or if (as is more likely) it contains insufficient nutrients, it may not be strong enough to maintain fermentation. Wine-makers should ensure that they either use special yeast formulae which incorporate the required nutrients or make up their own nutritious starter bottle.

3. Excessive sugar. The original must should never have a specific gravity of more than 1.120. Sugar syrup should be added only when the SG has dropped to 1.005, and when yeast activity slows down it should be added carefully in small quantities: if the yeast is reaching the limits of its alcohol tolerance it will not be able to cope with more sugar.

4. Excessive sulphite. The addition of more than one Campden tablet or more than one teaspoonful of sulphite solution to each gallon (4.5 litres) of the original must will inhibit or stop fermentation.

It is not easy to 'unstick' a stuck fermentation, but there are methods to try:

1. Aerate it by pouring it from one jar to another several times so that it can absorb plenty of oxygen.

2. Add nutrient: a little yeast energiser plus a vitamin B_1 tablet and one teaspoonful of yeast nutrient may be effective.

3. Change its temperature. If fermentation has stopped because of over-heating, it is probable that the yeast cells have been killed off. However, a few live ones may remain and might be triggered into activity again if the must is transferred to a cooler place. If the yeast cells have become dormant through being too cold, moving the fermenting vessel to a warmer place may be enough to re-start fermentation.

4. Dilute it. The addition of water will cope with the problem of excess sugar and give the yeast a chance to start work again.

5. Blend it. The addition of another strongly fermenting wine of a similar type may re-energise the yeast.

6. Use the 'doubling-up' method, which is more complicated, but more likely to be successful. First, make up a fresh starter bottle. Then, using a hydrometer, test the specific gravity of the must. If it is suffering from too high a concentration of sugar, reduce the SG to 1.080 or less by adding a similar sugar-free must or water. Add fresh nutrients, then aerate, either by stirring vigorously or by pouring from jar to jar. Then add 1pt (575ml) of the stuck must to the yeast starter, cover closely and store at a temperature of 75°F (24°C) until it begins to ferment energetically. Add another pint of must, wait for fermentation, and go on repeating this procedure until ½gal (2.25 litres) is fermenting vigorously. Finally, mix the fermenting must with the remaining half-gallon of stuck fermentation. By that time the

whole quantity, with luck, could be active again and fermenting healthily. *See* Yeast starter.

FERMENTATION HEATERS

It is important to keep the must at an appropriate and *stable* temperature during fermentation: about 70°F (21°C) for aerobic fermentation and 60°F (15.5°C) for anaerobic. It is sometimes possible

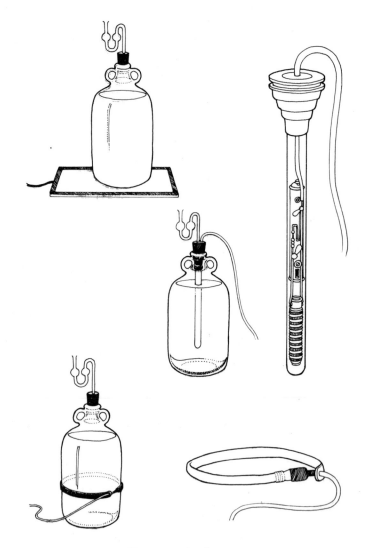

Fermentation heaters

to do this in a warm corner of the house: a shelf near a stove or radiator, an airing cupboard or beside the central-heating boiler. But with timed central heating which switches itself off during the day, and with carefully insulated hot-water tanks which keep the heat in instead of throwing it out, this can be difficult. Often during summer, when there is no constant source of heat in the house, it is impossible to find the right place for fermenting vessels.

However, there are now several types of thermostatically controlled electric fermentation heaters available. They include: immersion heaters, which are inserted into the must; fermenting trays, which range from the single demi-john size to one big enough to take six demi-johns; and heating belts which fit around the outside of a single demi-john. Most of these are reliable and safe, and they consume little electricity so are economical to use, although the initial expense is quite high.

It is also possible to buy 'black heat' space heaters that give heat without light, such as the Frostaway or Warmaway, and fit into a spare cupboard to give a constant source of heat. Again, running costs are low provided that the cupboard is well insulated, the door-surround fitted with draught-excluder and the door kept firmly closed. Many wine-makers use electric light bulbs to heat their fermenting cupboards, and this is a good idea provided that red wines are carefully protected from the light, preferably in amber-coloured demi-johns.

For those who are short of cupboard space, it may be necessary to make a special shelved fermentation chamber fitted with thermostat and heater or electric lamps, and designed to hold up to eight demi-johns at a time, depending upon output. Most do-it-yourself craftsmen will find this task quite straightforward, but *Woodwork for Winemakers* by C. J. Dart and D. A. Smith (published by Amateur Winemaker, 1971) gives a precise cutting list and construction details.

FERMENTATION LOCK *see* Air-lock.

FIGS

A basic flavour ingredient, particularly useful to the wine-maker in the creation of rich, dark, oloroso-type sherries; often combined with sherry-type concentrate and a sherry yeast. Bananas give the extra body required. Figs can also be mixed with tropical fruit cordial to make a sweet social wine, and are an excellent additive to anything that needs extra character, especially rosehips and cereals. The usual method of preparation is to mince or liquidise them and then to make an infusion with boiling water.

FILM YEAST *see* Yeast.

FILTRATION

Needed in wine-making to separate juice from pulp, and to clarify fermented wine of hazes, bacteria or yeast cells. Coarse filtration through a mesh cloth, bag or sieve is also called straining. Any finely woven cloth free of dye or starch is suitable for this, but polyester nylon is best since its fibres do not absorb liquid and it is easy to keep clean. Fine filtration can be carried out with a filter paper inside a funnel, but it is so slow that there is a high risk of severe oxidation of the wine. It is better to use a proprietary continuous wine filter. Filter systems on the market now are almost as effective as those used commercially. Some use exactly the same process of pushing wine through filter pads by air pressure. This method will clarify wines of all sorts, including those suffering from a protein haze. Different filter systems tend to use different filtration media, but asbestos has now been largely superseded by cellulose and silicon for health reasons.

Filtration is a controversial subject and many wine-makers argue that it causes a deterioration in the quality of wines, especially delicate ones, mainly due to oxidation and 'bottle sickness', and that top-quality wines should not be filtered except as a desperate measure. If clarification does not occur naturally it should be attempted by fining rather than filtering.

Filter-pad Flavour
When wine has been filtered mechanically through a filter powder or pulp it sometimes takes on an off-flavour. This usually disappears after maturation.

Filter Papers
Used, in conjunction with an open funnel, to clarify wine, but this method is not recommended. The rate of filtration is so slow that the wine will almost certainly become oxidised. Many better methods of filtering are now available.

Vacuum Filtration
A method of fast filtering to clarify hazy wines. It involves the use of a special filter funnel called a Buchner funnel which contains a filtration pad. This is connected to the domestic water supply which operates a water pump. A vacuum is then created and wine is sucked down through the pad. Owing to the speed of this operation it does not always remove the haze completely the first time and filtering has to be repeated, occasionally more than once.

98

FINING

The process of adding substances to wine in order to clarify a haze. It is not known exactly how a fining agent acts on the suspended particles which are clouding the wine, but it seems that the precipitate created by the agent has a positive electric charge, the other suspended matter a negative charge, and the two are consequently attracted together and then settle out, leaving a bright, clear wine.

In the past many agents have been used for fining: animal (such as egg-white, ox-blood, casein or milk, gelatine and isinglass), vegetable (such as alkalines) and mineral (such as bentonite and kaolin). Some of these are still used commercially but today most amateur wine-makers choose either bentonite or one of the proprietary wine finings to be found in wine-making supply stores because many of the traditional remedies can cause other complications. There is a great number of proprietary finings to choose from; some are better than others, some more expensive, but none is ideal. Practically all of them upset the chemical balance and the flavour of the wine by destroying its tannin content which has to be replaced by tea, tannic acid or grape tannin. The other danger is that if too much of the fining agent is used it might not do its work anyway and the wine will remain cloudy.

If all goes well, a properly composed and fermented wine should clear itself during maturation. If it does not clear, fining is the best method of clarification. If fining fails, the wine-maker may have to resort to filtration. *See* Filtration; Hazes.

FLATNESS

A vague descriptive term which means different things to different people. For instance, a flat wine can be defined as one that is under-acidic, lacking in tannin, low in alcohol or past its prime.

FLAVOUR

The most important quality of a wine, though bouquet runs it a very close second. Different types of wine should have different sorts of flavours. The flavour of a table wine should be restrained so that it does not dominate the food, but dessert wines can be more strongly flavoured than those chosen for the main course.

Social wines, often drunk without the accompaniment of food to enliven a convivial occasion, can be as powerfully flavoured as you wish, and it is in this range that ingredients like raspberries, pineapples, strawberries, rosehips and blackcurrants come into their own. Elderberry wine, considered by many too strong and fruity for the table, is an ideal social wine.

Aperitifs need a flavour that refreshes and cleanses the palate with a zesty tang, rather than one that leaves a distinctive taste which may counteract the taste of the food that is about to be eaten. Aperitifs frequently use the sharpness of citrus fruits and herbs to achieve the desired piquancy. *See* Blending – ingredients.

FLOCCULATE OR FLOCCULANT

Meaning 'composed of hair-like tufts', it describes the sort of consistency that is created in a wine when tannin combines with gelatine before forming a deposit, or the sort of condition that is encountered when a wine suffering from a pectin haze is mixed with methylated spirits as a method of testing.

FLOGGER

The simplest type of corker, just a shaped piece of flat wood with which corks can be beaten flush into the neck of the bottle for a perfect seal. It works on exactly the same principle as a wooden mallet which can be used as an alternative. Floggers and mallets can, however, cause breakages, or even physical injury, and today the commonest form of corking device is a wooden or plastic hand-corker which works on the plunge system.

FLOR *see* Sherry flor.

FLOWERS

Fresh or dried, these are valuable in wine-making primarily as a bouquet ingredient, but they can also impart a delicate flavour. On their own they lack nutrients and vinous quality, but they make a very desirable additive. The deeply coloured ones, like red roses, have the added advantage of heightening the final colour of a red wine.

Flowers of particular value are those that are strongly scented. The most prized include elderflowers, roses, white and pink hawthorn blossom, honeysuckle, especially the wild variety, white and pink clover and greater burnet. There is another group of flowers which are not exceptionally fragrant and yet still make excellent wine: they include coltsfoot, dandelion, gorse and broom. Strangely, all these yellow flowers have drawbacks. Coltsfoot and dandelion can impart a very bitter flavour to the wine unless every bit of greenery is removed, and this can be an exacting business. Gorse is tricky to gather because of the prickliness of the bush, and drinking wine made from either gorse or broom can cause an allergic reaction in some people. For this reason, it is wise to restrict the volume of flowers used to a maximum of 3–4pt (1.75–2.25 litres) per gallon (4.5 litres).

Primroses and cowslips, once staple fare for the country-wine maker, are now increasingly omitted from books of recipes because they have become so scarce that they should not be picked – especially not in the quantities that wine-making would require. Conservationists are rightly fighting a sturdy battle to discourage people from picking them. The keen gardener with enough ground and suitable conditions can buy seeds and grow his own; more practically, many wine-making supply stores sell the dried flowers.

A useful way of having a constant supply of flowers without having to rely on dried ones (which do not generally give such pleasing results) is to make a strong infusion of fresh flowers when they are in season and then to store the liquid, after it has been strained and sulphited, in a freezer until required.

Fresh flowers should be gathered on a dry sunny day after the dew has dried, when they are quite open, though not over-blown, and warmed through. Leaves and greenery should be discarded and the flowerheads washed in half a gallon (2.25 litres) of water sterilised with a crushed Campden tablet, then rinsed thoroughly before use.

Dried flowers are used in the same way as fresh ones, though in much smaller proportions. They should be added to the must in a muslin or nylon bag after the first vigour of the initial fermentation has died down, and left submerged for up to five days. The bag should be squeezed against the side of the fermenting vessel at regular intervals with a clean sterile spatula in order to release as much of the flower juices as possible.

The must of a good flower wine, rich in flavour, bouquet, body and vinosity, should include neutrally flavoured white grape concentrate; vitamin-enriched yeast nutrient; grape tannin; honey; white wine yeast starter; and acid mixture. As well as making flower wines, flowers are used to enhance the bouquet of many other wines and can even add a special quality to wine made from a basic kit. *See* Blending – ingredients.

FLOWERS OF WINE *see* Infections.

FORTIFICATION

The only legal and safe method by which amateur wine-makers can add to the alcohol content of their wines. Home distillation is illegal without a licence, difficult and also extremely unsafe. Fortification is one of the processes by which fortified wines such as port, sherry, Madeira and champagne are created. For these, fortifying brandy or eau-de-vie is used. For liqueurs, Polish spirit or vodka, as well as brandy, are used.

Table wines normally have an alcohol content of between 8 and 15 per cent. Distilled spirit can have as high an alcohol content as 95 per cent. Fortified wines (normally drunk as aperitifs or as after-dinner wines) are likely to have an alcohol content of more than 17 per cent.

Since distilled spirits are very expensive to buy, the home wine-maker should consider carefully whether a wine is really worth fortifying. Has it, before fortification, an alcohol content of at least 15 per cent? (To save expense the highest possible yield of alcohol should be reached by fermentation and careful feeding of the yeast, first of all.) Is it a good wine in its own right? Will it be noticeably improved upon by the addition of spirit? If in doubt, fortify one bottle and leave a control bottle unfortified. Both bottles should be given a few months in which to mature, then tasted and tested. If the fortified wine is noticeably superior, the expense of fortification is justified.

Distilled spirit for fortification should have a neutral taste so that it does not affect the flavour and bouquet of the wine. There is no need to go for a high-quality, high-priced spirit; look for one which provides the most alcohol and least taste for the lowest cost. When the appropriate wine is selected, and a suitable fortification agent chosen, all that remains is to calculate the proportions in which they should be combined. This can be done by using the Pearson Square. *See* Pearson Square.

Fortifying Brandy

This is distilled spirit. Much of it is produced by the distillation of wines, and the result is commonly known as eau-de-vie-de-vin. Wine used for this purpose may have been fermented specifically for distilling, or its quality may be too poor to be used either as a drinking wine on its own or for blending. Another form of fortifying brandy, eau-de-vie-de-lie, is made from the lees and rackings left over from the wine-making process. Fortifying brandy can also be produced from the used pulp or 'marc' which remains after the grapes have been pressed. The spent pulp is mixed with water, allowed to ferment and then distilled, and the result is called eau-de-vie-de-marc or marc brandy. Marc brandy can be quite good if it is carefully distilled and matured, and it is often sold as a cheap alternative to cognac rather than purely for purposes of fortification.

Depending upon the method of distillation, some fortifying brandies are neutral to the palate while others have quite a strong taste and can affect the bouquet and flavour of the fortified wine for which they are being used. This must be considered beforehand; you must decide whether you want to enhance your wine or simply to add to its alcoholic strength. Though it is normally considered wise to choose a spirit which will not affect the finished taste, it is possible to improve the quality of a port-type wine by choosing a brandy with a flavour that complements it.

FREEZING

Frozen fruit or fruit juice is perfectly acceptable in wine-making provided it is allowed to thaw before being added to the must. Freezing also allows some exciting combinations of wine-making ingredients that used to be impossible unless tinned or dried fruit was used. For instance, it is possible to combine frozen gooseberries with later fruits such as blackberries, to create a good rosé wine, and frozen elderberries mix deliciously with freshly picked elderflowers. It is also a good idea to infuse fresh flowers when they are at their best and then freeze the liquor until late summer or early autumn, when the complementary fruits are ripe.

The techniques of freezing can also be applied to distillation and the production of sparkling wine. *See* Distillation; Sparkling wine.

FRENCH BEANS *see* Beans.

FRIZZANTE

The Italian word for 'sparkling' used to describe wine.

FROZEN FRUIT *see* Freezing.

FRUCTOSE

'Fruit sugar' is a monosaccharide, one molecule of which combines with one molecule of glucose to form the disaccharide, sucrose. Fructose and glucose are the result of the work of the enzyme invertase on sucrose. They in turn are converted by another enzyme, zymase, into ethyl alcohol and carbon dioxide. Either fructose or glucose is usually the residual sugar in wine.

FRUIT

The most common main ingredient of wine, though country wines can also depend upon grains, vegetables, flowers, leaves and sap. Fruit can be used fresh, canned, dried, frozen or reduced to juice or concentrate. It gives both body and flavour and enhances bouquet. The grape, fresh or dried, also imparts vinosity.

Any type of fruit, provided that it is non-toxic, can be used to make wine, either on its own or blended with other ingredients. The grape is the best and the most used, but other useful and popular fruits are elderberries, peaches, apples, bilberries, gooseberries, apricots, bananas, blackberries, cherries, damsons, pears, raspberries and roseships.

Fruit is normally incorporated into the must after being extracted as juice (particularly recommended for white or sparkling wines); chopped and/or pulped and pressed for pulp fermentation (the normal method for red wine); or pre-cooked, a process that should only be resorted to when the other two methods are not adequate as, for instance, with bananas or dried fruits.

FRUIT FLY

Also known as the 'vinegar fly', its official name is *Drosophila melanogaster*. Though harmless in itself it is every wine-maker's enemy since it carries disease to wines, spreads infection and is irresistibly attracted to fermenting musts and any wine splashes or spills. The only way to prevent the immense damage it can do is to be scrupulously clean throughout all the processes of wine-making, taking special care with the sterilisation of equipment.

FRUIT JUICE

Already prepared and commercially available in bottles, jars, cans, plasticised packs or frozen, fruit juice is a useful way of incorporating fruit into a must. It can save hours of pressing, crushing, juice extraction or pulping. More economical to buy than canned or bottled fruit, fruit juice is sometimes cheaper even than fresh fruit.

The best-value fruit juices are usually pineapple, grapefruit and orange, as they are produced in large quantities; but wine-making supply stores can also provide elderberry, blackberry and rosehip juices and purées, as well as concentrated apple juice, blackcurrant juice and, of course, the invaluable grape concentrate. There is also an interesting range of compounds, linking grape juice and other concentrated fruit juices in such combinations as grape and strawberry, grape and gooseberry, grape and raspberry and so on – worth trying for a well-flavoured, country-style social wine.

FUCHSIA

The berries of the fuchsia can be made into wine. Freeze them as they ripen, until about 4lb (1.75kg) are available to make 1gal (4.5 litres); or, as not many gardens will yield enough, either collect some berries from helpful friends, or use only one-sixth of the recommended quantities to make just one trial bottle. Alternatively, part of the required fruit can be replaced by the appropriate amount of grape concentrate. The best type of fuchsia to use is *Procumbens*, since it has the largest berries, but any species will do, and the end product should be a light dry wine.

Recipe and method: Pour over 4lb (1.75kg) of berries 4pt (2.25 litres) of boiling water, and crush thoroughly; then leave to soak for two days. Add to the berry and water mixture 2lb (900g) of sugar in the form of strong sugar syrup, a teaspoonful of nutrient, the zest and juice of 2 or 3 oranges or lemons, and wine yeast. Ferment for five days, strain, then put into a fermentation jar, top up to about 7pt (4 litres) with cold water, and fit with an air-lock. Leave for ten days, then rack off. Add 8oz (225g) of sugar syrup and top up to the shoulder of the jar with cold water. As the gravity drops to 1.000 add the rest of the sugar syrup gradually, until fermentation stops and the wine tastes dry. Rack off again, sulphite, and put to one side to mature for about a year.

FUNGI

The simplest form of plant life, characterised by the fact that they do not form green chlorophyll. Yeast is just one of the many species of fungi. Their value to the wine-maker lies in their ability to break down sugars with the enzymes they secrete, and to produce alcohol. The fungus *Botrytis cinerea* is vitally important to the creation of Sauternes-type wine. Not all fungi are the wine-maker's allies. Wild yeast, for one, is a spoilage organism and source of infection. *See* Yeast; Bloom; Noble rot.

FUNNEL

A basic piece of wine-making equipment for transferring powder, granules or liquid from a container into a narrow-necked bottle or jar; and for pouring, racking and filtering throughout the wine-making process. The funnel can be made of glass, but is more likely nowadays to be plastic or polythene. Funnels are cheap, and you can have a range of sizes up to 1gal (4.5 litres) capacity. Plastic funnels should be kept for wine-making only, since they absorb odours and transfer them very easily. They should be sterilised before use, washed thoroughly afterwards and always stored clean.

FUSEL OILS

A mixture of higher alcohols, mainly isomeric amyl alcohols, which are produced during fermentation by the process called autolysis,

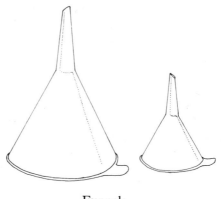

Funnels

which acts on dead yeast cells and spent pulp. In high concentration, fusel oils affect flavour and bouquet and can be toxic. The wine-maker must therefore take pains to prevent the formation of too much fusel oil, which is more likely to occur when potatoes and cereals are used in the recipe, or when an inadequate supply of yeast nutrients is provided. Preventive measures include racking the wine off the lees as soon as fermentation has finished; and feeding the must with yeast nutrients containing ammonium phosphate in the early stages of preparation.

GALACTOSE

A sugar which combines with glucose to form lactose, the main sugar in milk. Lactose is important to the wine-maker because it cannot be metabolised by wine yeasts and is therefore unfermentable. Consequently, it can be used to sweeten wine without re-fermenting it, which is a real problem if sucrose is used.

GALLON

It was common, until recently, to use the gallon as the wine-making unit in both Britain and the United States. However, there is a difference between the American and the British, or imperial, gallon and you should note whether a particular recipe is British or American. The imperial gallon is composed of 8pt, and each pint is made up of 20fl oz. The US gallon is also composed of 8pt, but each pint is made up of 16fl oz. So, the imperial gallon is the equivalent of 1.2 US gallons, or 4.5 litres. The US gallon is the equivalent of 0.83 imperial gallons, or 3.78 litres.

The move to replace the gallon by metric measures is gathering pace, and many recipes are designed to produce 4.5 litres of wine, but it will be many years before the old recipes and imperial measurements can be disregarded.

GAY-LUSSAC

A French scientist who first, in 1810, formulated the thesis that one molecule of sugar yields two molecules of alcohol and two of carbon dioxide. His name has now been immortalised by being used as the Continental expression of alcohol content: 1 per cent alcohol = 1 per cent Gay-Lussac. This is the scale marked on bottles of wine sold in France.

GELATINE

A protein obtained from animal skin, ligaments or bones. It is used as a fining agent to clear haze from wine. Gelatine, like other protein fining agents such as albumin and casein, is particularly effective in removing tannin, with which it forms an insoluble flocculate mixture which slowly settles. Consequently, there is a danger when using gelatine of deflavouring a wine and making it insipid. White wine is particularly vulnerable to this. If, however, a wine is over-astringent, gelatine can both clear and mellow it.

It is important not to use too much gelatine since it can itself form a haze or discoloration. Make a trial fining with a small sample before adding gelatine to the bulk of the wine.

Gelatine for fining is sold in wine-making supply stores and usually comes complete with instructions. A 1 per cent solution is used, starting with 1g (less than ¼tsp) in 25ml (almost 1fl oz) of cold water. After a few hours, when the water has been absorbed and the gelatine has swelled up, sufficient hot water should be added to make the volume up to 100ml (just under ¼pt). After the solution has been added to the wine, it takes at least 48 hours for a sediment to be formed that is firm enough for the wine to be racked off without dispersing it, but the sediment will become firmer if it is allowed to settle out at a low temperature. *See* Fining.

GINGER

The ginger used for cooking is the dried rhizome, root or 'race' of the plant *Zingiber officinale*. It is normally called 'root ginger' to distinguish it from 'sweet ginger', which is pieces of stem preserved in syrup and not used as a wine-making ingredient. Root ginger has a hot, spicy flavour. It can spice up a wine made from ingredients lacking in full flavour; or it can be used to make drinks, for example ginger beer, ginger wine or ginger cordial, in which it is the main flavour.

For a predominantly ginger drink, 2–4oz (60–115g) of root ginger are used for 1gal (4.5 litres). For flavouring a mild wine, about 2tsp are enough for a gallon. If just a hint of ginger is required, then ¼tsp will enliven a wine in such a way that the palate will respond more positively to its other flavours. Ginger is prepared for extraction by 'bruising' – beating the root with a mallet, pestle or heavy spoon.

Many root-vegetable wines are traditionally flavoured with ginger, especially beetroot and parsnip; carrot wine, however, is better if ginger is not allowed to obtrude, because the flavours are not complementary. Nettle, rice, parsley, sage, thyme and mint wines all benefit from the addition of ginger, but apart from these specific examples its inclusion is a matter of taste. It is, however, customary to spice up cereal wines with the extra buzz of ginger, peppercorns or caraway seeds, or a mixture of all three.

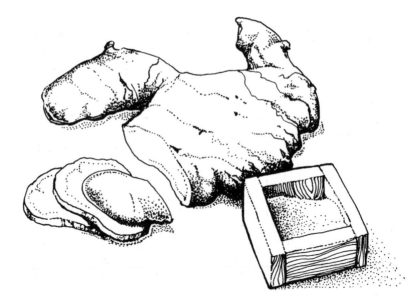

Root ginger

Ginger Beer

A country drink, traditionally used by farm labourers as a thirst quencher for hot-weather work. It is normally low in alcoholic content. The ginger-beer plant is a good way of introducing children to the principle of fermentation, and the idea that yeast is a living organism which acts upon sugar to change its nature. For a gallon

(4.5 litres) of ginger beer you will need:

  1oz (25g) fresh yeast, or ½oz (15g) dried yeast
  9tsp (45ml) sugar
  9tsp (45ml) ground ginger
  2lb (1kg) sugar
  2 lemons

Put the yeast into a clean jam-jar and pour over ½pt (285ml) of water. Stir in 2tsp of sugar and 2 of ginger. Cover the jar, and leave for 24 hours. The next day, add another teaspoonful of sugar and one of yeast. Feed the ginger-beer plant in this way for seven days in all. At the end of the week, strain the liquid through muslin, into a bowl, retaining the sediment from the muslin and the liquid separately. Put 2lb (1kg) sugar into a large pan, add 1pt (575ml) water, bring to the boil, stirring all the time with a wooden spoon, and boil rapidly for 2 minutes until the sugar has completely dissolved. Squeeze the lemons and add the lemon juice and the ginger liquid to the dissolved sugar. Then add 6pt (3.45 litres) of cold water and stir well. Pour the ginger beer into bottles, leaving a 2in (5cm) space at the top, cork and leave in a cool place for at least two weeks before drinking. Scrape the residue of the ginger/yeast mixture from the muslin into a jar, bottle or jug, and cover with ¾pt (425ml) of cold water. Mix well. Divide this into two jam-jars, and start feeding with 1tsp each of ginger and sugar every day as before. Now you have two ginger-beer plants, and can give one away to a neighbour.

Ginger Cordial
A liqueur made from raisins, lemon rind, ginger and water, and strengthened with brandy or whisky.

Ginger Wine
Strong, smooth and hot, with a higher alcohol content than Ginger Beer, it can be used as an aperitif or a social wine.

GLASS

Glass vessels are usually the wine-maker's first choice for most of the stages of fermentation and maturation of wine. Glass does not absorb odours or tastes, is impervious to air, easy to clean, transparent, easily available and cheap. Red wine should be kept in green or amber glass, or kept shaded, or it will lose its colour.

Glass does of course have its disadvantages – it can shatter if knocked or dropped, it can be cracked by rapid changes of temperature, and it is heavy – a vessel holding more than a gallon (4.5 litres) of liquid is too heavy to lift or move easily.

GLASSES

There is a strong connection between taste and good presentation, and the least you can do, if you have taken pains over making your wine, is to serve it in a glass that does it justice. There is a 'right' shape of glass for every type of wine, for which there is a good functional reason. A balloon-shaped brandy glass is designed to hold its bouquet; a liqueur glass is tiny because liqueur is drunk in small quantities; a stemmed glass makes it possible to drink wine that should be cool without raising its temperature by the heat of your hands; and so on.

Glasses should be transparent and colourless – apart from the stems – so that the colour of the wine can be appreciated. The goblet should curve inwards, directing the wine's fragrance upwards while holding some in reserve for continued enjoyment. The all-purpose glass which combines these features is the ubiquitous Paris goblet. Champagne and sparkling wines should *not* be served in a saucer-shaped glass; it allows the bubbles to escape too quickly. Use a flute or tulip-shape. A glass should be only half-filled to allow the air to reach the wine.

Take care of your glasses, when washing and storing them, if you want to protect the flavour of the wine. They should be washed in hot water without detergent, then stored upright, not upside down.

Glasses

GLOGG

The enchanting Danish name for mulled wine. This is a traditional Christmas Glogg. Mix together in a strong saucepan: 1 bottle of red wine; 1 bottle of port-type wine; 1 can of lager; 4tbsp of chopped candied fruit; 1 cup of sultanas; 1 cup of ground almonds; and 2 cups of brown sugar. Bring gently to simmering point, but do not allow to boil. Drink the wine hot, and eat the fruit with a spoon.

GLUCOSE

Another name for dextrose or 'grape sugar'. It is the most important monosaccharide in wine-making since it is a constituent of all the disaccharides encountered, including sucrose. It forms starch, cellulose and dextrins. It is active in the fermentation process by which ethyl alcohol is created. Either glucose or fructose is usually the residual sugar in wine.

GLYCERINE

A byproduct naturally formed during the early part of the fermentation process. It has the beneficial effect of giving wine a pleasant smoothness and adding body, because of its sweet, dense, oily nature.

For the home wine-maker, there are several occasions when extra glycerine might be added to advantage:

It can be added to an over-acid wine, using 4–6tbsp to each gallon (4.5 litres), to mask astringency or tartness. This, however, is only a cosmetic process, not a real remedy.

It *must* be one of the ingredients of a Sauternes-type wine recipe since the botrytised grapes used for genuine Sauternes are rich in glycerine. Add 2–3tbsp of glycerine to each gallon (4.5 litres).

It should be included in those liqueur recipes based mainly on Polish spirit and liqueur flavouring.

It may serve a useful purpose in the preparation of equipment. New hard corks should be softened before use and this is best done by soaking them for a few hours in a mild sulphite solution to which a few drops of glycerine have been added.

GLYCEROL

The chemical name for glycerine.

GOOSEBERRIES

A useful wine-making fruit, whether tinned, fresh or frozen, used either on their own or mixed with other base ingredients. They can be incorporated into the must to produce a dry white table wine; a white dessert wine; a sparkling wine or 'gooseberry champagne'; a rosé; or a Madeira.

For table wine, they are best used when green and unripe, because at this stage they have a more restrained flavour which does not overpower food. For a white dessert wine or Sauternes-type, fully ripe gooseberries are better. P. Duncan and B. Acton, in their book *Progressive Winemaking* (published by Amateur Winemaker, 1967), suggest that botrytised gooseberries would make an excellent base for Sauternes, since gooseberries are particularly vulnerable to noble rot.

Used on their own, gooseberries make a bright, fresh, golden wine. When they are mixed with blackcurrants, redcurrants, blackberries or raspberries they make a good rosé. Other successful combinations are gooseberry and orange and gooseberry and apple.

Since frozen fruit is perfectly acceptable in making wine, it is possible to buy or pick fresh gooseberries, and then freeze them until other ingredients are ripe and ready, whether in the garden or the greengrocer's.

GORSE *see* Broom.

GRAINS *see* Cereals.

GRAPE

The perfect fruit for making wine, since it can provide from within itself, and in an ideal balance, flavour, bouquet, body, sugar, nutrients, vitamins, acids, tannin, yeast from the bloom on its skin, sufficient juice to make extra water unnecessary in commercial production, and pigmentation to give colour to red wines. Also, by definition, vinosity. It is a fact that as a sole ingredient grapes make the best wines, and as an additive they improve every other wine. No other fruit can provide the complete range of wine-making requirements found in the grape, so country wines have to be made from combinations of flavour, body and bouquet ingredients, as well as additives such as nutrients, vitamins, acids, tannin, sugar and yeast.

The grape is now widely available to home wine-makers in the form of juices, concentrates and compounds; and many people with some suitable land are beginning to grow their own vines now that strains have been developed which can thrive in a chilly northern climate.

Both white and black grapes are used in wine-making. As a general rule, black grapes are used for red wine and rosé, and white grapes for white wine, but it is possible to make a white wine from black grapes provided that the skins are removed before the pigments are leached out by the alcohol during fermentation. The type of wine produced depends upon the particular variety of grape used; for instance, in Burgundy the best red wine is produced from the Pinot Noir, while the white wine that takes its name from Graves is usually made from the grape varieties Semillon, Sauvignon Blanc and Muscadelle. However, the grape is not the only factor that dominates the wine-type. It is also affected by the soil in which the vine grows, and its cultivation; the climate; and the whole wine-making process, from the initial composition of the must to the end of the maturation period.

GRAPE CONCENTRATE

Now readily available in supermarkets, chemists and wine-making supply stores, this has changed the nature of home wine-making and improved the body, bouquet, flavour and vinosity of the finished product. With it, even the novice wine-maker can produce palatable wines.

Concentrate can be used on its own as the main ingredient to produce a particular type of wine. This is quite expensive, however, and many wine-makers feel that it does not give enough scope to their own skills and creativity. The alternative is to use it as an extra ingredient, in the proportion of about ½pt (285ml) to 1gal (4.5 litres) of wine. One tin will then be enough for 3gal (13.5 litres) of wine, having been combined with other base ingredients such as flowers, vegetables or fruit.

Grape concentrate should never be undervalued. It is the best of the body-giving ingredients, it aids rapid maturation and gives a clean taste. It is a good idea to use it as a routine ingredient. The cheaper brands are perfectly satisfactory for use as an additive, and 1pt (575ml) will replace about 1lb (450g) sugar.

Grape concentrate is interchangeable with raisins or sultanas, 1pt (575ml) of concentrate being the equivalent of 2lb (1kg) of the dried fruit; but it is important to take into account the natural sugar content, which is higher in the concentrate. It is much better to add vinosity to flower wines with concentrate than with dried fruit, which is likely to overpower their delicate fragrance and flavour. Concentrate is also useful for sweetening an over-dry wine, and for topping up during fermentation. In the latter operation it should be diluted with about five times its own volume of cool, boiled water.

Concentrates are not only for use in making table wines. They are available to create fortified wines such as sherry, port and Madeira, as well as festive and social wines such as grape and gooseberry. *Winemaking with Concentrates* by P. Duncan (Amateur Winemaker Publications, 1976) is a useful book for the wine-maker who prefers to use a grape concentrate rather than a kit. It not only includes an excellent range of concentrate recipes, but also some straightforward advice about the principles and practice of wine-making.

GRAPE SUGAR

Another name for glucose.

GRAPEFRUIT

Bought either as juice or whole fruit, this is a useful wine-making

113

ingredient, though not to be used in too high a proportion, since it is very acidic. It can make a dry white table wine; a white dessert wine, especially of the Sauternes-type; or a tangy aperitif. It is also very good for producing an instant wine, when fermented with malt extract and vitaminised nutrient, which speed up fermentation and reduce the specific gravity to the mean (1.000) in about one week. If it is then sterilised, racked off, filtered, sweetened if necessary and stabilised, it will be ready to drink after another week's storage in a cool place, though it can, of course, be left for many months.

GRAVITY *see* Specific gravity; Hydrometer.

GREATER BURNET

Sanguisorba officinalis, the princess of wine-making flowers, surpassed only by the elderflower and rose. It blooms from June to September in damp places: water meadows, riversides and ditches. The blood-red blossoms give a deep ruby colouring and port-wine flavour. Sometimes the plant is hard to find, but it tends to thrive in dense little colonies once it takes a hold in the right place.

If flowers are scarce, it is possible to start the wine-making process by using just a few flowers, infused with water, sugar, fruit juice or grape concentrate and honey, to extract the aroma. More blossoms can be added as they become available during the following days, then the liquor can be strained off before the yeast is added and it is fermented out in the usual way. Cherish the plants and make sure some flowers are left to go to seed.

GREENGAGES

Can be used in any recipe that calls for plums, and are especially suitable as an alternative to yellow plums. They make a good base ingredient for an oloroso-type sherry; Madeira-type wine; or medium-sweet social wine.

GREEN VEGETABLES

Green vegetables, even cabbages, *can* be regarded as wine-making ingredients, but their value is limited as they lack essential acids and nutrients. Like root vegetables, they need to be boiled for about half an hour before the extracted liquor is added to the must. The finished wine will need a long period of maturation if it is to be of any value.

GYPSUM

Known as Plaster of Paris, and chemically as calcium sulphate, it is particularly associated in the wine-maker's mind with the creation oi good sherry. It is actually found in the soil in Jerez, but it is also sprinkled in powder form over sherry musts, in the proportion of 1tbsp per gallon (4.5 litres) to guard against infection.

The grape juice used in Spanish sherry, usually from the Palamino grape, has a high sugar content combined with low acidity, and therefore a very high pH. Plastering the pulp of the crushed grapes with gypsum, which is an acid, decreases the pH and kills bacteria. The lower pH also seems to aid the formation of sherry flor. Though flor can be created without gypsum, it certainly flourishes much more vigorously on musts to which it has been added. Wine-makers attempting to reproduce a sherry-type wine of the dry fino variety should incorporate it in the must. *See* Sherry.

HARSHNESS

A wine that can be described as harsh is one that is unbalanced, over-astringent or with the taste of alcohol predominating over the flavour of the ingredients. If the harshness is caused by excess tannin it can be removed by wine finings, but this method should be tried out with small samples of the wine first of all. About 1pt (575ml) should be taken from the bulk, and a small amount of fining agent added to it. The sample should be mixed up thoroughly, put to one side for 24 hours, then tasted. This process must be repeated until the balance is right. Gelatine is the most commonly used fining for excess tannin.

Alternative remedies include blending the harsh wine with one lacking in tannin; masking it with sugar syrup, glycerine or honey; and giving it a long period of maturation, at least two years.

Excess alcohol can be avoided by calculating beforehand the addition of sugar syrup appropriate to the type of wine required. Once the mistake has been made, it is difficult to rectify but blending and masking are probably the best solutions.

HAWS

Hawthorn berries are listed in wine-making books as a base wine-making ingredient, but they produce a bitter wine which has only a limited appeal to most palates. Try only a small quantity to start with to avoid possible wastage. Haws can be found in the hedgerows in abundance during the autumn or bought in their dried form from wine-making supply stores.

HAWTHORN BLOSSOM

The pink and white flowers of the hawthorn or may are exquisitely

Hawthorn blossom

scented and, like many highly fragrant flowers, make extremely good light wine. They appear in the hedgerows in May and June. The blossoms should be gathered fresh and fully opened, dry and warm from the sun, then stripped of their stalks and any greenery.

Used as the main wine-making ingredient, they will produce a dry table wine, white or rosé according to the colour of the blossoms, but when bananas are added to the must the result will be a medium-sweet social wine. Alternatively, combined with orange juice and champagne yeast starter, they form the basis of a sparkling wine.

The fragrant perfume of these sweet-scented flowers adds greatly to any white wine, including one made from a kit or tin of concentrate, provided that they are not added to the must until two or three days after the first highly active stage of fermentation. At this time the higher alcohol content and gentler action of the brew will extract and retain their fragrance more effectively, and the floral esters will not be vaporised. Hawthorn blossom can also make cheap brandy into a superb liqueur (*see* Liqueurs).

HAZE

Newly made wine is clouded for the period during which the yeast is working on the sugar to create alcohol, but if it is properly made from the correct balance of the right ingredients it should clarify itself given time and periodic racking. Unfortunately, this does not always happen. Things go wrong, despite every care being taken, and particles remain suspended in the liquid, giving it a cloudy appear-

116

ance. If the wine has not cleared after a few months, there are two simple tricks that might work.

1. The temperature can be dropped drastically for a short while. A few days in the refrigerator should do the trick, and then the wine can be racked again.

2. The wine can be sulphited. One Campden tablet should be crushed and dissolved in a little of the liquid first of all, then added to each gallon (4.5 litres).

If, after a few months, a wine still refuses to clear, and yet no lees or sediment is being formed, the cloudiness is probably due to one of the hazes discussed below.

Bacterial Haze

If the build up of bacteria in an infected wine is sufficiently intense it will become cloudy. The haze can be cleared in two stages. First, the bacteria must be killed off by sulphiting: 2 Campden tablets should be added to each gallon (4.5 litres) of wine. Then the wine should be racked off, after 24 hours or so in which the Campden tablets have been given a chance to do their work, so that the debris can be discarded and there is no danger of off-flavours developing.

Metal Haze

This should never be a good wine-maker's problem since one of the basic rules is to keep the must away from metal while it is being prepared and fermented. However, accidents do happen, and in the heat of the moment it is possible to seize a metal spoon and the damage is done.

If wine comes into contact with copper, iron, lead, tin or zinc, it may develop a metallic flavour and/or a white or coloured haze. As it matures, the haze will become hazier, but it can be treated by adding a small amount of citric acid before fining or filtering.

A word of warning! Some wine-makers, especially those who practise traditional country-wine making, like the idea of using beautiful old pottery fermenting jars or crocks, rather than glass demi-johns which do not look as attractive when standing in the kitchen. This lovely idea is unfortunately also a dangerous one. Many old pots are finished with a lead glaze which is toxic when leached out by alcohol.

Pectin Haze

Pectin is found in all fruits and some vegetables, and if these are boiled for wine-making, or even if they are merely infused in boiling water, the juice extracted will be very rich in pectin which will eventually, if it is not treated, cause a pectin haze in the wine. A pectin-destroying enzyme should therefore be added to the must when it is at room temperature, at the same time as it is sulphited, but 24 hours before the yeast is added. The enzyme is available from chemist shops or from wine-making supply stores in either liquid or powder form, but the liquid is preferable since it forms less sediment.

If the problem of pectin haze does arise, the enzyme can be added to the wine when it is finished. It will then need to be racked into a clean jar after having been allowed to settle out for a few days. Mix the enzyme first with a glass of the wine and then introduce it gradually into the bulk, stirring thoroughly all the time.

To ascertain whether or not a haze has been caused by pectin, combine 1 spoonful of wine with 3 spoonfuls of methylated spirits in a small container and leave for up to 2 hours. If a jelly-like precipitate or little clots are formed, the presence of pectin is confirmed.

Starch Haze

If a must contains cereals, potatoes, other root vegetables or apples, it may develop a starch haze unless it has had amylase added to it. To check for this particular haze, add a few drops of dilute iodine solution to a tablespoonful of the wine; if it turns a deep purple-blue colour, starch is the problem. The wine will need to be treated with a proprietary starch-reducing enzyme, available from wine-making supply stores and chemists. The addition of about $\frac{1}{4}$oz (7g) to each gallon (4.5 litres) should clear the haze. The enzyme preparation should be mixed with a small quantity of the wine first, and then incorporated into the bulk. Put the jar in a warm place until it clarifies, then rack off in the usual way. Quality and flavour will not be affected. *See* Amylase.

Unspecific Hazes

If a wine remains cloudy but tests and treatment indicate that the haze is not caused by live yeast, bacteria, metal contamination, pectin or starch, it should be treated preferably by fining, but as a final resort by filtering. These are drastic measures and should be avoided if possible because they can spoil the quality of a wine, and if a wine is over-fined, the haze might be stabilised instead of being dispersed. Filtering is even more dangerous since, unless filtration equipment is sophisticated, it may cause over-oxidation which will result in a flat or 'bottle-sick' wine, though it will recover given time.

HERBS

Flavour-enhancing ingredients which are important in wine-making on several counts. They can be used as the main ingredient in social wines such as parsley, sage, balm, mint and lemon thyme, in which they are often enlivened by root ginger, or as a flavouring for other social wines which may be rather lifeless. They can also flavour aperitifs, for example Dubonnet and Cinzano, or liqueurs, but their flavour tends to be too strong for table wines and would overpower the taste of the food.

If herbs are to be a base ingredient of the must, between 1¾ and 3½pt (1–2 litres) of herbs will be needed for each gallon (4.5 litres) of wine, extracted either by infusion or pulp fermentation. For adding flavour to a social wine or aperitif, 2oz (56g) of fresh herbs or 1oz (28g) of dried herbs will make a considerable difference to its taste. The herbs can be boiled for 20 minutes then strained before use, or added to the fermenting must as they are for pulp fermentation, or immersed in the wine in a small muslin bag after fermentation and allowed to infuse for a while until the flavour is strong enough. Several herb mixtures and flavourings, including Dubonnet, Cinzano, vermouth and Chartreuse, can be bought from wine-making supply stores.

Herb liqueurs are almost always made by the simple process of steeping herbs in spirit. The most popular is probably the famous mint liqueur, Crème de Menthe, but Chartreuse and Benedictine are also delicious, made from special combinations of aromatic herbs.

HONEY

A source of invert sugar which has the benefit of extra ingredients such as pollen, trace elements and floral esters. These all contribute to the bouquet, flavour and smoothness of the wine, and some wine-makers like to use honey instead of at least part of the sugar in the must. Despite its extra cost, the results are usually well worth it. As a general guide to substitution, 1lb (450g) of sugar is the equivalent of 1¼lb (565g) of honey.

Honey has many flavours, and the right sort should be selected with care to match the wine. Eucalyptus honey should be avoided because it is too strongly flavoured, and heather honey may well be overpowering for a delicate wine, but acacia honey is particularly delicious. Clover honey matches well with light white wine, and dark honeys are more suitable for rich sweet red wine. (The cheapest way of buying honey is in bulk, from wine-making supply stores or cash-and-carry centres.)

Honey tends to contain undesirable micro-organisms, such as wild yeasts and acetifying bacteria, so unless it has been pasteurised it must be sterilised before use. This can be done by boiling it in an equal quantity of water for at least 10 minutes or by sulphiting it. The latter method will do less harm to bouquet and flavour.

119

HONEYSUCKLE

One of the best wine-making flowers, especially if wild honeysuckle is used, because of its superb bouquet and flavour. It can be used to brighten up the bouquet of vegetable wines that may be rather dull, or as the main ingredient of a medium-sweet or sweet social wine of the Sauternes type. Two pints (1 litre) of blossoms, with every shred of greenery removed, will make 1gal (4.5 litres) of wine. They should be fermented with honey and white wine concentrate, as bland as possible, plus Sauternes yeast, vitaminised yeast nutrient, acid mixture and grape tannin.

The honeysuckle blooms in June and July in country gardens and hedgerows: do not be tempted by its poisonous berries.

HUCKLEBERRIES/HURTLEBERRIES *see* Bilberries.

HYDROGEN SULPHIDE

The chemical, traditionally beloved of schoolboys, which gives off the sulphurous smell of rotten eggs. It might afflict the wine-maker if wine is racked off and sulphited to put an end to fermentation too early in the process. The yeast may then act on the sulphur dioxide to turn it into hydrogen sulphide. This can be cured: 100ppm sulphite should be added every month until the smell has gone. Sulphur will be precipitated out and should be racked off.

HYDROMETER

An invaluable instrument for indicating the sugar content of a must by measuring the density, or gravity, of the liquid. If the density is measured before, during and after fermentation, it is possible to work out, with the use of a gravity table, how much sugar has been acted upon by the yeast and, consequently, how much alcohol has been produced from it.

The hydrometer is a long, slender tube with a bulbous lower end; it is made of glass or plastic, and is weighted at the bottom so that it floats upright in liquid. Its zero point is 1.000 because this is the density, or specific gravity, of water. The most useful hydrometer will be calibrated from .990 to 1.170. Pure alcohol has a specific gravity of .794 and therefore if it is present in water it will give a reading lower than 1.000.

Hydrometers are available which use 'sugar content' and 'potential alcohol' indications as well as specific gravity measurements, and this makes it possible to calculate the progress and eventual alcohol content of a wine without having to use tables.

Liquids to be measured should be at about room temperature (59°F/15°C), to avoid the possibility of inaccuracy, and measurement is usually carried out in a tall cylindrical hydrometer jar. The less dense the liquid is (or the less its gravity), the lower the hydrometer will sink into it. The more dense (or the greater its gravity), the higher it will float. Consequently, the small figures are at the top of its measurement scale and the larger figures at the bottom.

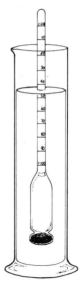

Hydrometer

How to use the Hydrometer

1. Clean and sterilise the hydrometer and the hydrometer jar, and fill the jar with a sample of the juices of the must before any sugar has been added to it.

2. Immerse the hydrometer into the must and spin it round to free it from bubbles which could cause a false reading.

3. When it comes to rest, take the reading with your eye level with the surface of the liquid. Note that, because of the meniscus or surface tension, the level of the liquid will be higher where it touches the hydrometer and sides of the jar. The reading should therefore be taken at the lowest point.

4. Check your reading against the gravity table. If, for instance, the hydrometer records a specific gravity of 1.050 this means that there is 1lb 5oz per gallon (136g per litre) of *natural* sugar in the must at this stage. If it were fermented out, the must would produce a wine of 8 per cent alcohol by volume. This is low for a table wine; therefore add extra sugar to the must so that the yeast can turn it into extra alcohol.

5. Decide what alcohol content you are aiming to produce. If you decide to make a wine of 12 per cent alcohol by volume, you will see from the table that you need an original specific gravity of 1.075 or a sugar content of 2lb per gallon (202g per litre). Since you already have 1lb 5oz (136g per litre) you will have to add 11oz (66g per litre). Part of this should be added straight away, part in gradual additions, using the feeding-the-yeast method. The original specific gravity should be between 1.060 and 1.100 at the maximum.

6. At this stage the yeast and nutrients should be added to the must and fermentation commenced.

7. As the fermentation proceeds, the specific gravity should be checked at regular intervals, partly to gauge when sugar should be added, partly to make sure that the fermentation has not stuck. The

specific gravity should drop quite rapidly at the beginning, and then slow down. The nearer it gets to zero the drier the wine will be. If the reading reaches 1.005, the wine will be slightly sweet; if it goes down to .995 it will be very dry.

Most beginners to wine-making find the hydrometer a frightening piece of equipment and are reluctant to use it. But it is perfectly straightforward and greatly improves wine-making success. When you buy one it will be accompanied by comprehensible instructions. *See* Yeast; Specific gravity; Fermentation, stuck.

IMMERSION HEATER

An immersion heater which will slip inside the fermenting vessel is a useful piece of equipment for keeping the must at the right temperature provided that it is fitted with a thermostat, and a rubber bung for use with a fermentation lock. If the demi-john is lagged with a quilted jacket less power will be used. Some fermenting vessels have their own built-in immersion heaters. Other forms of heating which are more reliable than the airing cupboard or kitchen shelf include electric trays, warming belts and fermenting cabinets. *See* Fermentation heaters.

Indicator Paper

INDICATOR PAPERS

Impregnated with chemical compound, they were formerly used simply to give an indication of the acidity or alkalinity of a must. Now they are more sophisticated, though simpler to use, and are combined with a coloured scale which shows pH. A drop of wine is laid on the paper, a colour develops as a result of the interaction of the wine with the chemical, and the pH is then read off the scale. pH is not, however, a highly accurate indication of acid content when compared with titration, and the papers themselves can be confusing: they sometimes produce a colour that is difficult to interpret, and which can be affected by the colour of the wine. Consequently, indicator papers are being used less and less by experienced wine-makers. *See* pH; Titration.

INFECTIONS

The most commonly encountered wine infections, caused by the entry of undesirable micro-organisms in the must, are:

Ropiness caused by lactobacilli
Flowers of wine caused by *Candida mycoderma*
Acetification caused by acetobacter, acetomonas
Mouse or mousiness caused by lactobacilli
Tourne disease caused by lactobacilli

Infection is almost always due to ineffective hygiene and sterilisation, and prevention is much better than cure, though most infections can be arrested if caught early enough.

Acetification

The process which usually occurs as the result of the bacteria *Acetobacter aceti*, also known as *Mycoderma aceti*, attacking the alcohol in wine and turning it into acetic acid. This is immediately noticeable by its vinegary taste and smell; finished wine affected in this way is usually only fit to be used as wine vinegar for cooking. If caught in time, acetification may be remedied by adding two Campden tablets, or ⅓fl oz (10ml) strong sulphite solution, to the must during fermentation.

Bacterial infection of this type may have been caused by the use of slightly decomposing or over-ripe fruit, by airborne spores or by the fruit fly – the so-called vinegar fly. As usual, prevention is better than cure, and acetifying bacteria can be kept at bay by using clean and sterile equipment; keeping container vessels well covered; keeping air-locks topped up with sulphite solution; making sure that vessels holding maturing wine are completely full so that there is no space in which aerobic infections can flourish; and by not allowing the temperature of the must or wine to exceed 80°F (26–7°C) because it is at that temperature that *Acetobacter aceti* flourish. Acetification is one of the commonest and most damaging of wine infections.

Aerobic Infection
Spoilage inflicted on the must or maturing wine by airborne spores or fruit flies. To avoid it, it is necessary to prevent the damaging organisms from gaining access to the liquid. Buckets, vessels and jars should be covered at all times, and air-locks should be kept topped up with sulphite solution.

At the beginning of a fermentation, the carbon dioxide will be effective in keeping out aerobic bacteria from the must, but when the initial vigour begins to decline the danger of infection becomes greater and it is important to make sure that air is excluded. Acetobacter, which cause acetification, and *Candida mycoderma*, which causes the infection 'flowers of wine', are probably the commonest airborne organisms with which the wine-maker has to contend.

Anaerobic Infection
Spoilage of the must caused by bacteria which thrive in the absence of air. To prevent it, careful hygiene must be practised at all times and sulphite used during the racking process. If bacteria still manage to damage the wine it may be saved by sulphiting. Lactobacilli, which cause ropiness and mousiness, are anaerobic organisms.

Flowers of Wine
Usually caused by the film yeast, *Candida mycoderma*, and recognisable as small whitish patches on the surface of the liquid or on the lees in the bottom of unwashed containers, which then form a grey-green scum. Proper hygiene and sterilisation should prevent the infection, and also fermentation of the wine in anaerobic conditions since *Candida mycoderma*, being an aerobic organism, needs air to survive. Treatment involves sulphiting the wine thoroughly and breaking up the skin. After a few days, the film will sink to the bottom, whereupon the wine can be racked off. The wine is therefore recoverable, though flavour may be impaired. *See* Candida; Yeast, film.

'Mother'
Rare term for infection by mould fungus lactobacilli.

Mouse or Mousiness
The name given to describe the after-taste caused by acetoin, an

unpleasant substance produced by the bacteria, lactobacilli. It is caused by inadequate cleanliness and sterilisation procedures during the wine-making process, and there is no cure for it. The only answer is to discard the spoiled wine and to start again.

Ropiness

An infection which makes wine thick and oily. It is caused by the bacteria lactobacilli, and is so called because the tiny organisms stick together and form long chains which can be seen in the wine. Proper cleanliness and sterilisation during the wine-making process will prevent ropiness, but if it does occur there is a cure. The wine should be sulphited with two Campden tablets to each gallon (4.5 litres), then thoroughly stirred so that the 'ropes' are broken up and dispersed. It should then be allowed to settle for about 24 hours before being filtered or racked off. The treated wine should be drunk as soon as it has completely settled, which will probably take a few weeks, rather than allowed to age. Its flavour and alcohol content should not be impaired either by the infection or the cure.

Tourne Disease

An infection caused by lactobacilli in wines that contain tartaric acid. It makes the wine taste bitter. It can be prevented by cleanliness and proper sterilisation during the wine-making process, and be arrested by sulphiting should it occur. Unfortunately, it will probably be impossible to eliminate the off-flavour. Blending may produce a better taste, but if this does not produce a palatable wine there is no alternative but to discard it.

INFUSION

The process of steeping a substance in warm or hot water, or preferably in an alcohol solution, in order to draw out flavour and colour, and to impregnate the liquid with its properties and qualities. The danger of using water is that if it is too hot it may drive off important esters, but if it is not hot enough the substances may not be volatilised. A reliable recipe, or personal experience, will indicate the best method of steeping specific ingredients.

Infusion is one of the first steps in wine-making, as it is the method of obtaining the components required for the must from fruits, flowers, vegetables and other materials.

INGREDIENTS

The base ingredient of a wine may be almost any vegetable, herb, fruit, leaf, bark, berry, sap or flower provided that it is known to be non-poisonous. To this is added yeast, sugar, acid, tannin, nutrients, vitamins and water, and perhaps other additives, such as enzymes and sterilising agents, depending upon the chemical make-up of the main ingredient. Good wine depends to a large extent not only on the quality of the base ingredient but also upon a careful blending of other ingredients too, in order to give flavour, body, bouquet and astringency, combined in the right proportions. *See* Blending – ingredients; Recipes for wine.

INOCULATION

Adding yeast to a must so that fermentation begins; in other words, introducing an organism into a substance in order to bring about a metabolic change. The old-fashioned and now largely out-moded technique was to sprinkle granules of dried yeast over the must. This was reasonably satisfactory with a must in a fermentation jar immediately sealed off from the air, but could be dangerous in a must containing crushed fruit left unsealed for a few days' pulp fermentation. There was a time-lag of some hours between inoculation with dried yeast and the formation of a blanket of carbon dioxide during which there was no protection of the must from infection by airborne organisms.

The better way to inoculate a pulpy must, and the one almost universally used today by skilled wine-makers, is to combine in it a yeast starter culture. In a starter culture the yeast is already actively fermenting so there is no delay between inoculation and the build up of carbon dioxide; the must therefore gets off to a healthy and vigorous early fermentation. *See* Yeast, starter.

INVERSION OF SUGAR

The first stage of the action of yeast on sucrose during which it secretes the enzyme invertase, and thus splits the disaccharide into two monosaccharides, glucose and fructose. Only when sucrose has been inverted can it be metabolised into alcohol and carbon dioxide. *See* Fermentation.

INVERT SUGAR *see* Sugar.

INVERTASE

An enzyme secreted by yeast which breaks down sucrose into its two components, fructose and glucose. In other words, it inverts sugar, which is one of the first stages of the fermentation process. *See* Sugar, invert.

IODINE

Can prove whether or not a wine haze is caused by starch. Add a few drops of iodine to 1tbsp of wine; if the wine turns purple, starch is indicated. *See* Haze, starch.

IRON

Should never come into contact with wine. If it does, the wine will develop a stubborn white or bluish haze and this may prove impossible to clear.

To test for iron haze, add a few drops of sulphite to a small quantity of the wine; if a yellow precipitate is formed iron is probably present. It may be possible to remove iron haze by adding 5 per cent tannic acid solution to the wine, but make a trial first with a small quantity. If the haze is not removed the wine should be discarded.

ISINGLASS

Fish gelatine. Still available from wine-making supply stores, but regarded as an old-fashioned protein fining agent, and rarely used because it is difficult to prepare and handle, and not always successful. It has been superseded by ordinary gelatine.

JELLY BAG

A useful and cheap piece of equipment for straining pulp. Traditional muslin has now been largely superseded by nylon, which is stronger, easier to clean and less likely to absorb odours or retain stains. *See* Straining.

JUDGING WINE

The wine-maker who becomes very skilled may eventually like to put his or her best fermentations into competitions. Success there may even lead to the next step of becoming a judge. In the UK there are several regional branches of the Federation of Amateur Winemakers, and each holds its own annual show, part of which is an open competition, with many different classes. Anyone can compete, whether or not a member of an official wine circle.

To become a national judge you must be a member of the Amateur Winemakers' National Guild of Judges. Judges must be highly proficient in the art of wine-making; knowledgeable about wine-making practice; conversant with the technique of judging; and successful in the demanding examination set by the Guild. Those interested should read *Judging Home-made Wines*, the official handbook of the National Guild of Judges, and *Be a Wine and Beer Judge* by S. W. Andrews. Both of these are available from Amateur Winemaker Publications.

People wishing to enter wine into a competition have to observe the rules laid down by the organisers. These are usually available from local wine circles (their details will be in the local library) if it is a small show, or from the Federation of Amateur Winemakers and the National Association of Wine and Beermakers for larger events.

The most important considerations, however, are as follows. The wine must be appropriate to the class for which it is entered. It should be perfectly clear and free from sediment and haze, and presented in a plain, clear, unblemished bottle with a capacity of approximately 26fl oz (728ml); there should be no identifying marks. The bottle should be filled to the exact level specified; it should be stoppered with a good-quality clean cork, flanged for ease of opening; and it should be labelled with the official label supplied by the organisers, properly positioned according to the instructions, and not written upon unless this is specifically requested. Marks are awarded for presentation, clarity, bouquet, and colour, flavour, balance and quality; these last four take about two-thirds of the total marks.

These are national rules and practices and may not be relevant to village flower shows and church fêtes which include wine judging as part of their programme; they do, however, apply to very many small local competitions, now that the technique of home wine-making has reached such a high level of expertise and excellence.

JUICE

Juice, and its extraction, form a vital part of wine-making, particularly of white wine. Juice extracted either manually or by a machine is superior for producing delicate and refined wines to juice extracted by pulp fermentation.

Most commercial wines are produced from pure grape juice, and this is the supreme juice for wine-making. Home wine-makers now have easy access to grape juice in concentrate form, as well as the fruits of garden and countryside to turn into juice themselves. Combinations of grape concentrate and country fruits produce excellent flavours. A wide range of top-quality juices is available in supermarkets and wine-making supply stores, whether tinned, bottled or frozen. Apple, orange, grapefruit and pineapple juice are all readily available throughout the year, and it is worth looking out for supplies of lime juice if a Sauternes-type wine is required.

Juice Extractors
Generally use either pressure or steam to extract the maximum juice from fruit and vegetables with the minimum of effort. Some are manually operated but the electric ones (though more expensive) are more convenient for some types of wine, since they can process firm-fleshed fruit, like apples, very quickly. For instance, 56lb (25.5kg) of apples can be turned into 3–4gal (13.5–18 litres) of apple juice in less than 2 hours. Electric juicers, however, are less good with soft fruits like peaches, which they turn into a messy purée rather than clear juice.

Juice extractor

Some electric extractors and liquidisers, like the manual mincer type of extractor, have a habit of breaking up seeds, and the oils that are released can give an extremely bitter flavour to the juice. Take care to avoid this or the wine may be ruined. Steam juice extractors are used by some wine-makers with great enthusiasm, while others insist that they give a cooked flavour to the finished wine.

The type of juice extractor chosen must depend upon the individual's purse, palate and preference. Some small-scale wine-producers find that a hand-operated model (or even an old-fashioned jelly-bag plus the back of a wooden spoon!) is more useful and versatile than an expensive powered machine.

Juice Fermentation *see* Fermentation.

129

JUNIPER BERRIES

Either fresh or dried, these are more often used as a flavouring for rice wine, in place of the more traditional spices, than as a main recipe ingredient.

KITS

By definition wine-making kits contain more than one item. But the range is enormous. Some kits contain only fruit juice – which may or may not be grape – and yeast compound, packed together, with instructions for making into wine printed on the labels. Others also provide steriliser and Campden tablets, sugar, enzymes, fining agent and various additives, plus bottle labels and corks. Express kits contain fast-working yeasts and finings to produce wine that will ferment quickly, clear rapidly, require no maturation, and be ready for drinking after two or three weeks. Beginners' kits contain ingredients and such equipment as a demi-john, a fermentation lock, bored demi-john corks, bottle corks, syphon tubing and tap, a funnel, even bottles – though it seems extravagant to pay for these when they can be so easily acquired from neighbours or from restaurants, pubs or wine bars if your own household cannot produce a supply of empties.

Most kits are designed to make 1gal (4.5 litres or 6 bottles) of wine, but there is a growing demand for larger ones which produce 28 or 30 bottles. Consider the advantages and disadvantages before you choose the larger size. The main advantages are that wine made from a 5gal kit is much cheaper, and that a large amount is made from only one fermentation process, so it is less complicated than having several demi-johns of different wines all at different stages of fermentation, and requiring different sorts of attention. The disadvantages are that you need to acquire extra equipment – bigger pans and preparation bowls or buckets, a large fermenting vessel and a heating space large enough to accommodate it, since the heating belts and trays are usually designed for demi-johns. Also, more physical strength is needed to lift or tip a large fermenter and to make sure that it is thoroughly agitated every day. If anything should go wrong, and the finished wine is tasteless or spoiled, there is a great deal of wastage. And you need storage space for all those filled bottles. But if you have the space for larger-scale wine making and storage, the equipment, the strength – and want a lot of wine – plus a recipe and technique which you know is reliable, giving consistently good results, a large kit makes sense and saves time and money. If not, especially if you are still at the trial-and-error stage, it is wiser to stick to the smaller size.

When you browse along the shelves of your wine-making supply store or supermarket, it's important to have decided what *sort* of wine you want, whether it is to be a table wine, and if so whether you prefer white, red or rosé, sweet or dry, and whether you are looking for a country wine or a grape wine. There are kits too for aperitif wines, fortified wines, dessert wines, social wines. Most people prefer to start with table wine, perhaps a gallon of red and a gallon of white. Once that is flowing it is possible to add to the cellar a few specialities, such as some peach or apricot, or a vermouth or Madeira type wine.

Deciding which *brand* to buy is largely a matter of experiment or recommendation. Boots' wine kits are reliable and reasonably priced; other shops may point you in the direction of a different manufacturer, such as CWE, Unican or Winemaster. Often the specialist wine-making supply stores have samples of homemade wine that you can taste, or at least assistants who can tell you about the various products from personal experience. Alternatively, wine-making friends, or members of your local wine circle, will be able to make their own suggestions and *Amateur Winemaker* magazine regularly reviews the kits available. But finally the choice is a matter of your own preference and purse. Sometimes, but by no means always, the more you pay the better the quality of the wine you make.

Many wine-makers begin by using kits, which provide a simple, safe, trouble-free introduction to the craft. Often, though, you want to be more creative, more adventurous, and to achieve better quality and more exciting results. For some people the answer is to stop using kits and to collect separate ingredients and recipes once they have mastered the methods. Others prefer to obtain a good basic kit and then to improve on it. This can be done quite simply by adding extra ingredients. For example, the addition of elderberries to a red wine can improve astringency, while elderflowers or orange blossom can enhance the bouquet of a white wine. Roughly 1pt (500ml) of fresh grapefruit juice substituted for the same quantity of water will prevent wine from tasting too bland, and will improve the flavour of a white wine provided that it is given a few months to mature. Sometimes if a wine tastes insipid and dull, one or two drops of tannin solution will bring it to life. Body can be improved by incorporating up to 1tbsp of glycerine to each bottle of finished wine, and with a red wine one cup of blackcurrant cordial can be added to the demi-john during the last stages of fermentation.

No kit wine will suffer from having tinned fruit added at the beginning of the fermentation process, provided that the amount of sugar it contains is accounted for. To allow for the syrup in a 16oz (0.5kg) tin of fruit, 8oz (250g) less sugar would be required for 1gal (4.5 litres) of wine. Finally, the maturing agent Sinatin 17 can be added. This is a concentrated extract of oak and can give wine the smoothness and taste of having been barrel-matured, provided that it is added to each bottle very carefully, just a drop at a time, until the flavour is right.

If you want to improve kits, the important thing is to make sure that you have a sound grasp of the basic principles of wine-making, and can control the various processes properly, and then to experiment. No recipe should be regarded as solemn law, simply as a guideline within which there is ample room for manoeuvre.

LABELS

Should identify and give vital information about the type of wine in each bottle, its main ingredient(s) and the date of bottling, all of which are necessary if the wine is to be drunk at the right time and on the right occasion. They also create a personal and decorative finishing touch. For show wine, special labels may be supplied with the competition entry forms, and instructions will be given on what should be written on them. The label should be placed midway between the seams of the bottle, a specified distance above the base.

For domestic use, you can buy cheap packs of self-adhesive labels which can be re-used by being peeled off and transferred from one container to another. More expensive, but also more fun, are the decorative labels produced by suppliers, wine-making clubs and by Amateur Winemaker Publications. These can make charming gifts for the wine-maker. The more artistic wine-maker, of course, might like to design and make his or her own personal labels.

For purely functional purposes, while wine is still in fermenting or

Labels

maturing vessels and demi-johns, before bottling, tie-on luggage labels are useful for identification and information. It is all too easy to forget basic details as time progresses and new fermentations are underway.

LACTIC ACID *see* Acid.

LACTIC ACID BACTERIA *see* Bacteria.

LACTOBACILLI *see* Bacteria.

LACTOSE

The main sugar found in milk. A useful sweetening agent since it is non-fermentable and will therefore not cause re-fermentation of a wine that has fermented out but is over-dry. Lactose is a disaccharide which is broken down into glucose and galactose by the enzyme lactase. It is particularly useful for making herb or flower wines, and is easily available from chemists or wine-making supply stores.

LAEVULOSE

An old name, occasionally found in wine-making books written many years ago, for fructose.

LAG PHASE

There is an apparent, but not actual, lag in activity between the time the yeast is added to the must and the time fermentation is obvious through movement and bubbles. During this 'lag phase' chemical reactions are taking place as the yeast cells divide up and use the oxygen dissolved in the must, the process known as aerobic fermentation. When available oxygen is exhausted, the yeast begins anaerobic fermentation, and this is the process which is so visible because of the production of carbon dioxide as a byproduct of the conversion of sugar to alcohol.

LEAD

This metal should never be allowed to come into contact with wine. It contaminates it and can cause a gradual build up of poison within the system. Though most people are aware of the dangers of lead poisoning, it is not always remembered that some old pottery, the sort that may well be considered desirable for wine storage, has a lead glaze. Salt glazes are perfectly safe, but if you cannot recognise the difference you should avoid earthenware crocks altogether because a lead glaze can *kill*. Less beautiful modern vessels are much safer.

LEAVES

Some leaves can be used as a base ingredient for wine. If gathered fresh, pour boiling water over them to kill any animal life. Leaves lack nutrients and acids, so these should be added to the must. Oak leaves are of particular value to the wine-maker, being rich in tannin. Others used for good traditional country wines, provided that they are tender and young, are walnut leaves, vine leaves, nettle tips and bramble tips. Tea leaves are also recommended.

LEES

The sediment at the bottom of a vessel or bottle containing must or wine. If it is composed of dead yeast cells and pulp debris, the liquid should be racked off without delay, otherwise off-flavours and fusel oils may be created. A certain amount of lees is acceptable in matured red wine, provided that it is composed of tannins precipitating out. It should not be present in white wine.

LEMON MINT

The plant that most people mean by this is not a true mint (*Mentha*) at all, but the lemon-flavoured balm (*Melissa*). This is a good perennial herb for making wine, and for flavouring iced drinks, alcoholic or otherwise.

LEMONS

An important fruit for the wine-maker as a source of citric acid. The juice from one lemon is equivalent to about ¼oz (7g) of citric-acid powder, but since lemons vary so much it is impossible to be precise. Fresh lemon juice is more expensive and less convenient to use than crystal or powdered citric acid, but some people prefer to use natural fruit. A combination of the two is a good idea when making wines based on root vegetables, grains, flowers, bananas and dried fruits, which are lacking in acid.

As an added flavour ingredient, lemons can give zest and tang to fruit wines such as elderberry, quince, apricot, bilberry, date and fig; vegetable wines such as broad bean, celery, parsley, parsnip and potato; nut and spice wines such as almond, clove and ginger; flower wines such as clover, cowslip, dandelion, honeysuckle, marigold and rose petal; and grain wines such as barley, hop, rice and wheat. Some of these, especially the flower wines, need extra lemon juice not only to boost their acid content but also to give a stronger flavour and extra 'bite'.

LICENCE

In the United Kingdom a licence is not necessary to make wine, but it is required by anyone wishing to *sell* wine. Homemade wines can be given away but never sold, not even for charity or a good cause. No duty has to be paid if a wine is not sold, but it is payable if the wine is offered at parties where there is an admission charge, or if it is included in a raffle or auction. There is one other embargo: wine cannot be given away if the gift is to the donor's advantage, for instance if it is being used to promote business ventures or as an incentive to buy something.

A licence is necessary for distilling spirits, and heavy penalties are imposed on those who set up illicit stills.

LIFESPAN

The length of time a wine will last once it has finished fermenting. Unless made from express kits, nearly all wines need to mature, some for much longer than others, but once they have reached a certain level of maturity they will not get any better – they will, in fact, begin to deteriorate quite rapidly.

Full-bodied wines with a high tannin, alcohol and acid content have the longest lifespan because these substances slow down deterioration. Light white wines mature quickly and require only about six months to a year in storage vessels for satisfactory maturation. They will, however, need another three months once they are bottled to recover from 'bottle sickness'. Fuller-bodied sweet white wines and Sauternes-type wines have a long lifespan because of their high alcohol level, and need one to three years in storage vessels. They will then last for a long time in bottles if storage conditions are right, perhaps for two or three more years. The high tannin content of red wines causes most of them to mature slowly. Clarets need particularly long and loving care: it might take them twenty years to reach perfection. Similarly, fortified wines – port, sherry and Madeira – will live and improve for very many years because their high alcohol content will inhibit the growth of most micro-organisms.

There are no hard and fast rules, but generally quality wines go on improving with age while mediocre wines may not get much better. The wine-maker should be sufficiently strong-willed to keep back at least some of his or her better fermentations to give them a few years

135

to mature. All wines, apart from instant ones, should be kept for at least six months to get rid of harshness and to be given a chance to improve. Then the less impressive ones can be drunk as *vin ordinaire*. It is wise not to make a decision about a dry red wine too soon, because it might take it a year or more to show its potential. Elderberry wine, for instance, can be almost undrinkably harsh after a year, but after two or more, when the excess tannin has matured out, the same bottle can be superb. *See* Maturation.

LIGHT

Red and rosé wines, in particular, will lose their colour if exposed to light. Store them in amber or green bottles or jars, or else they must be shielded. The simplest way of doing this is to cover them with black polythene bags, or to make them conical 'hats' of sturdy paper or lightweight cardboard. The best place for storage is in a dark cellar, cupboard or a darkened room. A wine exposed to light, particularly sunlight, while it is maturing can lose flavour and bouquet as well as colour, and will eventually become stale.

LIME

Lime blossoms make a delicate flower wine. If it is impossible to find a supply of fresh flowers, dried flowerheads are available from most wine-making supply stores and health-food shops, since they are also used to make a good 'tea'.

Lime juice is a particularly valuable base ingredient for a fine, golden, Sauternes-type wine, but care has to be taken with the recipe used to balance its high acid content. If the wine is too acid despite all precautions, precipitated chalk will reduce the level. A measure of 2–3tbsp of glycerol added to each gallon (4.5 litres) will benefit lime wine, giving it the required smoothness. Lime-juice cordial can be used instead of pure juice, but if so it should be simmered for 3 minutes before it is incorporated into the must in order to remove any preservative.

LIQUEURS

Strongly alcoholic drinks made from distilled spirits with added sweetening and flavouring; usually drunk after dinner. By clever choice of flavourings, it is possible to concoct very palatable liqueurs for much less than one would pay for commercially produced equivalents – though you do have to purchase some distilled spirits. This is also a way of making cheap brandy, such as marc brandy, into a thoroughly desirable drink with a touch of the exotic. The range of natural flavourings for liqueurs is extensive and includes flowers, herbs, fruits, spices and honey. One of the most famous and popular, especially in the country where there is an ample supply of the fruit, is sloe gin (for the recipe, *see* Sloes).

Egg Flip
Place 6 eggs, in their shells, in a bowl, and add the juice of 6 lemons. Turn every day until the shells have dissolved. This will take about a week. Strain, then add 5fl oz (140ml) of cream and 4oz (115g) of demerara sugar, and beat thoroughly. Add a quarter of a bottle of cheap brandy, bottle, and seal tightly.

Hawthorn Brandy
Cut dry fresh hawthorn blossoms with as little stalk as possible, press them down gently into a large jar and shake over them 2tbsp of sugar. Fill the jar with brandy, seal tightly, and store it in a warm cupboard for two or three months, agitating it gently at regular intervals. Decant into bottles, and keep them well stoppered to prevent evaporation. As an alternative flavour, use carnation petals, plus a small stick of cinnamon and a clove.

Cherry Brandy-type Liqueur
You can make liqueurs similar to commercial ones by using liqueur flavourings or extracts available from wine-making supply stores and combining them with Polish spirit or vodka, sugar syrup, glycerine and appropriate wine, either bought or homemade. For instance, a good cherry brandy-type liqueur can be made by mixing together 4fl oz (115ml) of Polish spirit with 5fl oz (140ml) of sugar syrup and 1tbsp of glycerine. Put these into a measuring jug and make up to 13fl oz (370ml) with dessert elderberry wine. Add cherry-brandy liqueur flavouring to taste, combine well and store for a month or two before drinking. Making liqueurs is a sensible way of using up wines that are drinkable but bland and boring. It does not matter what colour liqueurs are, but they should have a basic alcohol content of 16 per cent by volume.

For an absinthe, or aniseed liqueur, put 12fl oz (345ml) of Polish spirit into a measuring jug and add 2tsp of T. Noirot Anisette extract. Mix well and pour into a standard wine bottle. To this add 5fl oz (140ml) of sugar syrup. Tip a little white wine into the jug and swirl it around to collect up the last traces of spirit and flavouring, and add to the bottle. Finally, top up the bottle with white wine and shake thoroughly. The liqueur is now ready for drinking.

Slivovitz or Plum Brandy

For this you could use a red table wine, but a plum or damson social wine would give better results. Use the same technique as for absinthe, but combine the following ingredients:

11fl oz (308ml) 140° proof cheap brandy
1fl oz (28ml) sugar syrup
2–3tsp of T. Noirot Mirabelle extract
Wine for topping up

By using the same method but different liqueur flavourings and wines, it is possible to create, very easily, a whole range of excellent liqueurs. For a more detailed look at this mouth-watering topic the liqueur-lover would do well to acquire *Making Inexpensive Liqueurs* by R. Bellis (Amateur Winemaker Publications, 1976) and to read the relevant chapter in *Home Brewing and Wine-Making* by W. H. T. Tayleur (Penguin, 1973).

LITMUS PAPER

Formerly used to determine whether a wine was acid or alkaline, but not an adequate check for the needs of today's more sophisticated wine-maker. So pH papers are now used as indicators, bought in small books or rolls with a colour chart included in the pack. A leaf is removed and dipped into the wine or must, and when the colour has changed it is compared with the chart. This does determine the approximate pH, but for various reasons it is not as accurate or useful as titration – the method adopted by most experienced wine-makers who do not want to take chances. *See* pH; Indicator papers; Titration.

LIVELY

A term of praise for a wine with a satisfying, fresh and mature bouquet and flavour. The opposite of 'dull' or 'flat'.

LOAF SUGAR *see* Sugar.

LOGANBERRIES

Make a useful basis for red table wine, being virtually interchangeable, in wine recipes, with blackberries or raspberries. Also a useful source of malic acid.

LUMP SUGAR *see* Sugar.

MADEIRA

Madeira is not one but a group of tawny fortified wines which are given their characteristic colour, bouquet and flavour by being heated before maturation, a process which causes some of the residual sugar to caramelise. The only genuine Madeira is the product of the island of Madeira, situated in the Atlantic Ocean. The main types of Madeira are: Sercial (amber coloured, dry to the palate and drunk as an aperitif); Verdelho (golden coloured, slightly sweet and useful as an aperitif or a table wine); Bual (full-bodied, tawny coloured, medium sweet and drunk as a dessert wine); Malmsey (very full-bodied, tawny coloured, sweet and suitable for a dessert wine). The difference between these four Madeiras depends upon the type of grape used in their manufacture.

Since most Madeiras are full-bodied wines, the home wine-maker attempting to recreate a wine of that type should include a large proportion of bananas in the recipe as a body-giving ingredient, as well as raisins or white-grape concentrate for vinosity. In addition, useful ingredients include blackberries, gooseberries, yellow plums, greengages, peaches and parsnips. The usual method of dealing with them is by pulp fermentation. As much alcohol as possible should be produced in the first instance by natural fermentation. This is made comparatively easy by the use of a nutritious Madeira yeast starter, which should give 16–18 per cent alcohol provided that the yeast is fed regularly with sugar syrup. When the fermentation has ceased, the wine should be racked off and then fortified with distilled spirit to increase its alcoholic strength by about 1 per cent. The fortification will speed up clarification and improve the quality of the wine. It should then be stored for a few months and racked at least once more before the heating process.

In commercial production, heating is carried out in *estufas*, specially heated chambers where the temperature can be carefully controlled. The amateur must make his or her own type of estufa, perhaps a shelf in the airing cupboard, boiler-room or greenhouse, anywhere that it is possible to maintain a temperature of 90°F (32°C) plus, for a long time. The best container for this process is a glass vessel, not completely filled at first, to allow for expansion. Since fermentation may be lively in the early hours of the process, the vessel should be plugged with cottonwool to start with. When the carbon dioxide has been driven off, top up the container with warm wine, then firmly cork it to prevent evaporation.

While the wine is in the estufa (this period can last anything from three months to a year, the longer the better) it should be racked off regularly. When it is brought out it may have developed an off-flavour known as 'estufa flavour'. This can be removed by powdered charcoal:

mix ½–1oz (15–30g) of charcoal with each gallon (4.5 litres) of wine, allow to settle, then rack off. If the charcoal refuses to settle out, the wine will have to be filtered or, preferably, fined with a proprietary fining agent. Finally, the wine should be allowed to mature for another year, if possible in a wooden cask, before being bottled and kept for as long as possible before drinking, to allow the full rich Madeira flavour to develop. *See* Estufas; Topping up.

MAGNESIUM SULPHATE

Magnesium sulphate or magnesium salts, commonly known as Epsom Salts, is a soluble form of magnesium. It is necessary for some of the chemical reactions in fermentation. In hard-water areas it is present in sufficient quantities in tap water, but wine-makers who live in soft-water areas will need to add a pinch of magnesium sulphate to each gallon (4.5 litres) of the must.

MAIZE

Like other cereals, maize can be incorporated into a must as a body-giving ingredient, but it is not highly recommended as it can impair the wine and cause haziness. It can also be used as a base ingredient for a cereal wine in which grape concentrate and amylase are included to improve flavour and shorten the maturation period. Again, this is not a particularly worth-while fermentation; maize wine is inferior to barley or rice wine. Maize is best as a beer-making ingredient and is not greatly valued by wine-makers. *See* Cereals; Haze, starch.

MALIC ACID *see* Acid.

MALO-LACTIC FERMENTATION *see* Fermentation.

MALT

This is barley which has been heated and partly germinated so that the starch has been converted into maltose. Malt extract forms one of the ingredients of yeast starter, as well as being a separate ingredient in some wine recipes. Malt extract is the 'secret ingredient' in homemade 'instant wine' recipes. If it is combined with vitaminised nutrient, it accelerates the fermentation of tinned or bottled fruit juices, syrups and concentrates, and enables the yeast to work upon the sugar (which should have been inverted first of all) and other fermentables, and reduce the gravity to zero in just over a week. For 1gal (4.5 litres) of wine, 8oz (225g) of light dry malt extract can be used without affecting flavour. Most juices can be used, but among the most satisfactory are grapefruit, orange, lemon, apple, pineapple and pear, grape concentrate and blackcurrant and rosehip syrups.

MALTOSE

The principal sugar produced from barley. It is fermented very slowly by wine yeasts.

MANDARINS *see* Tangerines.

MANGOLDS *see* Turnips.

MANNITOL

An apparent paradox, a bitter-tasting sugar. It is produced by a species of lactobacilli, and may be formed if a sweet wine develops a malo-lactic fermentation. It is one of the byproducts which give the infected wine an off-flavour. *See* Bacteria, lactobacilli; Fermentation, malo-lactic.

MARC

The French word for 'pressed pulp'. Marc from spent grape pulp may be used to make cheap brandy, known as marc brandy or eau-de-vie-de-marc, which can have an alcohol content as high as 47 per cent. This is used either for fortifying wines or – as Marc-de-Bourgogne – as an alternative to the more expensive cognacs and armagnacs.

MARIGOLD

The flowers, either fresh or dried, can be used for making a pleasant, amber-coloured table wine. The marigold blooms from July to September, and about 4pt (2.25 litres) of the fresh petals, gathered when quite open and dry and stripped of any greenery, are enough for 1gal (4.5 litres) of wine.

MARROW

Marrow or pumpkin can be used to make a sweet social wine. It should be peeled, then diced or grated and placed in a fermenting bucket with minced sultanas or grape concentrate, orange juice, citric acid, sugar syrup, yeast, yeast nutrient and cold water. It should then be left to steep for ten days, closely covered, at a temperature of 70°F (21°C). It should then be strained, fermented out, racked off and left to mature in bulk for six months before bottling.

MATURATION

The change in the quality of wine between the time when fermentation stops and the point at which it has reached perfection – or as near perfection as it ever will – and is ready for drinking. During this period many things happen to the wine. If the acid balance is right, the succinic and malic acids will form esters which will enhance its bouquet and flavour. If it is over-acid, it will mellow. Unfortunately, if wine is lacking in acid, maturation will have the opposite effect and give it an unpleasant taste. Fusel oils will be broken down to form acids and aldehydes. Acetic acid will be produced, and the aldehydes will join with alcohol to form acetals. If it is a red wine (for which careful maturation is particularly important), the tannin content will be reduced and astringency lessened, reducing any original harshness.

Wine can be matured in bulk or in small quantities. The best results come from slow maturation, which is most effectively carried out in a very large cask or vessel as this admits less oxygen in proportion to the volume of liquid, and consequently oxidation reactions are slow and thoroughly satisfactory. Unfortunately, not many of us possess such large containers and have to be content with smaller ones.

Wine matures better in wood than in plastic or glass because wood is porous and admits air, which is vital if oxidation is to do its work properly. Plastic and glass can nevertheless be used provided that the container is fitted with a cork bung and is racked at regular intervals. Maturing in a large wooden cask is both ideal and traditional, and every wine-maker should aim to have at least one, preferably made of oak, in which to mature the very best fermentations.

After a period in a large maturation vessel, when the oxygen has done its useful work, the wine should be bottled in order to slow down oxidation. It will continue to mature and esterify, and both bouquet and flavour will improve.

Maturation should take place in a dark, dry and cool environment. A cellar is fine, but most of us have to make do with a garage, a cupboard under the stairs, the corner of the utility room or even a space under the floorboards. The most important thing, apart from the amount of light, is the temperature. It should remain at about 50°F (10°C), no more or maturation will be too fast to give satisfactory results.

There is no hard and fast rule about the time required for full maturation, except that white wine needs less than red. Most recipes will give an indication of how long the wine should be left; but taste at regular intervals to judge whether a wine is still improving or has reached its peak. While it is maturing the wine should be racked off whenever any yeast debris appears in the bottom of the vessel, probably at two- or three-monthly intervals at first. If this task is neglected, off-flavours will develop and the finished wine will be impaired.

MEAD

A very ancient alcoholic drink, perhaps dating back to 10,000 BC. Once immensely popular, its popularity waned, but it is now coming back into favour and is often part of the wine- and beer-maker's repertoire. It is made from fermented honey in water. The longer it is kept, the better it tastes, and it should probably be kept for a minimum of twelve months. It is generally drunk as a refreshing social drink, either before or after a meal.

MEASUREMENTS *see* Gallon; Scales.

MEDLAR

Now quite a rare fruit, though once widely grown. They look like small brown-skinned apples and are suitable for wine. They are ready

Medlar

for harvesting in October, and the fruit should be very ripe but not beginning to rot. It should be fermented on the pulp. Only sugar, yeast and citric acid need to be added, along with water; 6lb (2.75kg) of fruit are enough for 1gal (4.5 litres) of wine.

MELOMEL

Originally a simple, traditional country wine, made with fermented honey in place of sugar, with fruit added. Now, because of its honey content, it is more often classified as a type of mead.

MELON

This fruit makes a good wine provided that it is combined with banana gravy for body and with white grape concentrate for vinosity and flavour.

For 1gal (4.5 litres) of wine, you will need about 4 average-sized melons. These should be de-seeded and thoroughly mashed to a fine juicy pulp. Add 'gravy' made from 2 or 3 average-sized over-ripe bananas, hot sugar syrup and grape concentrate, cover, leave for 24 hours, and then add citric acid, tannin, yeast starter, pectin-destroying enzyme and water. Ferment on the pulp for five days, then strain and ferment out in the usual way. It should be ready for drinking after about six months.

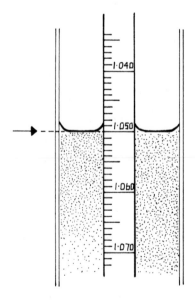

Meniscus

MENISCUS

The curved surface tension on the top of a liquid. When the must is poured into a trial jar for a hydrometer reading, the level of liquid will be seen to be higher at the edges of the jar and against the tube of the hydrometer, because of the effects of surface tension. Hydrometer readings should therefore be taken where the level of liquid is at its lowest, away from the edges. The reading should be taken with the eye at surface level for the greatest possible accuracy.

METABISULPHITE

The sterilising chemical from which Campden tablets are made. When it is put into water it is broken down into bisulphite, and sulphur dioxide gas is given off. It is this gas which kills or inhibits bacterial infection. Wine-makers usually refer to metabisulphite as sulphite or bisulphite, and it is usually sold in the form of Campden tablets, or sodium or potassium salts. *See* Campden tablets; Sulphite.

METABOLISM

A change, or chemical reaction, in an organism or single cell by which either nutrient material is built up into living matter, or protoplasm is broken down into simpler substances in order to perform special functions. Wine is created by the metabolism of its initial ingredients, basically sugar and yeast in water, to create alcohol.

METAL

Contaminates wine, giving it a distinct metallic flavour, and often causes haze. Metals should never be allowed to come into contact with acidic fruit juices, musts that are fermenting, or wines that are maturing. This means that metal equipment and storage containers should be avoided in favour of wood, plastic or glass. Metals which are particularly liable to cause damage are brass, copper, tin, iron, zinc and, especially, lead, including pottery with a lead glaze, and chipped or cracked enamel.

When it is necessary to boil ingredients in water it is permissible to use stainless-steel containers or *completely sound* enamel saucepans. If the ingredients are low in acid content, like bananas or root vegetables, aluminium pans are acceptable. The reason for this embargo on metal is that the acids which exist in fruit juice and wine dissolve metal and absorb some of its particles into the liquid. No wine should be subjected to prolonged contact with any type of metal, because some sort of chemical reaction will take place and the quality of the wine will almost certainly suffer from contamination. *See* Haze, metal.

METHEGLYN

A type of spiced mead, originally peculiar to Wales and drunk purely for medicinal purposes. It was often flavoured with herbs, but it is now more usually based on fermented honey to which ginger, cloves, cinnamon and nutmeg are added. It is at its best served at room temperature, and should not be chilled.

METHYL ALCOHOL *see* Alcohol.

MICRO-ORGANISMS

Single-cell plants or animals which are invisible to the naked eye. Those most important to the wine-maker are yeasts and bacteria. Both can be either useful or damaging. *See* Yeasts; Fungi; Bacteria.

MILK

The source of the protein casein, and a simple but effective fining agent. Only a few drops (find out how many by trial and error with a small sample of wine) are required to fine a gallon (4.5 litres) of clouded white wine. It is not suitable for red. It is also the source of the useful non-fermentable sugar, lactose.

MINT

A useful herb in aperitif wines, liqueurs, summer punches and fruit cups, and mint julep, in which it is combined with whisky.

An aperitif wine can be made by fermenting 1½pt (850ml) of mint leaves with dried fruit or grape concentrate, honey, ginger, yeast and nutrients. An alternative, and probably better method, is to infuse mint into a standard white wine base *before* the yeast is added and is fermented out. For this you need 2oz (56g) of fresh, or 1oz (28g) of dry, chopped mint put into a muslin bag which is suspended in the must for about 2 hours. If it is left longer than this the flavour will be overpowering.

Mint-flavoured liqueurs include the popular Crème de Menthe and its close rival, Mint Chocolate Liqueur, but it is probably wiser to make these from T. Noirot mint extract or other proprietary essences and flavourings rather than from the fresh herb, unless liqueur-making is one of your particular specialities.

For a summer punch try *Pineapple Cup*. Peel one small fresh pineapple, slice it into a bowl, sprinkle over 2tbsp of sugar and a miniature bottle of Kirsch liqueur, and leave to infuse for about an hour. Pour over it two bottles of dry white wine, and the juice of one large lemon, stir well, decant into a sparkling glass jug, and serve with ice cubes and sprigs of mint floating in it. To make *Mint Julep*, simply drop one large sprig of mint into a glass with a spoonful of sugar and some crushed ice, then top up with whisky and chill before drinking.

MONOPOTASSIUM TARTRATE *see* Cream of tartar.

'MOTHER' *see* Infection.

MOULD *see* Fungi.

MOUSE OR MOUSINESS *see* Infection.

MOUSSEUX

The description which, according to French law, must be put on any champagne-type wine which is not made in Champagne. It simply means 'sparkling'.

MULBERRIES

A good fruit for making both wine and liqueurs. Unfortunately, they may be difficult to find nowadays, but loganberries can be used in their stead. Mulberries ripen in September, and ideally should not be gathered until they have fallen from the tree. A total of 4–6lb (1.75–2.75kg) will make 1gal (4.5 litres) of wine. Considerably less are needed for a liqueur, and the process is quite simple. Take half a bottle of cheap gin, steep in it the same volume of pricked mulberries, add a few drops of ratafia essence and sugar to taste (usually about half the weight of the fruit used). Leave this mixture to infuse for two to three months in a tightly stoppered jar which should be agitated daily, then strain and bottle. It will improve with keeping, so try not to drink it too soon.

MULLED WINE

A good winter drink, a splendid starter for a cold-weather party and a useful way of using up a red wine that is reasonably pleasant to drink but not quite up to scratch. This is *not* a way to use one of your best wines because the original flavour will be quite transformed. The verb 'to mull' means 'to make wine, or beer, into a hot drink with the addition of sugar, spices, beaten yolk of egg etc' – and the 'etc' can mean anything that takes your fancy. My favourite method is to mix together:

1 bottle of full-bodied red wine
1 glass of port
2 cups of water
2tbsp dark brown sugar
2tbsp honey
a sliced lemon
a dash of grated nutmeg
a sprinkle of aniseed
a stick of cinnamon

Heat gently without boiling. *See* Glogg.

MUSCAT

A sweet fortified wine made from the muscat grape in southern Spain. The raisin produced from the muscat grape is called a muscatel, and is considered of very high quality. The addition of muscatels to a Sauternes-type wine will enhance the flavour.

MUST

The combination of prepared juices, sugar, additives and yeast from the original extraction to the end of fermentation. By this time it is officially considered to be a wine, though it still has to go through further phases: racking, clarification, maturation and bottling.

The must – its make-up, preparation, care and control – is the absolute essence of a good wine, and the eventual quality of the finished wine depends entirely upon what happens to the must. This includes the quality and condition of the ingredients that go into it; the method used for preparation and extraction; the balance with which the ingredients are combined; the temperature at which the must is fermented; the time allowed for its various stages of fermentation; and the standards of cleanliness and sterilisation maintained to guard the must against bacterial attack or to cure infections that may occur. *See* Blending – ingredients.

MYCODERMA ACETI *see* Bacteria, *Acetobacter aceti.*

NECTARINES

A useful fruit since they can be used fresh or tinned to make either a good wine or a delicious liqueur. If tinned nectarines are used, approximately 1lb (½kg) is required for each gallon (4.5 litres) of light dry table wine. If you are lucky enough to have a supply of fresh nectarines the following recipe will give good results.

Take 6lb (2.75kg) nectarines and cut in half. Pour over them 1gal (4.5 litres) of boiling water. Allow to infuse for four days, then strain and measure. To each gallon of liquor add 3lb (1.36kg) of sugar, the juice of 3 lemons, and 1tbsp of Sauternes yeast, and ferment out in the usual way. Keep for approximately one year before drinking.

Nectarine Liqueur is made by chopping the fresh fruit and packing it in layers in a screw-top jar, covering each layer with a sprinkling of sugar, just enough to fill the spaces between the pieces of fruit. After three or four days drain off the syrup, pressing the fruit gently, and put the liquid into a covered jar in a cool place. Cover the fruit with brandy and after another three or four days strain it off, pressing the fruit once again. Combine the spirit with the syrup, add sugar to taste if necessary, then bottle the liqueur and leave to mature for six months. The nectarines can be used in a fresh-fruit dessert or compote.

NETTLES

A source of a good traditional leaf wine, as well as being excellent for making beer. For a gallon (4.5 litres) of a medium social wine approximately 4pt (2.25 litres) of nettleheads are required. Only the top 2in (5cm) of nettle should be used, early in the growing season while the plant is still fresh, young and tender. The nettleheads should be infused with sugar, grape concentrate, ginger and the juice and grated peel of two lemons, and then pulp fermented in the must for one week only, before the wine is finished in the usual way. Nutrients as well as acids must be added to all leaf wines.

NITRATE

Plants obtain nitrogen from nitrates which are naturally occurring salts. Yeasts are unable to metabolise these salts so more have to be added to the must in the form of ammonium phosphate and ammonium sulphate. These are sold as 'yeast nutrients' because they literally nourish, or feed, the yeast.

NITROGEN

Vital to yeast growth, though many amateur wine-makers are guilty of not giving their musts sufficient. Some nitrogen is present in the basic ingredients of most wines, but more should be added in the form of ammonium sulphate or ammonium phosphate, preferably the latter, which can be bought either in a proprietary yeast nutrient or separately from a chemist or wine-making supply store. If yeast is kept short of nitrogen, it will take it from decaying cells, with a consequent build up of fusel oils in the must. These will cause off-flavours, detract from the bouquet and even become poisonous if they are present in a large enough concentration.

NOBLE ROT OR MOULD

The common name for the fungus *Botrytis cinerea*, which attacks grapes growing in warm, humid conditions. It is called 'noble' because it can improve the wine-making qualities of some grapes, and in specific regions is actively encouraged. In the Sauternes region, for instance, the infection is welcomed because if there is a dry sunny period *after* the grapes have been infected the mould draws the water it needs from the fruit, leaving a grape with a greatly increased sugar content. Its growth is similarly encouraged in Hungary and parts of Germany.

Grapes attacked by botrytis (or 'botrytised grapes') have other qualities as well as added sweetness. Their acidity level is raised, but not excessively so, and they possess glycerol, which influences the flavour and quality of the wine produced. In addition the shrinkage of the berries, due to loss of water, loosens the skin from the pulp, making the business of pressing or juice extraction much easier.

The unique quality of Sauternes wine is totally dependent upon botrytis, and those years in which weather conditions are not conducive to the growth of the noble rot may produce an inferior vintage. Because of the part played by botrytis it is difficult, though not impossible, for the home wine-maker to create a truly Sauternes-type wine, since he or she is unlikely to have access to a supply of botrytised grapes, though there are recipes which show how it can be simulated. A careful blend of appropriate ingredients is vital, and these will include a light-coloured fruit to capture the golden colour, grape concentrate for vinosity, bananas for body, flowers for fragrance and bouquet, and glycerine for smoothness to the palate.

In other great wine-producing areas, such as Burgundy, botrytis is considered an unwelcome infection. The reason for this apparent paradox is that, given the wrong climatic conditions, which may well occur in the Burgundy region, it can damage the grapes, splitting their skins and allowing access to undesirable organisms which will make the fruit unusable.

NON-VINTAGE

In some years wines of exceptional quality are created, mainly because weather conditions have been right to produce perfect grapes with the ideal sugar and acid content. When this happens the wine is declared 'vintage' and the date is put on the label so that people will know that it is an exceptionally good product. In other years, when the wine is of a lesser quality, it is declared 'non-vintage' and the label bears no date. Sometimes a non-vintage wine is a blended wine. The terms 'vintage' and 'non-vintage' refer particularly to port and champagne but can be used for other wines as well.

NOSE

Bouquet.

NO-YEAST RECIPES

Wine is created by fermentation. Without yeast, no fermentation can occur and no alcohol can be produced. It is therefore a contradiction in terms to talk about a 'no-yeast' wine recipe: it would be more accurate to describe the recipe as having no *added* yeast.

Wild yeast exists naturally all about us, on fruit, in the air and on our skins. Occasionally it is possible to achieve fermentation through the spontaneous action of these organisms. However, this method is old-fashioned and has largely fallen out of use because wild yeast is unreliable, can cause bacterial spoilage and impair flavour. It is therefore better to avoid no-yeast recipes and go for those which give more hope of creating a successful and trouble-free fermentation. *See* Yeast, wild.

NUTRIENTS

Yeast works on sugar to ferment fruit or vegetable matter, but it needs trace minerals too, which are naturally present in the grape but are often lacking in other basic wine-making ingredients. Without them, the yeast may not be sufficiently active to reach its maximum alcohol tolerance, so it is important to add them to the must separately.

The nutrients most often lacking are nitrogen, phosphate and vitamin B_1. A combination of these, known as 'yeast nutrients', can be bought ready-prepared, and one teaspoonful should be added to each gallon (4.5 litres) of the must before the yeast is put in. For those who make a lot of wine it is cheaper to buy the ingredients separately in the form of ammonium phosphate or ammonium sulphate; potassium phosphate or potassium sulphate; and vitamin B_1 tablets.

Nutrient deficiency is one of the causes of stuck fermentation and the production of undesirable fusel oils. When the must lacks nitrogen the yeasts have to create their own by de-aminating amino acids, and these are consequently released into the wine damaging both its flavour and bouquet.

OAK LEAVES

Oak tannin is available commercially in powder form as an additive for wines deficient in astringency. Young oak leaves can be used to give a refreshing bite to a grape or raisin wine, and if they are picked about a month after they have emerged from the bud, in the late spring, they will be at their best for wine-making, though they can be turned into oak wine as late as August.

In country-wine recipes, the recommended extraction method is by hot water infusion. Pour boiling water over the leaves and allow them to soak overnight; drain the liquor off and add to the must. The quantity of leaves depends upon their age: the younger they are the more are needed but the better the flavour. In August, use too many and you feel as if your tongue will curl up! Old country traditions involve practical tests like looking through them at the sky: if it is possible to see the clouds moving then a gallon of leaves is needed to make a gallon of wine.

Oak leaves

The following recipe makes a delicate aperitif or social wine but is too strongly flavoured for use as a table wine. You will need ¾lb (340g) raisins or 7fl oz (200ml) white grape juice; the juice of one lemon; 1½lb (675g) sugar; yeast starter and nutrients; 2½lb (1.25kg) oak leaves (more or less). Prepare an oak liquor by hot infusion, then use half for pulp fermentation of the raisins and half to dissolve the sugar for addition to the raisin juice when this is strained off the pulp. (If grape concentrate is used the method will be by juice fermentation, of course.) When the oak-leaf liquor and the raisin juice are combined, add the lemon juice and yeast starter and nutrients, put into a fermenting vessel and ferment out. The wine should be ready for bottling in about two months, and ready for drinking about four months after that. *See* Sauternes.

OFF-FLAVOURS

Those tastes in wine that are caused by infection, poor fermentation or poor control of the must, and destroy the true flavour of the wine. Fusel oils are a common cause.

OILINESS

When wine becomes thick and viscous, almost the consistency of white of egg, it is a symptom of 'ropiness'. This is an infection caused by lactic-acid bacteria and it can be cured by sulphiting. *See* Infection.

ORANGE BLOSSOMS

These can be used fresh, dried, or in the form of an infusion, and make a useful additive to a white wine. They are almost as good as elderflowers for imparting a delightful, flowery bouquet, and are particularly valuable if used to enhance a rather dull white wine kit. The easiest way to incorporate them is to pack dried flowers into a small nylon or muslin bag and to suspend it in the must for two or three days during fermentation. Half an ounce (14g) is sufficient for 1gal (4.5 litres) of table wine, twice that amount for dessert wine.

ORANGES

A good wine-making fruit which can produce an excellent aperitif wine, rather like a dry sherry; a splendid Sauternes-type dessert wine; or a light white table wine. Oranges should not be used in too great a proportion since they are rich in citric acid. The pith should be carefully excluded because of its bitter taste.

To get the best of an orange, the peel should be grated, boiled for 5 minutes in 1pt (575ml) of water, and left to steep for a day. The fruit should be squeezed, then added to the strained rind liquid. At this point it is ready to be included with the other recipe ingredients. Alternatively, tinned, bottled or frozen orange juice makes a perfectly acceptable substitute for fresh oranges.

Orange Wine Cup can be made with orange wine. Mix together one bottle of the wine with two small measures of brandy and the juice from a small tin of mandarin oranges. Chill well. Just before serving add a small bottle of cider, ice cubes, mandarin oranges; sweeten to taste and stir well.

Curaçao-type Liqueur: Soak the grated peel of one large orange overnight in 5fl oz (140ml) of Polish spirit. Strain, and add to the liquor 5fl oz (140ml) of sugar syrup, 1tbsp of glycerine, 1–2tsp of curaçao extract, and make up to 13fl oz (370ml) with orange wine.

ORGANISATIONS

Though wine-making is often considered an individual hobby, it can be a convivial pastime if wine-makers join the various organisations that exist to share and exchange advice, experience, information, recipes and equipment. Most areas possess a wine circle; details of this should be available from the local library or advertised in the local press. Many wine circles belong to a regional branch of the Federation of Amateur Winemakers, which organises an annual wine-makers' festival with demonstrations, competitions and social events.

Individual wine-makers, wine circles and federations may belong to the National Association of Wine and Beer Makers, which puts on a weekend national show known as 'the National'. It is normally held around Easter, at a different venue each year, but usually in the south of England. The awards presented to the best wines at the National are very highly prized since competition is keen.

Workers' Educational Associations, local Colleges of Further Education, catering departments, cookery schools and organisations like the Women's Institute also arrange classes in wine-making. If there is one in your area, it may well be worth investigating since there you can meet all types of wine-makers, from beginners to national judges, and their pooled experience is an immensely useful source of ideas and information.

OXALIC ACID

A toxic acid present, for instance, in rhubarb. Rhubarb can nevertheless be a good wine-making ingredient, provided that it is not mechanically pressed or subjected to infusion or pulp extraction, and provided that the leaves are discarded. The acid is then not present in sufficient quantities to be dangerous.

OXIDATION

Some fruits oxidise and turn brown almost immediately their skins are removed and they make contact with air. These include apples and pears. When these fruits are being prepared for wine-making they should be put into cold, sulphited water as soon as they are cut and not left standing on a chopping board even for 5 minutes or so. If the fruit is crushed and pressed to extract juice, the juice should be treated at once with 100ppm sulphite.

Wine Oxidation
Oxidation of the must should be prevented since it will cause brown enzymic discoloration and haze, and may ruin the finished wine beyond saving. However, if the wine is looked after carefully; the fermentation vessel sealed with an air-lock; the racking conducted with the minimum of splashing; the jar topped up completely after racking; and the wine sulphited after the first two rackings, oxidation should be avoided. Some methods of filtration which expose the wine to the air for any length of time can cause over-oxidation, and consequent 'bottle sickness', but the more modern and sophisticated techniques such as continuous filtration, or pressure filtering, minimise oxidation and do less damage.

In some cases, oxidation can have beneficial effects on wine. Red wines which are harsh and astringent when young, due to excess tannin, will mellow when they are oxidised. For this reason they cannot be properly matured in glass, which is not porous and will not admit air. They should be bulk-matured in casks of the right size so that the surface area, affected by oxygen, is in the correct proportion to the volume of the wine. In a small cask the surface tends to be too large and oxidation is consequently too rapid.

Wines that begin to show signs of oxidation (apple wines in particular) can be converted into sherry-type wines. The oxidation should be arrested by the addition of sulphite and the wine left for 24 hours so that any discoloration will be bleached out.

Oxidative (or Oxidassic) Casse
A brown discoloration of fruit caused by an enzyme called o-polyphenyloxidase which is present in large quantities in over-ripe fruit, especially in pears and apples, and which oxidises tannin to brown pigments.

OXYGEN

Needed during two stages of wine-making: first, it is necessary for primary (or aerobic) fermentation to allow the yeast colony to become active; secondly, it is needed, in *small* amounts, during maturation to allow oxidation reactions and to help the wine to mellow. Oxygen should be excluded during the secondary (or anaerobic) phase of fermentation to prevent airborne infections and spoilage.

PALATE

Commonly used to refer to the seat of the sense of taste. In fact, the palate and the rest of the mouth combine with the nose and the brain to appreciate taste, and when the nose is not functioning properly taste is affected too. A good wine is said to 'appeal to the palate', and when wine is being judged it is moved around the judge's mouth so that it contacts all parts of the palate, so that its flavour, balance and quality are completely assessed before being spat out.

PARMAGOOSE

It is almost worth making this wine for the charm of the name alone, though it is very palatable in its own right. It is simply a combination of parsley, marrow and gooseberry wine mixed in equal proportions.

PARSLEY

One of the best wine-making herbs, with a flavour very similar to that of elderflowers. It can be the base ingredient for an aperitif or medium white table wine. Two pints (1.25 litres) of freshly picked parsley for 1gal (4.5 litres) of wine produces the best taste and bouquet, and though many recipes recommend the boost of ginger this is not necessary. It *is* important to add acids and nutrients since these are lacking in the plant.

PARSNIPS

One of the best wine-making vegetables although they contain a great deal of pectin, which is released during boiling, and this can give rise to clarification problems unless the must is treated with a pectin-destroying enzyme. Parsnips can be used for a Sauternes-type wine; an oloroso sherry-type wine; a Madeira-type wine; a white table wine; or a blending wine. They are very useful for the latter function since they are bland but provide body; they make the perfect complement to a wine that tastes satisfactory but is a little thin.

Parsnips are best lifted from the ground after a short hard frost; January is often a good month. Parsnip wines must have slow maturation and will not be at their best until they are at least a year old.

PASTEUR

The famous French chemist, Louis Pasteur, is important to wine-makers because he pioneered the idea that yeast caused fermentation as well as proving that wines that were maturing needed oxygen. His name has gone into the language as the verb 'to pasteurise' and the noun 'pasteurisation'. Wine, like milk, can be pasteurised, or sterilised, by being heated to a temperature of 140°F (60°C) for 3–4 minutes. This will kill nearly all the bacteria, and therefore arrest fermentation, but it will also prevent maturation since the enzymes will be destroyed.

PEACHES

An excellent wine-making fruit, whether used fresh, tinned or as diluted juice, and available all the year round. They are very versatile and can make a good, medium-bodied, delicately flavoured, white table wine; a fino-type sherry; a Sauternes-type social wine; a Madeira-type wine; or peach liqueur and peach punch. Since they provide little body, it is necessary to use a body-giving ingredient such as bananas, which are an excellent complement in both colour and flavour. As peaches are rich in pectin, use a little pectin-destroying enzyme in the must to avoid later problems in clarification.

Peach Liqueur: for an economical peach liqueur, mix together 14fl oz (400ml) peach wine with 4fl oz (115ml) sugar syrup and 4fl oz (115ml) cheap brandy, stir thoroughly, steep together in a sealed bottle for a couple of months, and then use.

Peach Punch is also delicious as a summer 'cup'. Drain a small tin of sliced peaches, and put the juice into a bowl. Add some ice cubes to the juice along with two bottles of red wine and two cups of undiluted orange squash, then stir in the peach slices. Just before serving, add two cups of soda water or lemonade, and float thin slices of cucumber on top.

PEAPODS

When fresh, young and fleshy, peapods make an excellent white table wine, and have the double advantage that the peas themselves can be eaten since they are not required in the wine. The pods should be boiled until tender, and then the strained liquor fermented out. The

157

pods provide almost as much body as raisins, but they lack flavour, sugar and tannin, so raisins, sultanas or, preferably, grape concentrate should be included in the recipe. Peapods can also be used as the base for flower wines and are especially good with elderflowers. This is convenient since their growing periods overlap. Peapod wine benefits from a minimum storage period of six months.

PEARS

A versatile fruit which can make perry, dry white table wine or an excellent sparkling wine. As pears are a hard fruit, they need to be crushed, sliced and pressed to extract the maximum juice. Pulp fermentation is not to be recommended for delicate and refined white wines. The flavour will be enhanced if the pears are pressed while ripe, but still firm, before they have become completely mature.

Like apples, pears are also rich in the oxidative enzyme o-polyphenyloxidase which catalyses the oxidation of tannins to the production of brown pigments which can ruin the appearance of the wine. They should therefore be sulphited during the preparation process, and sulphite should also be added to the extracted juice.

PEARSON SQUARE

Those wishing to fortify their best home-made wines should have a working knowledge of the Pearson Square, a simple method of calculating how much spirit should be added to the wine.

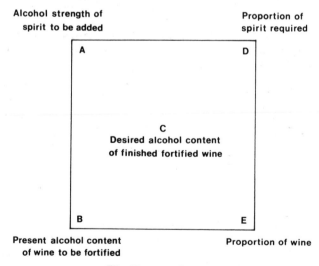

The Pearson Square

To use the square, write against A, B and C their strength *either* as a percentage of alcohol by volume *or* in terms of proof. Never mix the two systems! Then, to find D, subtract B from C; to find E, subtract C from A.

Suppose you are making a port-type wine from an elderberry wine, which you wish to fortify with Polish spirit containing 80 per cent alcohol, according to the label on the bottle. You have measured or calculated the alcohol content of the elderberry wine, which will probably be about 15 per cent, and you are aiming for a content of 20 per cent, which is normal for port. So fill in your Square like this:

To find D (the proportion of Polish spirit needed), subtract B (15 per cent) from C (20 per cent), and you have 5. To find E (the proportion of elderberry wine required), subtract C (20 per cent) from A (80 per cent), and you have 60.

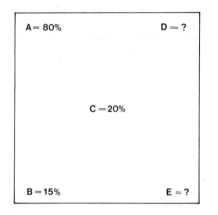

```
A = 80%                    D = ?



             C = 20%



B = 15%                    E = ?
```

Consequently, 5 parts of spirit should be mixed with 60 parts of wine, or they should be blended in the proportion of 1:12 in order to reach the desired alcohol strength.

```
A = 80%                    D = 5



             C = 20%            = 1:12



B = 15%                    E = 60
```

PECTIN

A substance found in the cell wall of plants, constituting the gelatinising agent in fruits and vegetables. While it is useful to the jam-maker, it can cause problems for the wine-maker if it is present in sufficient concentration to form a jelly. It is more soluble at higher temperatures and is therefore more likely to cause problems if pectin-rich fruit and vegetables, such as parsnips, peaches, plums, citrus fruits and apricots, are heated or boiled. Boiling also puts pectinase out of action, the naturally occurring pectin-destroying enzyme. The only remedy therefore is to add commercially produced pectin-destroying enzymes to pectin-rich materials while the must is being prepared, before fermentation. Since enzymes are destroyed by heat, they should only be added when the must is at room temperature. They will also procure a greater juice yield.

If a pectin haze develops in the finished wine, pectin-destroying enzymes may clear it, without affecting its quality. A precipitate will form which should be racked off. This process is usually more successful with red wine than white wine. It is quite simple to test wine for the presence of pectin. One part of wine should be combined with three parts of methylated spirits in a glass. If pectin is present it will gel within about 2 hours, forming little clots. *See* Haze, pectin.

PEEL

Fruit peel, especially that of oranges and lemons, adds zest to wine, particularly to aperitifs. Grate the peel off the fruit, carefully removing all pith, simmer in a little water for 5 minutes, then leave to infuse overnight. After straining, add to the must.

Peel extract has an inhibiting effect on yeast, so fermentation may be slow to start; if too much is used, it may prevent it altogether. This is because the peel excretes an oil which forms a layer on the surface of the must and keeps out the oxygen which the yeast needs for its aerobic fermentation period.

Pear peelings are rich in tannin. The peelings of six pears will provide enough tannin for 1gal (4.5 litres) of wine, if added to the must.

PERRY

Not a wine but pure pear juice (just as cider is pure apple juice) slightly fermented and weakly alcoholic.

PETILLANT

A French word used to describe a slightly sparkling wine which is fizzy on the tongue because of the bubbles of carbon dioxide which burst against it. Other words with the same meaning and used descriptively on wine labels include perlé, perlant, perlwein, crémant, spritzig and frizzante.

pH

A measure of the acidity or alkalinity of a solution. The pH factor gives the concentration of hydrogen ions, and this concentration depends upon its acidity. A pH factor of 7.0 signifies a completely neutral solution. Factors less than 7.0 indicate an acid solution, the lower the figure the more acidic the solution. Solutions with a pH factor of more than 7.0 are alkaline, higher figures being more alkaline than lower ones. Indicator papers can be bought which measure the pH of a solution when they are dipped into it and the colour compared with a standard colour chart, but this is not a very accurate or reliable technique and most experienced wine-makers will prefer to titrate for acid.

It is useful to know the pH factor of a must *not* primarily to determine its acid content but to assess its liability to bacterial infection and to judge its potential for a healthy fermentation. Many bacteria cannot grow in a must with a pH below 3.4; if it is less than this there is little likelihood of bacterial spoilage. Vigorous yeast growth, however, is likely to be inhibited if the pH is below 3.0. An ideal pH level is between 3.0 and 3.4. This should be achieved without difficulty if the wine-maker has prepared a properly balanced must. *See* Indicator papers; Acidity testing; Titration.

PHOSPHATES

Release energy in wine-making chemical reactions, and are usually introduced into the must in the form of nutrients and additives. *See* Ammonium phosphate; Potassium phosphate.

PINEAPPLE

Can be used in wine-making fresh (peeled and diced), tinned, in the form of squashes and cordials or as fruit juice (frozen or in tins or jars) to make either a social wine or a medium white table wine. Tinned fruit, juices, squashes and cordials, however, may contain preservatives and will need to be simmered for 3 minutes to remove them. Exotic fruit wines of this sort are better drunk young than mature.

For a *Pineapple Liqueur*, thinly slice a large fresh pineapple, sprinkle with sugar and leave it for 24 hours. Then squeeze out as much juice as possible, and measure it. Take an equal amount of cheap brandy, and add sugar in the proportion of 1tbsp to each ½pt (285ml). Combine the juice and sweetened brandy, put into a tightly sealed jar with a few pieces of pineapple, and leave for about a month, then strain and bottle.

PIPETTE

A calibrated tube used with a burette when titrating for acid. A wine-maker will usually use a 10ml pipette. *See* Titration.

PLASTERING

Covering the must with gypsum in the production of sherry, which increases the acidity and decreases the pH factor, and therefore minimises the risk of bacterial spoilage which might occur if the pH is high. The amateur wine-maker will add cream of tartar: ½–1oz (15–30g) to each gallon (4.5 litres) of must. It should be stirred in very thoroughly or it will not dissolve. *See* Gypsum; Sherry.

PLASTIC

Though not as attractive as wood or cork, plastic equipment has much to recommend it and is becoming more and more part of the wine-maker's stock. Its main advantages are that it is cheap, lightweight, virtually unbreakable, easily sterilised and readily obtained. It does have disadvantages, though. Yellow plastic should be avoided since it contains a poison called cadmium, minute amounts of which can be absorbed into the wine. Lightweight plastic containers may have such porous walls that oxidation could occur, and plastic often has an odour of its own (or that of its previous contents) which might ruin the bouquet of a new wine.

Plastic vessels, barrels, lidded buckets and bins should therefore be tough enough to be described by the retailer as 'food grade', and they should be odourless. Then provided that they have been thoroughly cleaned and sterilised, they can be used for short-term storage or fermentation, as well as preparation.

Plastic is also used to make 'corks' of various shapes and sizes. Though more expensive than those made of natural cork, they can be used repeatedly, so they are economical provided that they fit properly. Unless they are tight the wine will seep out if the bottles are laid on their sides for storage. Most modern funnels are plastic, though some people prefer glass. Avoid metal funnels, which may give off-flavours to the wine and cause metallic haze.

PLUMS

Plums, and their close relatives, the sloe, damson and greengage, as well as prunes, which are dried plums, can all be made into wine.

Plums are usually classified as culinary or dessert. Culinary plums are not only cheaper than dessert plums, they are generally considered better for wine-making. Wait until they are slightly over-ripe when they will give the best results. Culinary plums have a fairly high sugar content and a substantial amount of pectin, so pectin-destroying enzyme should be added if the fruit is prepared with boiling water. They are also high in acid, rich in vitamins and most nutrients, but contain little phosphorus, so include ammonium phosphate in the recipe. They are well provided with tannin, especially in the skins, but if you are aiming at a slow-maturing red wine add extra tannin to the must to improve the final product.

Plums

Plums are usually used to make a medium table wine or a sweet social wine. Red plums yield a rosé or golden wine, yellow plums a white one. A very special drink is a full, heavy plum wine with bananas incorporated for body and brandy for fortification.

There are some danger points, however, which need attention. Plums may have a waxy bloom on their skins and this can cause a haze. It should be removed by pouring boiling water over the fruit *while the skins are unbroken*. Plum stones should be discarded; they do not improve the wine, and can be harmful. Wine made from plums alone lacks body and will taste thin unless ripe bananas are incorporated in the recipe.

163

POISONS

Though most plant material can be used for wine-making, some of it is toxic, even deadly. Unfortunately no two wine-making authorities agree about what is safe. But should you be tempted, avoid making wine with: aconite; alder; azalea; berberis; bluebells; buttercups; clematis; cyclamen; deadly nightshade (belladonna); delphiniums; foxgloves; fungi; hemlock; holly; honeysuckle berries; irises; ivy; laburnum; laurel; lilac; lobelia; lupins; mistletoe; narcissus (including daffodils); poppies; privet; rhubarb leaves; rhododendrons; sweet peas; wood anemones; yew. If in doubt – don't.

Lead is also toxic, so avoid fermenting wines in earthenware crocks which may have a lead glaze.

POLISH SPIRIT

A type of vodka. As a general rule, 140° proof Polish spirit is the best spirit for fortification purposes. It combines a neutral flavour with great alcohol strength, and is consequently a better fortifying medium than brandy or gin. As these are only about 70° proof, more is needed to achieve the desired level of fortification. *See* Pearson Square; Fortification.

POLYSACCHARIDES

Sugars composed of many sugar molecules as distinct from monosaccharides, which are one-unit sugars, such as glucose and fructose, and disaccharides, which are made up of two monosaccharides joined up together, like sucrose and maltose. Polysaccharides include starch and glycogen. Yeast cells use the latter, and store it as a food reserve as part of the fermentation process.

PORT

A fortified wine originally produced in northern Portugal, in the region around Oporto, which gives it its name. Most port is sweet and red, but white port, either dry or sweet, is also produced in smaller quantities. It is thought that the character of port wine is due to the soil of the Upper Douro Valley which is rich in manganese and titanium. The true quality of port wine is also derived from fortification in the early stages to stop fermentation as soon as the must has achieved the required colour and alcohol content, and before all the sugar has been metabolised by the yeast, so that the result is a sweet, full-bodied, fruity wine. Long maturation is also necessary in cask and bottle to bring out the fullest possible flavour and quality. The home wine-maker must take note of both these requirements if he or she attempts to make a good port-type wine.

Most commercially produced port is blended – older wines with younger ones, harsh wines with smoother ones – to achieve a uniformity of character and a consistently high quality. There are five main types of port:

Vintage: deep ruby-red, full-bodied, with a fine bouquet and flavour. This should not be drunk until it is at least ten years old, but preferably twenty or thirty.

Crusted: similar to vintage, but not of quite the same high standard.

Ruby: a ruby-red port that has spent seven or eight years in the cask and has then been blended with other wines. It is fruity, with a vinous flavour, and is ready to be drunk almost as soon as it is bottled, though it may improve if kept for about five more years.

Tawny: this colour develops in port that has been left in the cask for fifteen years or more and become paler with the passing of time. The best genuine tawny ports have been blended with younger wines and fortified with old brandy to replace alcohol lost by evaporation. Some ports that are simply a combination of white and red ports are called 'tawny' but they have nothing of the character of a true tawny.

White: made in the same way as red port, but from white grapes. It can be either sweet or dry. A sweet white port is similar to ruby in character, but different in colour.

To make a reasonably inexpensive port, the home wine-maker must produce most of the alcohol, about 16–17 per cent, by natural fermentation, and to achieve this the yeast must be adequately supplied with nutrients and fed with sugar syrup. Fermentation should be conducted at a temperature of between 65° and 75°F (18° and 24°C) nearer the top of the range during the later stages. If it does not reach the required alcohol content, it can be fortified with brandy or Polish spirit as soon as fermentation has ended. If the wine improves dramatically after spending a year in a cask, then, and only then, it might be worth considering fortifying it to 20 per cent. The wine should be racked about every three or four months during storage both to clarify and oxygenate it. If it remains hazy after six to nine months it should be fined with a good proprietary fining agent. When it is twelve months old racking can be reduced to once every six months.

Port-type ruby wines can only be made with deep red juicy fruits such as cherries, elderberries, bilberries and blackcurrants. Bananas, raisins and red grape concentrate, preferably all three, should be added to give body, and elderflowers for bouquet. The following recipe is a possible guide.

3lb (1.5kg) elderberries
1lb (450g) bananas
1lb (450g) raisins
1pt (575ml) red grape concentrate
½pt (285ml) elderflowers
port yeast starter and yeast nutrients
sugar as required
1dtsp pectin-destroying enzyme
water up to 1gal (4.5 litres)

Make banana gravy by boiling the bananas in 5pt (3 litres) of water. Crush the elderberries and mince the raisins, and pour the hot banana gravy over. Add nutrients, cool, then combine with the concentrate, yeast starter and enzyme. Pulp ferment for two days, strain, and press lightly. Add the flowers to the liquid, leave for three days, then strain again. Add ¼pt (145ml) of sugar syrup every time the gravity drops to 5 (SG 1.005) or below until fermentation has ended (as instructed under Feeding the yeast, *see* Yeast). After fermentation, rack off and sulphite, then continue racking first at three-monthly intervals, then at four-monthly intervals, finally at six-monthly intervals, till perfectly clear. Now for the hard bit! Mature the wine in a cask for two to three years, and then in bottles for one or two more. The classic feature of a good port is lengthy maturation, so there should be no cheating. *See* Fortification.

POTASSIUM

Plays an important part in yeast reproduction and the fermentation process; if it is lacking from the must there is the danger of a stuck fermentation. If too much is added, however, it may combine with tartaric acid and form cream of tartar which could cause a haze. This is not a serious problem since cream of tartar haze can easily be precipitated out by chilling the wine. Potassium is usually added in the form of potassium salts, potassium phosphate, in the proportion of between a quarter and a half teaspoonful to each gallon (4.5 litres).

Potassium Benzoate *see* Acid, benzoic.

Potassium Carbonate
Can be used, like precipitated chalk, to reduce the acidity of a wine or must. Slightly less than ¼oz (7g) should be added to each gallon (4.5 litres). Though wine treated in this way will not have a chalky taste it may have a slightly salty taste, so take care. It is usually considered better wine-making practice to reduce acidity through blending rather than by adding chemicals.

Potassium Metabisulphite
Usually known simply as sulphite, it is now the most widely used sterilising agent, most frequently in the convenient form of Campden tablets.

Potassium Phosphate
A nutrient necessary to provide the must with potassium and phosphate to ensure healthy fermentation. It is vital for yeast growth and activity and the consequent prevention of harmful fusel oils.

Potassium Sorbate *see* Acid, sorbic.

Potassium Tartrate *see* Argols.

POTATOES

Can make a full-bodied, sweet dessert wine which improves with keeping. It benefits from being made with demerara sugar, and can have oranges, lemons, wheat and raisins or grape concentrate incorporated into the must. Spices are often added for flavour. A good combination is made up of ginger with caraway seeds, peppercorns or cloves. A variation is potato and prune wine, using 3lb (1.5kg) of potatoes to 1lb (450g) of prunes for each gallon (4.5 litres) of wine.

POTENTIAL ALCOHOL *see* Alcohol.

POURRITURE NOBLE *see* Noble rot.

PPM

Used in instructions for sulphite dosage: 'parts per million'.

PPT

Used as the unit for acid measurement: 'parts per thousand'.

PRECIPITATE

A noun and a verb. A precipitate is a sediment or deposit which is formed in the wine and sinks to the bottom of the vessel as a result of two compounds combining, through a chemical reaction, to form an insoluble compound. Since it is insoluble it cannot be dissolved in the wine and therefore it precipitates out (the verb), and can be racked off.

Precipitation is therefore a useful way of getting rid of unwanted substances, and is the basis of the fining technique of clarification. For instance, bentonite, which is a hydrated aluminium silicate, will combine with particles of protein in wine and precipitate them to the bottom of the vessel. *See* Fining.

PRECIPITATED CHALK

Calcium carbonate, used to reduce the acidity of a must, and obtainable from any chemist's shop. One teaspoonful should be added to each gallon (4.5 litres) of wine and stirred in thoroughly, then tried for taste after a day or two. Guard against initial frothing which may cause the wine to overflow its container.

If the wine remains too acidic to the palate, the procedure should be repeated but only half a teaspoonful should be added each time until the balance is right. A fine white precipitate of insoluble calcium salts will settle into the bottom of the vessel and can then be racked off. If the wine is very acidic, chalk is not the right remedy; it would have to be added in such a quantity that the finished wine would taste chalky. Instead, use potassium carbonate or blend the wine very carefully.

PRESSES

Several types of fruit press for the home wine-maker are available from wine-making supply stores. These are valuable aids, but expensive to buy, and the competent craftsman might prefer to make one. Better still, a small wine circle could build its own press for communal use. They are best constructed from oak or another hard wood, and work on the simple principle of gradually bringing increasing pressure to bear on fruit pulp, usually through screwing a board tightly down onto it so that it is firmly squeezed. The pulped or crushed fruit should first be wrapped in cloth or put into a jelly bag to prevent the nooks and crannies of the press becoming clogged with particles of vegetable matter which would make it difficult to clean. Do not aim for maximum pressure immediately but build it up gradually after each extraction of juice. This saves the press from too much strain on its working parts, and produces more juice in the long run.

A handmade press consists of three basic components. (1) The tray on which it stands, made from external quality plywood and drilled to take a short length of polythene tubing. (2) A sturdy square bucket, tough enough to withstand pressure, which stands in the tray. This too can be made from external ply. (3) The pressing equipment itself, made from a 16in (40cm) vice screw, available from any good

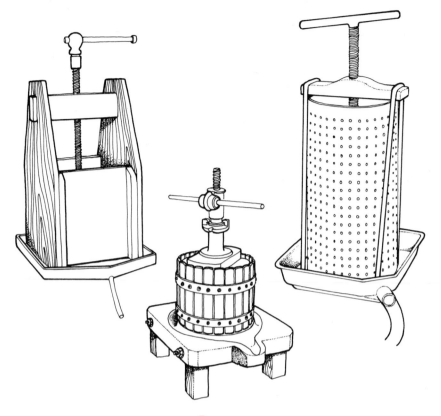

Presses

ironmonger, with a plywood pressure plate at the bottom end, firmly fixed. For construction details see *Woodwork for Winemakers* by C. J. Dart and D. A. Smith, who say that it can be built in an evening and will give years of service (published by Amateur Winemaker, 1971). The finished assembly should be carefully rubbed down and varnished with three coats of polyurethane to prevent bacteria from entering the wood and causing spoilage.

Among the commercial wine presses now available two are particularly good. Walker Desmond makes one of nylon-coated steel, supplied with a base which can be screwed down onto a bench to resist movement when pressure is applied. Fruit is loaded into a filter bag, which then goes inside a cylinder positioned on a plastic tray. A heavy plate is screwed down onto the fruit by turning a handle fitted onto a piston. As the plate squeezes the fruit, juice pours out into the tray and overflows through a plastic extension tube into the receiving vessel. The press has a capacity of 10½pt (6 litres). Sanbri's classic peasant-style wine press works on the same system but is made of traditional wood and is very handsome. It is available in a range of sizes to suit any wine-maker's needs, graduating from the tiny 4pt (2.5 litres) model to the 10gal (45 litres) press suitable for club use.

PRESSURE COOKERS

Can be used by the wine-maker to sterilise equipment and to cook ingredients that cannot be prepared by infusion or cold water extraction. These include very hard fruits, most dried fruits, root vegetables and bananas.

The fruit or vegetables should first be cut up or the dried fruit minced. Next, put them into a nylon jelly or straining bag, tightly tied round the top. Lay this in the pressure cooker with about 2pt (1 litre) of water, and cook at 15lb pressure. Hard fruits and vegetables will need about 5 minutes' cooking time, dried fruits 15–20 minutes.

Many people believe that pressure-cooked ingredients retain more flavour than those cooked in an ordinary pan, even one that is lidded tightly. It certainly saves cooking time and therefore cost.

PRIMARY FERMENTATION *see* Fermentation.

PROOF *see* Alcohol content.

PRUNES

Good wine can be made with dried or canned prunes, but they will not substitute for plums in plum wine. Wine made from tinned prunes can taste rather like sweet sherry if it is allowed to stand for a while in a half-filled container to allow oxidation to occur. The stones must be removed or they will affect the flavour adversely, and glycerine should be added, 1tbsp to each bottle, for smoothness. Prune wine can be drunk after maturing for only a month but it will go on improving for about a year.

Dried prunes can be made into a medium social wine, but it is essential to prepare the fruit carefully. The prunes should either be boiled in an open pan for 20 minutes, or pressure-cooked for 5 minutes, until they are soft. Then crush them, add a little water and cook them again for the same length of time. Finally, the liquor should be cooled, strained off and fermented out in the usual way.

Prunes mixed with the same weight of fresh ripe cherries make a good red table wine. They can also make a social wine if combined with potatoes: use one measure of prunes to three of potatoes.

PULP FERMENTATION *see* Fermentation.

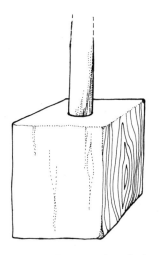

Mallet for crushing fruit

Walker Desmond Pulpmaster

PULPING OR CRUSHING

Crushing fruit to a pulp before pressing improves the eventual juice yield, and is vital for hard fruits such as apples and pears. Crushing can be carried out manually using a pestle and mortar, a mallet or hammer or an old-fashioned mangle. Nowadays, however, there are commercially produced fruit crushers available, such as the Walker Desmond Pulpmaster. The Pulpmaster comprises a stainless-steel

171

cutting blade and spindle which fits into a nylon cover with a central bearing. It is designed to be used with a 2gal (9 litre) bucket with a 10in (25cm) diameter, plus an ordinary handyman's electric drill. Fruit or vegetables are chopped up and put into the bucket with water, the lid is fitted tightly, and the drill is inserted into the spindle. When it is switched on, the blade will pulp the fruit in 10 seconds.

PUMPKIN *see* Marrow.

PUNCHES

Can be either long, cool, fruity drinks for summer or warm, spicy drinks for winter, concocted on a wine or spirit base. Ideally, they should be served in a punch bowl, but any large bowl will do provided that it has a lid to keep in the aroma and flavour. Homemade wines, either red or white, make excellent punch bases. For cold punch add sugar, fruit juice and lemonade, and float on the top chunks of apple or orange, berries, tinned fruit slices, citrus rind, slices of cucumber, or sprigs of mint or lemon balm, and serve with ice cubes. For hot punch, take care not to overheat or the alcohol will be driven off. When the temperature is raised just high enough to make a good warming drink, add sugar, lemon juice, cinnamon, cloves, nutmeg, honey, ginger or what you will. Extra spirits, especially rum and brandy, chase the chill from the coldest day.

A good *Christmas Punch*: for each person fill a wine glass two-thirds full with red wine, then fill half the remaining space with orange juice. Pour the wine and juice into a saucepan and begin to heat gently. Add to the liquid half a teaspoonful for each person of cinnamon, mace and ginger, mixed in equal proportions, as well as two cloves and one dessertspoonful of brown sugar or (preferably) honey. Stir well, taste and add more sugar if required. When the liquid begins to bubble round the edges it is ready for drinking. Pour into heat-proof glasses (or ordinary glasses with metal spoons in them to absorb the heat) and add a generous dash of brandy for a warming, euphoria-inducing, festive tipple.

QUINCES

Not easy to find, but if you have a supply of quinces (*Pyrus cydonia*) they can be turned into a golden dessert wine. Grate them into a pan, having discarded the core, then boil for about 15 minutes. Next, ferment them on the pulp for about ten days to extract the maximum amount of juice and flavouring. The liquor should then be strained off and fermented out in the usual way.

Quince

Chaenomeles japonica, known as Maule's quince, is grown in many gardens for its flowers, and if you later have a lot of the fruits they can be used as an alternative to the genuine quince. It is important to wait until they have turned yellow, usually from October onwards.

RACKING OFF

Removing the wine from the deposit, sediment or lees in the bottom of the fermentation vessel and transferring it to a clean and sterile container. This helps clarification, flavour and quality. It plays a very important part in good wine-making and should never be neglected.

Wine can be racked simply by pouring, but this is not satisfactory as it is almost impossible to prevent some of the lees being poured off with the wine. It is much better to siphon off the wine through a siphoning tube that is bent upwards at the bottom, and held well clear of the lees, so that the latter cannot be sucked up.

It is not only the method of racking that is important, but also the timing. The first racking should be carried out as soon as fermentation has ceased, otherwise the yeast debris will be converted by autolysis and off-flavours and fusel oils will develop. For a sweet wine, racking can be carried out before the ending of fermentation to prevent all the

173

sugar from being converted into alcohol. To do this, add sulphite, and then rack two or three times. This should destroy and remove the yeast colony. It is good practice to add sulphite anyway, in the proportion of 100ppm at the first racking and half that strength at later rackings. This process performs two functions: it prevents the yeast from re-establishing itself and re-starting fermentation, and it prevents oxidation.

For a red wine the racking routine should go on for up to two years, being performed approximately every three months until the wine is properly matured. Since white wine matures more quickly, racking need only be carried out for six to twelve months. After the first racking, the wine will need to be topped up. This can be done with a topping-up wine or with water, but the latter will cause dilution which must be accounted for. Immediately after topping up, the wine will still be cloudy because of yeast particles and plant matter suspended in it, but after a few weeks, depending upon the wine type and the temperature at which it is being stored, these particles will settle down at the bottom, and a second racking will be necessary. At this stage it is important to avoid splashing which would absorb oxygen and cause oxidation. The pouring end of the siphon tube should be held below the surface of the wine rather than splashing on to it from above.

After the second racking, the wine should be topped up a second time, then put in a cold place 40–50°F (5–10°C) to assist clarification. Subsequent rackings need to be carried out when more yeast deposit appears, and only when the wine is completely clear should the air-lock be replaced with a plain cork.

Any wine which fails to clarify despite careful racking and storage procedures probably has a haze due to some fault or infection, and curative measures should be taken. *See* Siphoning; Haze; Topping up.

RAISINS

More or less interchangeable with sultanas in wine-making recipes. Being dried grapes, they are important for giving vinosity to a wine made from ingredients other than grapes. They are also a valuable body-giving ingredient, as well as adding flavour.

There are various methods of using raisins. For pulp fermentation, they should be minced or liquidised, but since the seeds are bitter care must be taken not to crush them. For juice fermentation, the raisins should be minced or liquidised and then cooked in water and strained.

Raisins used to be vital to country-wine making but many people now prefer to use grape concentrate; 2lb (1kg) of raisins are roughly equivalent to 1pt (575ml) of grape concentrate, and this is enough for 1gal (4.5 litres) of must to give it that extra special vinous quality.

Nevertheless, raisins still have their place in wine-making. They make many good wines when used as a base ingredient and, according to the recipe used, they can produce a white table wine, a sweet dessert wine or a strong Madeira-type social wine. *See* Sultanas.

RASPBERRIES

Ready for eating from the middle of July but they will be cheaper and sweeter for wine-making in August, and even into September. Some raspberry canes yield a second crop in late September and this may be even better than the first for wine-making.

The very strong flavour and aroma of raspberries make them a superb fruit to eat but can be overpowering in wine, producing a drink more like an alcoholic fruit cordial. If treated properly, however, raspberries can make a refreshing dry rosé, a red table wine, a sweet dessert wine or a fruity port-type wine.

In addition to their powerful taste, they have a high level of acidity so it is better to use only a smallish proportion of raspberries in the must, making up the rest of the required fruit ingredient with a different fruit, grape concentrate or sultanas. A combination of raspberries and redcurrants is particularly good. Normally, no extra acid needs to be added but if the fruit is very ripe a pinch of malic acid can be included, as the raspberry has a high preponderance of citric acid. Raspberries are very low in tannin, however, so even for a rosé wine more needs to be added, and it is a sensible precaution to use a pectic enzyme in the recipe. Include nutrients and vitamin B_1, too, to start and maintain a healthy fermentation. If grape concentrate is to be added, white juice should be used rather than red, since red does not mix well with the raspberry flavour.

A few words of warning. The aroma of raspberries is volatile and easily lost. If the fruit is crushed before water is added, the raspberry flavour may disappear. The fruit should be crushed under water, and then strained. Pulp fermentation is not suitable because of the off-flavours produced by the pips. Over-ripe berries are just as good as firm ones for wine-making, but are liable to house insects. These can be removed by covering the berries with water so that the insects float to the surface and can be skimmed off. The fruit must also be sterilised before fermentation to keep the wine free from infection. Finally, the colour of raspberries fades easily through contact with air or with sulphite solution. However, the change can reverse itself, given time.

RECIPES FOR WINES

Many people interested in wine-making have an insatiable desire for more and more exciting recipes. They feel that a good recipe will automatically produce a good wine, that a prize-winning recipe will create a prize-winning wine. Sadly – but more interestingly – wine-making is not as simple as this. It does not depend upon formulae but upon the quality and proportions of the ingredients and their careful control through the stages of extraction, fermentation, clarification and maturation. Poor-quality elderberries will not make fine wine, no matter how sound the recipe. Nor will a good recipe produce a fine fermentation if hygiene has been careless, if temperature control has slipped, if oxidation has been allowed to take place, if the cap has remained unbroken, if there has been no checking of alcohol content and acidity.

Recipes have their uses, of course. They prevent you from mixing ingredients that should be kept apart, such as malic acid and apples, or oak tannin and immature elderberries. They can advise about the addition of ingredients which might have been overlooked, such as nutrients and acids when making leaf wines. They can help with the creation of special wines, such as aperitifs and liqueurs, which use ingredients not needed in table wines. And they assist with wines such as sherry-types that have special requirements, both in the use of gypsum and the management of the flor. Also, they can suggest happy combinations, eg redcurrants with peaches, guavas with bananas.

All the wine-maker really needs to know is the sort of ingredients required, the proportions that work best and the pros and cons of the various methods. With experience, and with knowledge of the type of wine being aimed at and its specific characteristics, he or she will learn to calculate: the type and quantity of fruit or vegetables to use; whether or not a pectic enzyme is required; how much grape concentrate should be added for vinosity; whether extra body-giving ingredients are required; whether flowers should be added for bouquet and, if so, in what proportion; the sugar requirement, and whether this should be provided in the form of household sugar, demerara, honey, or a combination of two or three of these; whether acids should be added and, if so, what sort and how much; whether extra tannin is needed, or whether the tannin content is going to be so high that it will need to be reduced; what sort of yeast starter will give the best results; what sort of nutrients and additives will be required to ensure a healthy and vigorous fermentation; and whether it is necessary to add water and, if so, how much. A few recipes nevertheless have something different to offer, and several are given in this book. For one or two good books of recipes *see* Books.

RECORDS

Much of the success of wine-making depends upon careful control and timing. To get the timing right, and to save too much strain on the memory, it is helpful to keep both a record card index and a diary. The former will tell you not only what ingredients have been used, but also what has been done: the date of the beginning and end of fermentation, details of the various rackings and the treatment of any infections, the putting down to mature, and the first date for drinking. This will help future fermentations by enabling you to avoid mistakes a second time around and to repeat successes.

The diary is useful for jogging your memory about future activities. If it is kept up systematically, a glance at any day will inform you whether any jobs are due to be done and, if so, what. Any diary will do, but it is helpful to use the *Wine and Beer Maker's Diary* produced by Collins in association with Amateur Winemaker Publications. This not only provides sufficient space for your notes, it also has useful information and month-by-month recipes, and makes an ideal gift for the wine-maker.

REDCURRANTS

An easy wine-making fruit because of their high acidity. The juice needs to be diluted with water to reduce the acid content, but then the body is diminished, leaving it thin and watery. So to avoid this, combine with raisins, sultanas, grape concentrate and bananas, for the best results. Redcurrants blend deliciously with another problem fruit, the raspberry, and they can also be blended with honey to make a pleasing melomel.

REDUCTION

A chemical process which usually occurs naturally when wine is being matured in the bottle, and is particularly important for its effect on red wine since it mellows the wine and precipitates tannin.

RED WINE

A term normally applied to red table wine rather than to wine that is red in colour but drunk on other occasions (eg port). Commercially produced red table wines (the most famous are probably Beaujolais and Burgundy) usually have an alcohol content of 10–12 per cent alcohol by volume and taste dry to medium-dry to the palate. They are generally rich in tannin and are consequently harsh when young, but they mellow through long maturation which precipitates the tannin. Red wine is usually drunk at room temperature, to accompany red meats.

For the home wine-maker aiming to produce red table wine partially or wholly from fruits other than the grape, the best choices are elderberries, bilberries, red plums, damsons, cherries and sloes; all these are best combined with red grape concentrate and a red-wine yeast. These fruits contain tannin in their skins, as well as red pigments, which should be extracted by alcohol since most of them are insoluble in water. For this reason, pulp fermentation is the correct method to use with red fruit. As alcohol is produced, colour is extracted. Once sufficient colour has been achieved (bearing in mind that some colour will be lost if the wine is diluted with water for topping up), the fruit pulp should be removed from the fermentation vessel in order to avoid the production of too much tannin.

Raspberries, loganberries and blackcurrants all give a good depth of colour but because of their fruitiness they are not suitable for a table wine when used on their own; they can be incorporated with other fruits to make good social wines. Blackberries make a tawny rather than a red wine.

If the season has been poor, the fruit will almost certainly possess excessive acid and tannin and the wine should be allowed at least two years to mature. The acidity should be between 3.3 and 4.3ppt measured on the sulphuric acid scale.

REFRIGERATION

A useful method of clarification. For instance, cream of tartar will be deposited if a wine suffering from excess tartrate is chilled to just above freezing point for a few days. Since the tartrate is totally insoluble at such a low temperature the wine can be racked off leaving the sediment in the vessel. Other proteins too are precipitated by cooling, and it is always easier to clarify wines at a low temperature than at a high one.

Some white wines and sparkling wines need refrigeration before serving. *See* Temperature.

RESIDUAL SUGAR *see* Sugar.

RHUBARB

A difficult wine-making ingredient since, though its chief acid is malic, it also contains poisonous oxalic acid. The quantity of oxalic acid is, however, very small and a great amount of rhubarb wine would have to be drunk before any ill effects (other than intoxication) were felt. Nevertheless, *discard the leaves* entirely and use only *young* stalks; extract their juice with cold water so that much of the oxalic acid is left behind in the pulp. Never use hot-water extraction or pulp fermentation, or the acid will be retained in the must. The next step is to reduce the acidity of the rhubarb juice by precipitated chalk and to dilute it.

The best method of preparing the rhubarb is to cut it up and crush it. Cover it with cold water to which a crushed Campden tablet has been added, and leave it for three days, stirring frequently. Then strain, and add the chalk to the juice (remember that it will fizz!). By this stage, the excess oxalic acid should have been disposed of and the juice can be fermented out in the usual way, along with yeast and nutrients, lemon juice, sugar, tannin and pectin-destroying enzyme, to produce a rosé table wine. Alternatively, rhubarb can be combined with beetroot, wheat and ginger for a different flavour. It also goes well with raspberries or apples.

RICE

Can make a strong dessert wine or a white table wine. Sake is a highly potent and famous Japanese rice wine; rice wine is also drunk in China.

Rice has two major problems. First, it has a very high starch content, so that it is necessary to use a starch-reducing enzyme as well as a pectin-destroying enzyme to make sure that it will not develop a haze. Secondly, it can smell extremely strongly during the fermentation process. It is important to use the right sort of rice: long-grain, wholemeal or paddy rice, not polished rice.

When immature, this wine is harsh; it will not be at its best until it has matured for at least two years. If it is possible to keep it for twice as long it will taste twice as good. Rice is also incorporated into some recipes as a body-giving ingredient, but because of its starch content the advantages of this can be outweighed by the disadvantages, and there are other body-giving ingredients, such as banana gravy, which are easier to use. *See* Cereals; Haze, starch.

ROHAMENT P

An enzyme which can be incorporated into a pulp fermentation to break down fruit into purée and is particularly useful for hard fruits that are difficult to crush but should not be boiled. It is widely available from wine-making supply stores; the preparation comes complete with full instructions for use.

ROPINESS *see* Infection.

ROSEHIPS

A suitable ingredient for a rosé wine; they also make a good social wine. The rosehips should be washed thoroughly, minced or liquidised, simmered for 10–15 minutes, then crushed and fermented on the pulp for five days. Then they can be strained and the liquor fermented out in the usual way.

Rosehip syrup can be used as an alternative to the fruits, but this seems a shame because they are just about the only wine-making ingredient really at their best in December, when they have been softened by the frost but not yet devoured by the birds. Consequently, rosehip wine-making is a pleasant winter activity which can become a traditional part of the end-of-year festivities: a wine to be made one Christmas and drunk the next.

Rosehips

ROSE PETALS

Second only to elderflowers as a bouquet-enhancing ingredient; they may be available fresh from June until October, and can be bought in dried form all year round. Their scent is so strong that they must be

Rose petals

used in moderation. Depending on their fragrance, you need only between one and three cupfuls of petals to each gallon (4.5 litres) of must. Red roses must not be used in the making of white wines or the colour will be spoiled, though pink and yellow are suitable. Rose petals are particularly valuable in the production of the powerful bouquet of Sauternes-type wine. You can combine rose petals with elderflowers in roughly equal proportions because they complement each other splendidly.

Apart from being an extra ingredient for other wines, rose petals can make a white table wine when used as the basic ingredient, provided that they are mixed with grape concentrate and/or raisins for body. Pick the petals when the flower is overblown, but before they have begun to wither. There is disagreement about the best method of extraction, whether hot-water infusion, cold-water extraction or slow pulp fermentation. Experience and taste alone will make the final decision for each individual wine-maker.

ROSÉ WINE

A light, fresh, fragrant, fruity and prettily pink wine. Despite its colour, it is more like a white wine to the palate than a red. Some rosés, like the famous Mateus, are slightly sparkling. As a rule they have an alcohol content of approximately 10 per cent of volume, and are drunk slightly chilled, with delicate food, salad, hors-d'oeuvre, white meat, fruit and so on.

The pink colour should not be the result of blending white wine

181

with red, but of pulp-fermenting red grapes for only a short time (between 6 hours and 2 days), until the desired depth of pigmentation is leached out of the skins. The home wine-maker aiming to produce a good rosé should choose fruit or fruits from the following list and combine them with grape concentrate (red if it is necessary to deepen the colour; otherwise white is preferable): redcurrants, rhubarb, apricots, gooseberries, rosehips, peaches and cherries – all excellent as a base.

Cold-water extraction and a cool, slow fermentation are important to retain fragrance, and this should be heightened by the addition of rose petals and/or elderflowers. Acidity should be between 3.5 and 4ppt with a slight predominance of malic acid. If a pectin-destroying enzyme is included in the must it will help the wine to clear without having to be fined or filtered, either of which would impair its delicate flavour. Rosé wine is normally ready to drink after six months in the bottle but will go on improving for up to two years.

SACCHAROMYCES

The generic name given to yeast fungi which are essential to wine production, since they turn sugar into alcohol; from 'saccharo' meaning sugar and 'myces' meaning fungi. There are very many types of yeast fungi, including baker's yeast and brewer's yeast. The specific name for wine yeast is *Saccharomyces ellipsoideus*.

SACROMETER OR SACCHAROMETER

A simplified form of hydrometer used to estimate the amount of sugar in a solution by specific gravity and, consequently, its progress towards fermentation. Simplification of the process is achieved by the use of coloured bands to indicate the desired sugar level for the beginning of fermentation and the levels that should be reached if a dry, medium or sweet wine is desired.

SAGE

A richly flavoured herb which can make the basis of a good dessert or aperitif wine. Try combining 2oz (60g) of fresh sage with ½oz (15g) each of mint and rosemary, infused together for 24 hours. Then add

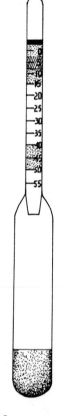

Sacrometer

raisins or grape concentrate, sugar, yeast and nutrients, and ferment out in the usual way. Alternatively, a herb infusion can be added to a standard wine. Take 2oz (60g) of fresh sage, put it into a muslin bag and suspend it in the fermenting vessel of the must of a basic white wine for about 2 hours at the beginning of the fermentation process. Remove the bag after 2 hours or the flavour will be overpowering.

SALTS

Formed when metals combine with alkalines. Some salts are vital to yeast growth and activity, and have to be added to the must to ensure a healthy fermentation. They are usually called 'nutrients'. Those most commonly needed in wine-making are ammonium phosphate, magnesium sulphate, potassium phosphate and vitamin B_1.

SAP *see* Birch sap.

SATSUMAS *see* Tangerines.

SAUTERNES

Probably the best-known sweet white wine; it comes from Sauternes in the Bordeaux region of France and has a distinctive golden colour and high alcohol content. It is made from grapes that have been left on the vine until almost shrivelled. Legend has it that it was discovered by chance when the owner of a vineyard forgot to tell his workers to harvest the grapes and they were neglected until over-ripe, only to produce, eventually, a superb wine, full-bodied and with an almost overpowering bouquet. Sauternes is served chilled as a dessert wine, though it can sometimes be drunk as an accompaniment to strongly flavoured fish, fowl or game, when there is no danger of it overwhelming the flavour of the food.

A unique aspect of the production of Sauternes is that the grape is deliberately exposed to the attack of the fungus *Botrytis cinerea*, known as the noble rot. This draws water from the grapes while they are growing and therefore leaves within them a very concentrated sugar content. The shrivelling of the berry also loosens the skin so that juice extraction is easier. Grapes attacked by botrytis have a high glycerol content, and this gives the finished wine an attractive smoothness.

Amateur wine-makers can create a Sauternes-type wine if they can achieve the right balance of ingredients in the must to reflect its sweetness, high acidity, full-bodied quality, bouquet and colour. The recipe must include a large proportion of bananas and white grape concentrate, as well as yellow fruit such as greengages, grapefruit, oranges, apples, limes or lime juice, apricots, peaches, ripe gooseberries, and so on. Young oak leaves tend to bring out the flavour, as do muscatel raisins, and the bouquet is enhanced by the inclusion of sweet-scented flowers, either fresh or dried, particularly elderflowers, yellow rose petals and honeysuckle, combined with succinic acid for esterification. Additives should include glycerol, malic and tartaric acid, and tannin if it is not possible to obtain oak leaves. Finally, a special Sauternes yeast starter should be used. Sauternes needs a long period of maturation. Two years in a wooden cask plus several in the bottle are ideal.

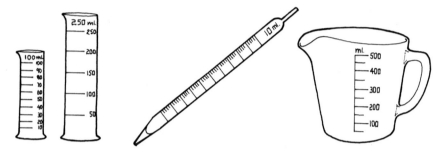

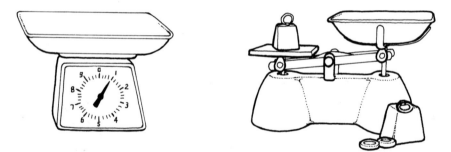

Measuring equipment

SCALES

Accurate measuring containers are a vital part of the wine-maker's equipment. It is necessary to be able to weigh out both solids and liquids, to measure large quantities and tiny amounts, and to do this in both metric and imperial measurements. Good kitchen scales and a measuring jug and spoon are perfectly adequate for most purposes, but there are one or two jobs where these are inadequate. For instance, it is difficult to measure really minute amounts and it is usually a good idea to make up ingredients like tannin and acids into stock solutions. Graduated measuring cylinders, such as a hydrometer jar, are a useful addition to normal household equipment, since they can perform many functions. They can be used for taking samples, preparing tests and trials, adding sulphite solution to the must, and so on. They are easily obtained from wine-making supply stores. A pipette is also useful; it is a small calibrated tube used to measure an accurate volume of solution (necessary for titration).

SECONDARY FERMENTATION *see* Fermentation.

SEDIMENT *see* Lees.

SETTLING OR SETTLING OUT

The process by which, in some wine-making procedures, the fruit pulp is given time to fall out of suspension, after being pressed and sulphited, so that the clear juice can be racked off the deposit and fermented. The fruit is first stoned and crushed; the juice extracted and treated with 100ppm sulphite to prevent browning and inhibit bacteria. Then it is transferred to a glass container, sealed and left to stand in a cool place for 24 hours without disturbance. The juice can then be carefully racked off and transferred to another container, ready to incorporate in the must.

'Settling out' is also used to mean simply falling out of suspension and forming a deposit on the bottom of the jar. Hazes are dispersed, for instance, by persuading the particles floating in the liquid to settle out so that the wine can be racked off and removed from the matter which has been clouding it.

SHARP

The taste of an over-acidic wine. Many wines benefit from having a certain hint of sharpness, 'bite' or 'edge', but this should never be over-done.

SHERRY

A fortified white wine, originally from the Andalusian area of southern Spain, around the town of Jerez which gives it its name. The true sherry flavour occurs through a combination of the excellence of the grapes used; the gypsum-rich soil in which they are grown; the plastering of the must with gypsum; the carefully controlled oxidation to which the wine is subjected through its long, slow maturation period; and, in the case of fino sherries, the formation of sherry flor. It is difficult for the amateur to make a good-quality sherry because it is very easy to spoil it by over-oxidation. However, it is also possible to convert some wines which have begun to oxidise slightly of their own accord into reasonable sherries, provided that they have been made from appropriate ingredients. Apple wine is a prime example. Some wine-makers prefer to buy sherry-type wine-making kits, finding they produce a passable drink which has some of the genuine sherry flavour.

The wine-maker wishing to make a good sherry-type wine from scratch must select the right ingredients and follow the correct procedure. Yellow plums, apples, greengages, peaches, apricots and figs are all acceptable fruits, preferably combined with raisins, sultanas and white grape concentrate for vinous quality, and bananas or parsnips for body. Gypsum and cream of tartar also play an important part, as does a good-quality sherry-yeast starter.

The treatment of the wine after fermentation is a vital factor in its eventual quality. It should be racked into a container, preferably a wooden cask, only five-sixths filled, and the bung plugged, not sealed. This allows the entry of oxygen but prevents infection. It should then be left undisturbed for two to three years before bottling. If a flor develops the wine will not need to be sweetened and will be a good fino. If it does not develop, or develops only patchily, the wine will be more like an oloroso sherry and should have some grape concentrate added to sweeten it and to deepen its colour.

After maturation the wine should have sufficient spirit added, if necessary, to bring it up to 18 per cent alcohol by volume for a fino, or 20 per cent for an oloroso. Neither should be drunk for about a year after bottling, but an oloroso will continue to improve in the bottle for several more years. A dry sherry makes an excellent and popular aperitif. Sweeter sherries are highly acceptable social wines.

Sherry Flor
A creamy skin of yeast which sometimes grows on a sherry-type wine, eventually darkening and becoming wrinkled. Its growth can be encouraged by allowing large amounts of oxygen to reach the sherry after it has been racked, and for this reason maturing sherry is not sealed but merely plugged to prevent infection. If only a few patches of flor develop, rather than a complete crust, oxidation is not completely prevented and the wine darkens but acquires a characteristic sherry flavour, like an oloroso. If the flor covers the surface of the wine, the liquid will remain pale and taste dry, like a fino. It is impossible to guarantee the development of flor; much depends upon

the wine having the correct balance of alcohol, pH, tannin, sugar and sulphur dioxide. The maturing vessel should have sufficient empty space left (about one-sixth of the volume of the container) above the surface of the liquid to encourage its growth.

SIEVE

Useful to the wine-maker for straining fruit pulp after pulp fermentation. The best sort is made of fine-meshed nylon and is at least 6in (15cm) in diameter. Nylon is easy to keep clean and sterile, as well as being strong. For a final straining, when minute particles still remain, the sieve can be lined with firmly woven straining cloth or a jelly bag.

SINK

A vitally important item to the wine-maker for the constant washing, cleansing, emptying and sterilising of bottles, containers and equipment as well as for the preparation of ingredients. The sink is usually in constant use during a wine-making session and can cause domestic irritation if there is a conflict of interests and need. The ideal solution is to have a second sink for wine-making. Some houses have a utility room, an old-fashioned scullery or a spare bedroom fitted with a sink or hand-basin, and any of these could be converted to a winery. Alternatively, it might be possible to screen off part of a garage or workshop and fit it with its own sink. If none of these is a practicable answer to the problem, the wine-maker must be aware of other household needs and choose his or her time carefully before monopolising the sink to prevent a pleasant pastime from becoming a source of friction.

SINKER

A perforated plate which sits on the top of the fruit cap, pushing it below the surface during pulp fermentation, and preventing infection from reaching the must through contact with the air. It also makes sure that all the juice and colour are extracted from the pulp. Sinkers are rarely used by home wine-makers. Most simply break up the cap twice a day and stir it vigorously into the must.

SIPHONING

The best way of racking off wine from the lees or for transferring it from maturation vessels to bottles. (*See* Racking off.) Siphoning equipment includes a sterile, empty demi-john; a length of plastic siphon tubing with a U-bend at one end and a tap (optional) at the other; and a clothes peg. The method is as follows:

1. Put the full container onto a work surface, and put the empty demi-john (or alternative receiving jar) on a surface below it. (Most people use a table and chair for the two surfaces since one is just about the right height above the other.)

2. Place the end of the tube with the U-bend into the wine just above the lees, being very careful not to disturb the sediment.

3. Clip the clothes peg at the spot where the tube comes out of the neck of the demi-john so that it will not drop down.

4. Suck the other end of the tube until you feel the liquid in your mouth, then cover it with your finger and insert it into the *bottom* of

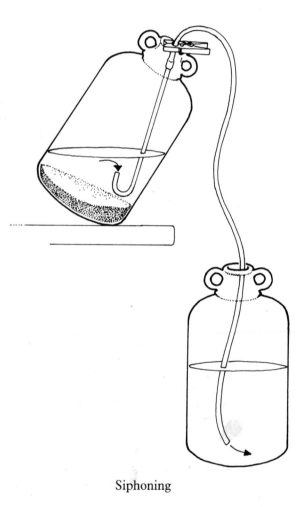

Siphoning

the empty demi-john so that the wine will flow in gently without too much splashing.

5. Allow the flow of wine to continue smoothly until the U-bend is *above* the surface of liquid in the upper container. When it has nearly stopped the jar should be tipped very gently so that as much as possible of the wine is removed but none of the lees.

6. Remove the tubing and put to one side for cleaning and sterilisation.

7. Since the lower jar will not be quite full it should be topped up either with water or with topping-up wine to just below where the bottom of the cork will be, otherwise there will be the danger of aerobic infection.

8. Fit the newly filled jar with an air-lock or cork, depending upon whether or not fermentation has ended.

If you are bottling wine and the last bottle is only half full it should not be topped up with water because the dilution will be too great, but neither should it be stored or it will go bad. Use it for cooking, or blend it with a finished and complementary wine, or drink it as 'plonk' if it is palatable.

Siphoning is a lengthy and time-consuming business because the wine flows quite slowly through the narrow tubing. Some wine-makers enjoy the quiet respite this provides, but others find the enforced wait tedious and irritating and succumb to the temptation to fit in other small jobs once the flow has begun. This is a dangerous policy which often ends with spilt wine and a mopping-up operation. If siphoning is one of the routines you find dull, it might be wise to invest in a siphon pump.

Siphon Pump
The main advantage over the 'suck-and-flow' technique is that the wine is less likely to become oxidised. The disadvantages of the siphon pump include the initial expense and the problem of having yet another, and not entirely necessary, piece of equipment to find storage space for. Wine-making supply stores can provide siphon pumps; telescopic siphoning tubes which are sufficiently versatile to fit any container; siphon kits which include PVC siphon tubing, glass tubing and a siphon tap; and a large range of glass and plastic tubing, taps, U-bends and clamps with which the wine-maker can make up his or her own siphoning equipment.

SLOES

The fruit of the blackthorn or wild plum ripens in October and November, and is excellent as a wine-making fruit as well as for making Sloe Gin. Sloes should be left on the bushes for as long as possible before picking, because the young fruit is rich in acids and tannins, while the mellow fruit has more natural sugar and is better balanced. It is not always easy to find blackthorn bushes in the autumn, so mark them out in the spring when they are covered with white blossom.

For a good, well-coloured, medium red table wine, combine sloes in a recipe with honey, red grape concentrate and red rose petals, and mature *slowly* in wood, if possible, for the first year, and then for two more years in the bottle.

Sloe Gin

For a superb sloe gin, combine 8oz (225g) of the fruit, pricked over with a fork, with 1pt (575ml) of gin and add 6 whole, unpeeled almonds, slightly bruised with a pestle. Add 2tbsp of sugar. Pour into a bottle, topping up with gin to the bottom of the neck if necessary, and cork tightly. Store for three months, agitating daily for the first week or two, then strain, and re-bottle. Seal tightly, and keep for a year before drinking. The gin-soaked sloes should not be discarded. Make them into liqueur chocolates instead. Simply chop up the flesh and mix into dark chocolate which has been gently melted. Pour into tiny petits fours cases and put in a cold place to set. Delicious!

SOAKING *see* Cold extraction.

SOCIAL WINES

Those intended to be drunk on a social occasion rather than as an aperitif, table wine or dessert wine. They generally have a distinct flavour and full sweetness which are pleasant but could overpower the taste of food. They usually bridge the gap between table and dessert wines in body and alcoholic strength. Most 'country wines' can be used as social wines, depending on the recipe. These include fruit wines, such as apricot, elderberry, raspberry, cherry; vegetable wines, such as parsnip, beetroot, carrot; flower wines, such as rose petal, dandelion, clover, elderflower; and herb or spice wines, such as fennel, sage, parsley and ginger.

SODIUM ASCORBATE *see* Acid, ascorbic.

SODIUM BENZOATE *see* Acid, benzoic.

SODIUM CARBONATE *see* Washing soda.

SODIUM HYDROXIDE

A strong alkali used for the titration of wine when measuring acidity. *See* Titration.

SODIUM HYPOCHLORITE

The basis of domestic bleach.

SODIUM METABISULPHITE

The wine-maker's sterilising agent, usually referred to as sulphite or Campden tablets.

SORBIC ACID *see* Acid.

SORBITOL

A useful sweetening agent. Since it is not fermented by wine yeasts, it can be added to fermented wines after fermentation has stopped to attain a desired level of sweetness without any danger of re-fermentation.

SOURNESS

If a wine tastes sour, vinegary or very acidic, it has almost certainly been infected and acetified. There is no way of remedying this but the wine can be used for cooking.

SPARKLE

A fresh, fizzy, bubbliness in wine due to the presence of dissolved carbon dióxide. *See* Sparkling wine.

SPARKLING WINE

The prince of sparkling wines is undoubtedly that joyous celebratory drink champagne, but there are many other good ones, including the popular Mateus Rosé and Asti Spumante. It is difficult for the novice wine-maker to achieve a good sparkling wine by intention, but occasionally they occur by happy accident. This can happen when wine has been bottled before fermentation has ceased or as a result of a malo-lactic fermentation through infection. Apple wine is particularly prone to the latter and many wine-makers produce splendid sparkling apple wine without even trying.

Until recently, the safest and most reliable way for the home wine-maker to create a sparkling wine was by skilfully controlled bottle fermentation combined with a great deal of care to avoid accidents through the build up of pressure within the bottle. It was a dangerous business, demanded great precision concerning the sugar level, and could not be attempted without a hydrometer and commercial sugar-testing kit. In the simplest and most basic of outlines the method was as follows.

1. The wine was fermented in the usual way, using a champagne yeast.

2. Sugar was added and the wine was bottled in champagne bottles, sealed with champagne corks and fermented again.

3. Then the business of *remuage* began, the gradual twisting and turning of the bottles upside down so that the yeast debris fell down on to the cork.

4. The next step was *degorgement*, the freezing of the necks of the bottles, followed by the releasing of the corks with the yeast debris frozen on to them in solid plugs.

5. Finally, the bottles were topped up with fortifying brandy and sugar syrup, recorked and securely wired.

This technique is thoroughly described in *How to Make Wines with a Sparkle* by J. Restall and D. Hebbs (published by Amateur Winemaker, 1972), and it is recommended that anyone who wants to make them should first study this useful book.

Fortunately, the recent invention of a special champagne cork may make producing sparkling wines a safer and easier procedure. It is fitted with its own pressure valve which releases excess carbon dioxide once the pressure has reached $60lb/in^2$. It also has a nylon thread through the top of the valve so that the wine-maker can release pressure at will. This clever device makes *degorgement* perfectly safe, simplifies the whole technique and can be used to turn express wine made from kits into sparkling wines, provided that a champagne yeast is used. The champagne cork has been commercially produced since the middle of 1983 and should be available from good wine-making supply stores, which will order it if it is not in stock.

SPECIFIC GRAVITY

The specific gravity (SG) of a liquid is its density, compared with the density of water. This density is expressed by a number. When the liquid is a wine must (which is essentially a solution of sugar) you can calculate from the specific gravity, with the aid of gravity tables like those on pages 194–5, how much sugar the must contains. When the liquid is a spirit (which is essentially a solution of alcohol) the specific gravity can be used to calculate how much alcohol is in the spirit.

Water has a specific gravity of 1.000. A typical wine has a specific gravity in the range of 1.065 to 1.120. A dry wine has a specific gravity of 0.996 and strong vodka about 0.890. The specific gravity of a must is given by the number 1, followed by a decimal point, followed by three figures of decimals. It is only the three decimal figures which matter to wine-makers and these three figures are often used on their own, disregarding the figure 1 and the decimal point. In this case they are called simply 'gravity'. For example, a specific gravity of 1.089 is called a gravity of 89; a specific gravity of 1.004 is a gravity of 4; a specific gravity of 0.995 is a gravity of −5.

Specific gravity is measured by a hydrometer. It is, of course, possible to make wine without using a hydrometer to establish the precise level of specific gravity but it does give much greater control over the wine-making process, and has four main uses:

1. To ascertain the initial sugar content. When a wine must has been prepared from fruit with a certain amount of added sugar it may need yet more if it is to reach the desired alcohol strength. By measuring the SG and consulting Table 1, it is possible to judge how much sugar is in each litre of must.

2. To determine when to add more sugar using the 'feeding the yeast' system of gradually incorporating sugar solution as fermentation progresses instead of including it all at the beginning. Normally a first addition is made when the wine has an SG of about 1.010 and further additions when it has dropped to 1.005.

3. To check whether fermentation has finished. As the wine ferments and the sugar is converted into alcohol, the SG falls rapidly at first, perhaps from 1.080 to 1.020 in the course of about ten days, and then more slowly. It is unsafe to bottle a wine before the end of fermentation but this may take weeks, or months, and if you rely merely on the absence of bubbles to indicate that fermentation has ended it may start up again after bottling. A low SG, below about 0.996, is a first indication that fermentation is over, and if the same reading is obtained at the same temperature a week later it is safe to assume that the wine is finished and ready for racking.

4. To estimate the alcohol content of a finished wine. The SG at the end of fermentation is normally called the *final gravity*. This is not on its own sufficient to indicate the alcohol content because it is due to a mixture of alcohol, residual sugar and flavouring substances. However, it is possible to estimate the alcohol content fairly accurately from the *gravity drop*; that is, the difference between the *original gravity* and the final gravity. The original gravity, when no more sugar is added after the yeast, is the gravity of the must at the start of fermentation. When sugar is fed to the yeast during fermentation, the original

gravity is the gravity the must would have had if all the sugar had been present in the first place (see Table 2).

Specific gravity varies with temperature: as the liquid gets warmer it expands, and because it expands it becomes less dense. Consequently, it is important to make hydrometer readings at the same temperature, otherwise correction factors should be used according to Table 3. Potential alcohol, as given in Table 1, is an estimate of the alcoholic strength you can reasonably expect to get from a must of a known specific gravity, but it is only a rough estimate.

Table 1.   Potential Alcohol

Specific gravity	Gravity	Balling or Brix	Twaddell	Baumé	Weight of sugar oz/gal	g/l	Potential alcohol (% by vol)
1·000	0	0·0	0	0·0	½	4	0
1·005	5	1·7	1	0·7	2¾	17	0·8
1·010	10	3·0	2	1·4	4¾	30	1·7
1·015	15	4·3	3	2·1	7	44	2·5
1·020	20	5·5	4	2·8	9	57	3·3
1·025	25	6·8	5	3·5	11	70	4·1
1·030	30	8·0	6	4·2	13¼	83	4·9
1·035	35	9·2	7	4·9	15½	97	5·8
1·040	40	10·4	8	5·6	17½	110	6·5
1·045	45	11·6	9	6·2	19½	123	7·0
1·050	50	12·8	10	6·9	21½	136	8·3
1·055	55	14·0	11	7·5	23¾	149	8·8
1·060	60	15·2	12	8·2	25¾	163	9·6
1·065	65	16·4	13	8·8	28	176	10·4
1·070	70	17·6	14	9·4	30	189	11·2
1·075	75	18·7	15	10·1	32	202	12·0
1·080	80	19·8	16	10·7	34¼	215	12·8
1·085	85	20·9	17	11·3	36½	228	13·6
1·090	90	22·0	18	11·9	38½	242	14·4 ·
1·095	95	23·1	19	12·5	40½	255	15·2
1·100	100	24·2	20	13·1	42¾	268	16·0
1·105	105	25·3	21	13·7	45	282	16·8
1·110	110	26·4	22	14·3	47	295	17·5
1·115	115	27·5	23	14·9	49	308	18·3
1·120	120	28·5	24	15·5	51¼	321	19·1
1·125	125	29·6	25	16·0	53¼	335	19·9
1·130	130	30·6	26	16·6	55½	348	20·7
1.135	135	31·6	27	17·1	57½	361	21·5
1·140	140	32·7	28	17·7	59¾	374	22·2
1·145	145	33·7	29	18·3	62	387	23·0
1·150	150	34·7	30	18·8	64	401	23·8
1·155	155	35·8	31	19·4	66	414	24·6
1·160	160	36·8	32	19·9	68¼	427	25·5

NB The names Balling, Brix, Twaddell and Baumé denote other scales of measurement which may be encountered in some wine-making books.

Table 2. Estimated Alcohol by Gravity Drop at Temperature of 59°F (15°C)

Gravity drop	Potential alcohol % by volume
80	10·6
85	11·4
90	12·0
95	12·7
100	13·3
105	14·0
110	14·7
115	15·5
120	16·0
125	16·7
130	17·3

Table 3. Temperature Correction Factors

Temperature °C	°F	Specific gravity correction	Gravity correction
10°	50°	−0.001	−1
15°	59°	None	None
20°	68°	+0.001	+1
25°	77°	+0.002	+2
30°	86°	+0.003	+3
35°	95°	+0.005	+5
40°	104°	+0.007	+7

SPICES

Can be added to various types of alcoholic drinks, but particularly to aperitif wines, liqueurs, hot punches and mulled wines, and metheglyn. Those most commonly used are cloves, cinnamon, ginger and nutmeg. They should be used sparingly as their strong flavours can be overpowering.

SPIRIT

Distilled alcohol. The alcohol content is raised by the driving off of liquid. Distilling is illegal without a licence, and the offence carries severe penalties. Wine-makers tend to use a comparatively neutral-flavoured spirit to fortify wines when they wish to increase their alcohol level. Polish spirit or vodka is the most common addition, but fortifying brandy can also be used. *See* Fortification; Pearson Square.

SPOILAGE

The spoiling of wine by infective micro-organisms (bacteria, yeasts and moulds); photochemical deterioration and loss of colour due to light; or metal contamination. If wine is carefully made from good-quality fruit, in hygienic conditions, in clean, non-metallic containers and equipment which have been thoroughly sterilised, and then protected from the light when maturing, it should be safe from spoilage. This counsel of perfection is difficult to adhere to in an imperfect world! Consequently, most wine-makers have to cope with a certain amount of spoilage. Much of it is treatable, but sometimes the wine has to be used for cooking or discarded.

The pH of a must will give some indication of how susceptible it is to bacterial spoilage. Many bacteria cannot survive in an acid wine with a pH below 3.4. For this reason, among others, sherry is plastered with gypsum. The low acidity of the Palomina grape makes it particularly vulnerable to infection unless its pH is decreased in this way. Also bear in mind that no matter how hygienic preparations are, the pulp cap which forms on the top of a must during primary fermentation is a favourite breeding ground for airborne spoilage organisms, and this should be broken and mixed vigorously into the must two or three times a day for safety's sake. *See* Bacteria; Light; Metal.

SPRITZIG

A descriptive word for a semi-sparkling wine.

SQUASHES

Squashes and cordials, commercially produced concentrated flavouring for drinks, can be used as a flavour ingredient for wines, provided that they are supplemented by ingredients which provide body, vinosity and bouquet. Those most useful are the top-quality, well-flavoured ones. Some enhance or complement a basic recipe ingredient; for example, tropical fruit cordial gives an extra zest to fig wine; orange and pineapple squash complements apple wine; grapefruit and pineapple cordial makes a good addition to sultana wine.

Squash or cordial can also be used instead of fruit juice or whole fruit. Lime cordial can be used to make a lime social wine or a Sauternes-type wine. Strawberry or raspberry cordial can take the place of strawberries or raspberries. Pineapple and grapefruit squash can substitute for pineapple juice or grapefruit juice. Remember, though, that these concentrates contain preservatives and must be simmered for 3 minutes before being incorporated into the must, in order to drive off any inhibiting substances.

196

STABILISERS

Substances which stop fermentation and prevent a wine from re-fermenting due to the presence of residual sugar. Benzoic acid and potassium sorbate are the most commonly available and frequently used stabilisers for home wine-making.

STARCH

Contained in cereals, potatoes, other root vegetables and apples, all ingredients frequently used in country-wine making. As wine yeasts do not possess an enzyme capable of breaking it down, starch may well cause a haze in the wine which should be treated by the starch-reducing enzyme, amylase. *See* Amylase; Haze, starch.

STEAM

Occasionally used for juice extraction. Fruit subjected to steam pressure will be broken down so that the juice flows freely, but the steaming process must not last too long or the juice will receive a 'cooked' flavour which can ruin a good wine. Though some wine-makers use commercially produced steam juice extractors and recommend them highly, others complain that they impair the final quality. It is therefore worth tasting the results of steam extraction before investing in a piece of equipment of this sort.

STEEPING

A method of extracting juice. *See* Cold extraction.

STERILISATION OF EQUIPMENT

This, along with thorough cleansing, is vitally important. Only if all equipment is scrupulously clean and sterile will the wine resist oxidation, bacterial and fungal attack, and remain free from acetification or other equally damaging and troublesome infections. The most convenient sterilising agent is sulphite, either in the form of sulphite solution made from crystals of sodium metabisulphite or Campden tablets. Sulphite crystals are cheaper to buy but Campden tablets are more convenient to use. To make *stock sulphite solution* dissolve either 5 Campden tablets or 1tsp of crystals in 1pt (575ml) of warm water. (Stored in a tightly lidded bottle it will last for a few months.) Pour a little of the solution through a funnel into the container that is to be used and swirl it around so that it comes into contact with every part of the interior, then leave it to stand, covered, for a few moments.

Pour out the solution but do not discard it since it can be used again. After a quick rinse with tap water, the sterilised containers are now ready for use.

Any containers not in use can be kept sterile by storing them, firmly stoppered, with a small quantity of stock sulphite solution in the bottom of them. Other pieces of equipment can be sterilised by washing them with a cloth soaked in sulphite. Similarly, a sulphited cloth should be used to wipe the outsides of fermentation vessels, to clean up any spillage of wine that has been racked or bottled, and to sterilise splashed surfaces.

STERILISATION OF MATURING WINE

Either 1 Campden tablet or 1tsp of strong sulphite solution should be added to every gallon (4.5 litres) of the wine after the first and second racking, to prevent oxidation and bacterial action. If the wine still becomes infected, a double dose should be added, but no more than 3 Campden tablets or their equivalent in strong sulphite solution should be introduced into the wine or the flavour will be ruined. *See* Sulphite, strong solution.

STERILISATION OF THE MUST

It is not always understood that the ingredients from which wine is made are as likely to cause infection as non-sterile equipment. Fruit (over-ripe fruit in particular) is covered with wild yeasts, moulds and bacteria; flowers, grains, vegetables and other natural ingredients carry their own micro-organisms which could spoil the wine. Consequently, it is important to sulphite the must. This is done by adding 1 Campden tablet or 1tsp of *strong* sulphite solution to each gallon (4.5 litres) of the must 24 hours before adding the yeast. These 24 hours will give time for the action of the sulphite to abate sufficiently so that it will not inhibit the action of the yeast.

STOCK SOLUTIONS

Stock solutions of acids, tannins and sulphite enable the home wine-maker to add minute quantities of these materials to a must. For instance, it may be necessary to add one-fifteenth of an ounce (about 2g) of grape tannin to a gallon (4.5 litres) of must. The best way to do this is to make a solution of ½oz (15g) of grape tannin in ¾pt (420ml) of boiled water, so that the necessary tannin will be contained in 2fl oz (56ml) of solution, an amount easily measured. In this way even one-sixtieth of an ounce (0.5g) can be provided.

Similarly, with acids 1oz (28g) in 1½pt (850ml) of water gives a solution of which 1fl oz (28ml) contains 1g of acid.

STOCK SULPHITE SOLUTION *see* Sterilisation of equipment.

STONES

Fruit stones, pips and seeds all contain oils that can add a bitter flavour to the must. When using a fruit crusher or juice extractor, make sure that seeds and stones are not broken.

STORAGE *see* Maturation; Cellar.

STRAINING

Separating fruit juice from fruit pulp by means of a colander, sieve, strainer or jelly bag. Since it can be a time-consuming process, the biggest problem is to find a secure method of suspending the straining

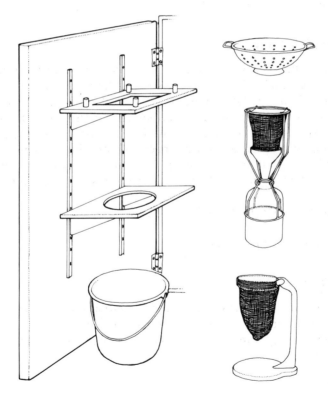

Strainers

equipment over the receiving vessel. An old but still valuable homespun method is to turn a kitchen chair upside down on the table and hang a straining cloth from the four legs, putting a bowl or bucket under it, on the upside-down seat of the chair, to catch the juice as it drips through. Alternatively, a bag can be slung from a board bridging two surfaces at an equal height, with a bucket standing on the floor beneath. More sophisticated variations are commercially available. They include a metal frame which can clamp onto the top of a bucket or demi-john holding a bag firmly in position while the juice flows, or an oak filter bag unit, as illustrated.

The handyman may prefer to make his or her own. A neat idea I have seen is a straining stand which fits onto the inside of a cupboard door. The door is fitted with an adjustable shelving system, two uprights and two pairs of brackets. The upper brackets hold a shelf with a square hole cut out of it and four pegs from which to suspend a bag. The lower brackets hold a shelf of the same size with a circular hole into which a large funnel can be fitted. A container stands on the floor below. When not in use the shelves are removed and packed away but the shelving system remains in position, ready for use.

STRAWBERRIES

A difficult fruit for the wine-maker to use because of the overpowering flavour. According to some connoisseurs, though they are unsuitable as an ingredient for table wine, they do make a pleasant social wine with a good rosé colour. It is important to use only sound, firm strawberries – none of them should be over-ripe or beginning to decay. There is no need to use a pectin-destroying enzyme.

Strawberry Liqueur can be made quite simply by combining strawberries with sugar and brandy, steeping, straining and maturing.

STUCK FERMENTATION *see* Fermentation.

SUCCINIC ACID *see* Acid.

SUCROSE

The commonest of sugars used for wine-making and our ordinary household granulated sugar, derived from sugar cane or sugar beet. It is a disaccharide, composed of glucose and fructose. *See* Sugar.

SUGAR

Essential to wine-making since, apart from grapes, no fruit has a high enough sugar content to be turned into alcohol by yeast. The best method of adding sugar is to turn it into sugar solution, begin the fermentation process with a proportion of the full amount specified in the recipe, and then to 'feed the yeast' gradually with what remains until the fermentation has died down and the specific gravity has reached the desired level.

For most recipes, the best and cheapest type of sugar to use is ordinary household granulated sugar, derived either from sugar cane or sugar beet. Some recipes refer to special sugars such as candy sugar, loaf or lump sugar, but these usually date from a time before household sugar was as pure as it is today, and need not be strictly followed. Demerara sugar should be used only in wines where its effect on colour and flavour is an advantage, such as Madeiras, sherries and ports. It is also good in some kinds of vegetable wine (potato, for instance) but is unsuitable for light table wines. Honey is a source of invert sugar which has advantages over sucrose because of the natural additives it contains, and many wine-makers provide at least part of the quantity of sugar required in the form of honey, which creates a smoother, mellower wine.

Brown Sugar
Sucrose obtained from sugar cane or, less commonly, sugar beet, which has not been purified to the same extent as white sugar. The impurities which colour and flavour brown sugar contain valuable yeast nutrients, so it can be preferable to white sugar for use in a starter culture.

When making red wine, it can be an advantage if up to half the sugar required is brown, but not more than that proportion or the caramel flavour will predominate over the flavour of the fruit. Even a little brown sugar will ruin the colour of a white wine. In practice, most wine-makers prefer to play safe and use it only in the production of sherry, port and some dessert wines.

Candy Sugar
May be listed as an ingredient in old-fashioned wine recipes compiled at a time when candy sugar was purer than ordinary household sugar. Nowadays household sugar is as good as candy sugar, though some people still argue that the latter gives a better flavour.

Cane Sugar
The solid obtained from the juice of the sugar cane, which has the highest sucrose content of any plant. The juice is a milky liquid which can be bought in cans as a drink. It can be fermented simply by adding yeast to it to turn it into wine. The solids of the juice are purified by

repeated crystallisation to provide either white granulated sugar, which is about 99.5 per cent sucrose, brown sugar which is about 96 per cent sucrose, and molasses which is about 30 per cent sucrose. Cane sugar is almost indistinguishable from beet sugar, and the two are interchangeable in wine-making.

Cube Sugar *see* Loaf sugar.

Demerara Sugar
Originally a partly refined brown cane sugar from Demerara in Guiyana. Today, it is more often London Demerara, which is fully refined white granulated sugar coated with a partly refined sugar. The main advantage of using real demerara in wine-making is in the creation of those dessert wines for which a golden brown colour is required, such as a Madeira. It is also useful in wines made principally from vegetables to enhance their flavour.

Grape Sugar
Another name for glucose.

Invert Sugar
A solution of sugar in which sucrose has been broken down into its components, fructose and glucose. Some wine-makers maintain that invert sugar produces better wine, but this is controversial. Invert sugar can be bought or it can be produced by boiling 2lb (1kg) of household sugar in 1pt (575ml) of water, to which 1tsp of tartaric or citric acid has been added, for about 10–15 minutes, until the syrup is straw-coloured. However, since yeast contains the enzyme invertase which will invert sucrose of its own accord, the preliminary inversion of sugar seems to be an unnecessary step, except in the production of sparkling wines. If invert sugar *is* used, it is necessary to incorporate half as much again as the amount recommended for household sugar. Invert sugar is only two-thirds as sweet as household sugar on account of the water in the solution.

Loaf Sugar
Otherwise known as lump or cube sugar. For adding to a must, this is an expensive, fiddly and time-consuming type of sugar, as it has to be dissolved before it can be used. Though occasionally recommended in old-fashioned wine-making recipes it does not seem to have any beneficial effect. It is more sensible to use the cheapest form of household sugar.

Lump Sugar *see* Loaf sugar.

Residual Sugar

The sugar which remains in the wine after fermentation, when most of the sugar originally used has reacted with the yeast. It is the amount of residual sugar, expressed in terms of specific gravity, which is responsible for the definition of a wine as medium or sweet. A medium wine usually has a specific gravity of between .998 and 1.005; a sweet wine has a higher specific gravity, of between 1.005 and 1.025. A measurement above that figure indicates a stuck fermentation.

Sugar Beet

The source of most of the sugar used in Britain and, of more significance to the wine-maker, also one of the vegetables that can be used as a basic ingredient for wine. It is frequently used in Madeira recipes, for instance, as an alternative to parsnips.

Sugar Cane

Cane sugar is refined from the juice of this plant. It used to be our only source of pure sugar but it is now being largely replaced by sugar made from sugar beet. *See* Cane Sugar.

Sugar Solution

Sugar dissolved in water for easy implementation into the must. *See* Sugar syrup.

Sugar Syrup

Made by heating 2lb (1kg) of household sugar in 1pt (575ml) of water, then allowing it to remain just under boiling point for a few minutes until it has clarified. It is ready for use as soon as it is cool. One pint (575ml) of this syrup will provide 1lb (450g) of sugar.

It is good wine-making practice to add sugar to the must in the form of syrup since it can be more easily assimilated into the must and the liquid measurement can be more easily assessed. If sugar is added as a solid, it may sink to the bottom of the fermenting jar and form a layer which could inhibit the activity of the yeast. Where the yeast is fed regularly during fermentation, sugar should always be added as a syrup. The syrup can be stored in a refrigerator for several weeks if it is kept in a sealed, sterilised bottle.

SULPHITE

The wine-maker's name for sodium metabisulphite or potassium metabisulphite. When either of these salts is dissolved in water it releases sulphur dioxide, which acts as both an anti-bacterial agent and an anti-oxidant, and is the most significant sterilising agent used in home wine-making. If sulphite is added at the racking stage, it will combine with acetaldehyde to prevent oxidation reaction and bottle sickness. The sodium salt is preferable for wine-making usage, because the potassium salt can form insoluble compounds with the acids in the wine, and these precipitate in the form of argols. *See* Sterilisation of equipment, etc.

Strong Sulphite Solution
Used for sterilising musts, preserving maturing wines, stopping re-fermentation and arresting infection. It is for adding to wine, not for sterilising equipment. It is made by dissolving 2oz (60g) of sulphite crystals in ½pt (285ml) of warm water and then topping up with cold water to 1pt (575ml). One teaspoonful (5ml) of strong sulphite solution is the equivalent of 1 Campden tablet. Like stock sulphite solution it can be kept for months in a tightly stoppered bottle.

SULPHUR

Yeasts need a certain amount of sulphur to do their work properly. They take this from the sulphite used for sterilising.

SULPHUR DIOXIDE

Released from sulphite; it kills or inhibits bacteria.

SULTANAS

Small, seedless raisins originally produced around Smyrna in Turkey, which can add vinosity, body and flavour to a wine made from plant material other than grapes. Now that grape concentrate is widely available at a reasonable price, sultanas (and raisins with which they are interchangeable) are less likely to be used for this purpose. However, they do have a value in their own right as the basic ingredient of a good social or Sauternes-type wine. *See* Raisins.

SWEDES *see* Turnips.

SWEET

'Sweet' wine can be defined as having a final specific gravity of between 1.005 and 1.025. Alternatively, wines can be described as 'sweet' if they taste sweet to the palate, but this is a very subjective judgement, depending upon the drinker's perception and preference.

SYRUPS

Thick sweet liquids consisting of a concentrated solution of sugar in water or fruit juice. Commercial fruit syrups, such as rosehip and blackcurrant, are useful base flavour ingredients for wine-making provided that they are brought to the boil and simmered for 3 minutes to remove preservatives before adding to the must. They need the addition of grape concentrate and bananas for vinosity and body. *See* Sugar syrup.

TABLE WINE

Red, white or rosé, normally with an alcohol content of between 10 and 12 per cent, and usually medium-dry and medium-bodied. Since it is meant to complement food, it is important that neither flavour nor bouquet should be overpowering. A table wine should be subtle in flavour, with a fragrant, vinous bouquet.

It used to be a rule of etiquette to drink white wine with delicately flavoured food such as fowl, fish or white meat, and red wine with stronger-flavoured dishes such as red meat or game, but that is no longer always observed. Self-confident gourmets choose the wine they prefer rather than the 'right' wine. White wines should be chilled before serving, while red wines should be brought to room temperature several hours before drinking, and the cork should be drawn about one hour before the meal to allow them to 'breathe'.

The home wine-maker can make table wine from the many kits available or from fresh ingredients. Good white wines can be made from flowers, or from vegetable or fruit *juice* rather than fruit fermented on the pulp. The best country red wines will usually be made from elderberries, bilberries, red plums, damsons, cherries and sloes, and for them pulp fermentation is required in order to extract tannin and colouring from the skins.

TANGERINES

Tangerines, satsumas, clementines and mandarins make excellent dry table wines. The small fruit tends to be very sweet and one tangerine can contain the same sugar as a large sweet orange. Consequently, in most cases they will contribute more sugar than the same weight of oranges. To avoid over-sweetness, the sugar required in the recipe for an orange wine should be reduced by about 5 per cent. If necessary, it can be made up at the end of fermentation. Fortunately, the pith of tangerines is less bitter than that of oranges so it is not quite as vital to keep every particle out of the wine.

TANNIN (Tannic acid)

A substance found in the skins of fruit, in association with the pigment, and needed in wine to give zest and assist in clarification and maturation. Too much tannin can make a wine over-astringent and harsh, but wine without tannin is insipid and uninteresting. It is not possible, when working to a recipe, to guarantee the astringency of the finished wine, so it is often easier, if the recipe calls for extra tannin, to add it after fermentation, according to taste and preference, in the form of the proprietary product.

Red Bordeaux, the better red Burgundies and many rough red 'plonks' from other parts of the world contain up to 0.3 per cent tannin which is considered on the high side. An average red wine contains 0.2 per cent. A white wine can be satisfactory with only 0.1 per cent. It may be that tannin is more easily detected in a cold wine. White wines low in tannin are normally drunk chilled, while full-bodied reds are consumed at room temperature. Many light reds, such as Beaujolais and north Italian wines, which are also low in tannin, are drunk young, fruity and slightly chilled. The same rule of thumb can apply to homemade wines.

Tannin from Fruit

Grapes contain roughly 0.5 per cent and are used to make commercial wine at the approximate rate of 16lb (7kg) per gallon (4.5 litres). Fruits that contain more tannin than grapes and do not generally need additional tannin (they can even be used to supply tannin to other wine-making materials) include apricots, bilberries, blackcurrants, damsons, elderberries (which have less tannin when very ripe), grapefruit, oranges, peaches, plums, apples and pears when fermented in their skins, rosehips, sloes, dried figs and raisins.

Some fruits, however, contain so little tannin that it always has to be added: these include bananas, unless their skins are included, dates, gooseberries, pineapples and strawberries. The same applies to rhubarb, root vegetables (except for swedes), flowers and grains.

Most other wine-making plants have just about enough tannin to look after themselves, but the amount of tannin in the must depends not only on the fruit used but also on the method of treatment. Merely pressing the juice, or steeping in cold water, extracts very little tannin. Pulp fermentation extracts nearly all of it.

Tannin from Other Sources

A regular ingredient in many old country-wine recipes is 'a cup of tea' for its tannin content, but this tends to be a hit-and-miss method, depending upon the strength of the tea and the length of time it has been brewed. Oak leaves are also a good source of tannin, but as with tea, it is difficult to control the amount of tannin since it depends upon the age of the leaf. The safest way to add tannin is in the form of proprietary grape tannin powder. On average, about half a teaspoonful per gallon is sufficient, but recipes give specific amounts. Since the powder is difficult to dissolve it is simpler to use it in the form of a ready-made solution, adding a few drops from the bottle as required.

Removing Excess Tannin

The best way of mellowing an over-harsh wine is by prolonged maturation in an oak cask. During the years the tannins precipitate out, and the wine becomes smooth and delicious. If this is not possible, then blend an over-astringent wine with an insipid one until the balance is right. Tannin can also be removed by fining with egg-white or gelatine, but take care not to over-fine or the wine will become dull and lifeless. Perhaps it is safer to use one of the proprietary preparations for tannin reduction. These are readily available, and come with detailed instructions.

Tannin is a natural constituent of wine and is important for its clear, bright appearance, astringent flavour and keeping qualities. Red wine contains more than white and consequently requires longer maturation and a different temperature for drinking. Astringency caused by tannin is masked by sweetness. Consequently, medium and dry wines require less tannin than sweet ones.

TANSY

A herb with yellow flowers and bitter aromatic leaves. The leaves can be included in the mixture of herbs used for making a vermouth-type aperitif.

TARTARIC ACID *see* Acid.

TASTE

The taste of a wine is made up of sweetness, sourness, saltiness and bitterness, and a wine that tastes good is one that has the balance right. The *specific* taste depends upon many factors, such as the quality, nature, mixture and proportion of the ingredients; the soil in which the fruits or vegetables were grown; the climate in which they ripened; and the method by which the wine was made and matured.

TEA

A source of tannin. An old-fashioned method of adding tannin to a must was to pour a cup of strong, cold tea into it, and some wine-makers still do this. A cup of tea made with one tea-bag should be adequate for 1gal (4.5 litres) of wine, but it is difficult to control the strength of the infusion. For greater precision, use commercially produced tannin.

Tea Wine is a stimulating, refreshing drink, attractively amber-coloured. It is best produced by making tea in the usual way, pouring 4pt (2.25 litres) of boiling water over 4tbsp of tea leaves, preferably a good-quality scented tea. This should be infused for 5 minutes, then strained, cooled and added to a combination of white grape concentrate, honey and citrus fruits. Ferment it out with a good sherry or Madeira yeast.

TEMPERATURE

A vitally important factor in almost every stage of wine-making. The must can be prepared by cold-water extraction, heat infusion or boiling, in order to get the best results from recipe ingredients, and fermentation needs to be conducted at the right temperature during its different stages. When fermentation has ceased, low-temperature storage is an effective means of clarification; and for some conditions needing correction, such as protein haze, refrigeration is the best cure. Maturation is most effectively accomplished when wine is kept in a cool place, such as a cellar. Finally, it is important to *serve* the wine at the right temperature.

Sweet white wine (eg Sauternes, Muscat) is served very cold – 3 hours in the refrigerator.

Medium-sweet white wine (eg Liebfraumilch) is served very cold – 3 hours in the refrigerator.

Medium-dry white wine (eg Graves, Riesling) is served cold – no more than 2 hours in the refrigerator.

Dry white wine (eg Mosel, Vinho verde) is served chilled – slightly less than 2 hours in the refrigerator.

Sparkling white wine (eg Asti Spumante) is served very cold – leave for a full 3 hours in the refrigerator.

Dry red wine (eg Bordeaux, Chianti) is served at room temperature.

Full red wine (eg Beaujolais) is served at room temperature or slightly chilled.

Slightly sparkling red or rosé wine (eg Mateus Rosé) is served chilled – leave for 2 hours in the refrigerator.

Wine should not be left in the refrigerator for more than 3 hours or it will lose flavour.

TESTS

The making of good wine depends upon good ingredients, careful methods and vigorous control, rather than on recipes. This control depends on regular testing of the progress of the must. Wine should be tested for its alcohol content, sugar content and acidity. It is also necessary to test for haze or infection.

You can test for pectin by adding methylated spirits to a sample of wine, for a starch haze by the addition of iodine, and iron haze by the addition of metabisulphite. Only if testing and tasting is conducted systematically throughout the wine-making process can the wine-maker know that he or she is creating a good wine. *See* Acidity testing; Haze; Hydrometer; Infection.

THERMOMETER

A wine-maker's thermometer is a very useful piece of equipment for the control of temperature during the fermentation period, the correction of specific-gravity readings and the making of syrups. Wine-making supply stores normally carry a range of types – floating, wall-mounted or stick-on – from which the wine-maker can select one or more for specific needs. Choose one with temperatures marked in both Centigrade and Fahrenheit degrees.

THERMOSTAT

Valuable for keeping the temperature of a fermentation stable. Most commercial electric heaters – whether they are cabinets, belts, trays or immersers – are fitted with thermostats.

THIAMINE HYDROCHLORIDE

Vitamin B_1, also known as aneurine hydrochloride. It plays an important part in yeast growth. It may not be present naturally in the wine-recipe ingredients, so it can be added in the form of vitamin B_1 tablets: 1 to each gallon (4.5 litres). Half a teaspoonful of Marmite is an alternative source.

THYME

The lemon-scented thyme, *Thymis citriodorus*, makes a good herb wine which can be drunk as an aperitif. Two pints (1.2 litres) of the leaves should be bruised with ½oz (14g) of root ginger, covered with 3½pt (2 litres) of boiling water, and left to infuse for 24 hours. The liquor should then be strained and fermented out with white grape concentrate, honey, acid mixture, tannin and a Chablis yeast. The addition of a pectin-destroying enzyme will prevent the possibility of a haze. The wine should be stored in bulk for a year, then bottled and kept for another six months before drinking.

TIN

Equipment made from tin should not be used in wine-making, since the acids in fruit juices and wine musts can dissolve it, causing metallic haze, or 'casse', and an unpleasant flavour. *See* Haze, metallic.

TITRATION

Measuring the acid content of a fruit juice or must, by adding an alkali, such as sodium hydroxide, and then assessing the end result with an indicator. This makes correct adjustment possible. Titration can be performed with an acid-testing kit, available with simple instructions, from wine-making supply stores. Alternatively, the wine-maker can collect together his or her own apparatus. This will include a 25ml burette, graduated in 0.1ml divisions, with a burette stand; a 10ml pipette; one or two conical flasks; decinormal sodium hydroxide solution; either phenolphthalein indicator or BDH universal indicator; and distilled water.

Titration Method

1. Measure out 10ml of wine or must with the pipette and transfer to a flask.

2. Dilute it with about 30ml of distilled water, rather more in red wine, in order to reduce the colour.

3. Add a few drops of indicator.

4. Rinse the burette twice with sodium hydroxide, then fill it above the zero mark, a few drops at a time, until the base of the meniscus of the surface of the liquid is at zero.

5. Pour very small quantities of sodium hydroxide solution into the conical flask, swirling continuously and adding it very gradually.

6. When a pale pinkish colour shows and lasts for more than 10 seconds, the 'end point' of the reaction has been achieved. Make a note of how much sodium hydroxide has been used from the burette.

7. Wash the burette thoroughly.

8. Refill, reset at zero, and repeat the process with another 10ml sample of wine.

Take the average of the two results obtained, and the acidity of the must is half of this average, expressed as ppt (parts per thousand) of sulphuric acid. (This is a universally accepted international standard of measurement for assessing acidity, though sulphuric acid itself is not of course used in wine-making.)

TOLERANCE

The amount of alcohol concentration a yeast can withstand before its activity is inhibited and fermentation ceases. Good yeast has a high alcohol tolerance and can be persuaded to have an even higher one if it is fed with small amounts of sugar solution during the fermentation process. Most wine yeasts will produce 12–15 per cent alcohol by volume. Some, such as Madeira yeast, can tolerate a higher alcohol concentration, up to about 18 per cent alcohol. A higher alcohol content than this is rarely produced by natural fermentation, and is likely to be the result of distillation or fortification. *See* Yeast.

TOMATO

An unusual, but very easy, novelty wine can be made for fun. Simply cut the tomatoes into quarters, put them into a fermenting vessel with sugar, cover with boiling water and allow to cool. Then add yeast and citric acid and maintain at a temperature of 70°F (21°C) for a week, before straining and fermenting out in the usual way.

TOPPING UP

When wine is racked a certain amount of volume is lost, and the bottle or vessel must be topped up to the bottom of the cork or air-lock to prevent an airspace where aerobic fermentation could flourish. A wine can be topped up with tap water but this will dilute colour, alcohol and taste; unless a recipe has made allowances for dilution, it is not a sound practice. Topping up is best done with a bland wine of the same alcoholic content and similar characteristics, neutral in flavour. Topping up wine can be specially made, or you can use one that has turned out to have too little character to be drunk on its own. Another possibility is to keep a 'top-up bottle'. To do this, prepare more must than the fermenting vessel will hold, and ferment the surplus separately in a smaller container; then use this to top up the main bulk of the wine after rackings.

TOURNE DISEASE *see* Infection.

TREE WINES

Good wine can be made from tree sap and from leaves. The most usual source of sap is the birch tree, though it is also possible to use the sap of sycamore and walnut.

Leaf wine can be made from the *young* leaves of the oak, the walnut and the vine. Old leaves are too rich in tannin and give a bitter flavour. Oak leaves also make a good addition to a grape wine and improve the flavour of Sauternes-type wines in particular. *See* Birch sap; Oak leaves.

TURNIPS

Turnips, swedes and mangolds can all be used for making a white table wine, but first remove any rough tops and roots. Then chop up the vegetable and boil in water for about an hour before straining. Discard the pulp and ferment out the liquid. Add pectin-destroying enzyme, and ½oz (15g) of dried hops added to every gallon (4.5 litres) of juice will improve the final quality of the wine.

TWADDELL

A scale of measurement of specific gravity. One unit equals five units on the SG scale. *See* Specific gravity.

ULLAGE

The airspace remaining in a container between the surface of the liquid and the bottom of the cork or bung. In a bottle, allowance should be made for ullage of ¼–½in (0.5–1cm). In other containers it should be the minimum sufficient to allow for expansion. In a vessel containing a maturing sherry the rule differs: one-sixth of the total space should be left empty to encourage the development of sherry flor.

U-TUBE

A piece of glass, plastic or glass-and-plastic tubing with a short U-bend at the end, used in the racking and bottling process. *See* Siphoning.

VACUUM FILTRATION *see* Filtration.

VAT

A cask of the size usually used for the commercial fermentation of wine.

VEGETABLES

Many vegetables can be used in wine-making, some more successfully than others. The list of possibles includes potatoes; marrows; carrots; parsnips; sugar beet; beetroot; turnips, swedes and mangolds; French, broad and runner beans; the pods of peas. Not all are to be recommended without some warning.

Parsnips, for example, can produce a wine so rich in pectin that it is extremely difficult to clarify, and beetroot can impart an earthy flavour. Root vegetables in general contain little acid, which can affect the quality of the wine, allowing unpleasant off-flavours to develop. They can also cause a starch haze, which must be prevented, or removed, by the addition of amylase. Wines produced primarily from vegetables often lack bouquet, and as most vegetables need to be boiled as part of their preparation this can produce a 'cooked' taste as well as excess pectin.

With the exception of peapods, which make an excellent dry table wine, vegetables should only be used as a proportion of the basic ingredient, generously augmented by grape concentrate, flowers and fruit for vinosity, bouquet and flavour. Their main advantage is their body-giving properties. They can therefore have an important part to play in the making of full-bodied wines such as sherries, Madeiras and dessert wines.

Vegetable Preparation

Always choose vegetables carefully, and check that they are in prime condition. If they are over-mature or damaged, they can ruin the flavour of the wine. They should be chopped up and boiled rapidly in an uncovered saucepan for between 10 and 30 minutes. This vigorous boiling serves a double function: it extracts the maximum flavour from the vegetable and drives off undesirable substances which would coarsen the taste of the matured wine. After boiling, the pulp should be strained off, pressed and discarded, and the vegetable extract used in exactly the same way as fruit juice. Since boiling will extract pectin from the vegetables, add a pectin-destroying enzyme to the must before it is fermented.

VENDANGE

The French name for the orgy of activity in late summer when the grapes are picked and the harvest is joyfully celebrated.

VERMOUTH

A popular fortified wine drunk as an aperitif, and made in France and

Italy under such brand names as Cinzano and Martini. Italian vermouth, once known as 'It', tends to be sweeter than French. Vermouth can be red or white, and its special flavour, which varies from one brand to another, depends upon a combination of aromatic herbs steeped in it after fermentation. It is then fortified, pasteurised, refrigerated and filtered.

Home wine-makers can produce their own 'vermouth' by buying commercially produced packets of vermouth herb mixture, packing a small quantity into a cotton bag and infusing them in a combination of a miniature bottle of brandy or vodka and an equal quantity of a good, strong homemade wine. After two days at room temperature, the herbs should be removed, the wine mixed into the bulk and fortification increased to 18–20 per cent.

VINE

The essential wine-making plant. Best grown – because of climate and geology – in France, Germany, Spain, Portugal and Italy. However, vines can also be grown to a high standard in Canada, America, New Zealand, Australia and Chile, and even Britain's cool climate has sprouted several successful commercial vineyards, making mostly white wines. Nowadays, more and more British home wine-makers with some space are cultivating their own plants, in greenhouses, but also in the open, especially in the southern half of the country.

Local nurserymen are best able to advise you which type of vine grows most effectively in your area. Be sure to give your horticulturist details of the soil-type, position and conditions of the spot in which the vine is to be planted. The best open-air situation is against a south-facing, sunny wall, or on a waist-high fence, sheltered from wind. Early-ripening hybrid vines are the best, as they are vigorous, prolific and disease-resistant.

Since the grape is borne on the wood of the previous season's growth, a spring-planted vine will take at least eighteen months to provide grapes, and should be allowed longer than that, with drastic pruning in the early stages, so that it can develop a deep, strong root system. If the right vine is chosen and planted in a suitable place, and if the plants are given careful attention, they should yield a satisfactory crop in any reasonably good summer, but may fail if the season is constantly wet. To discover more about growing vines read James Page-Roberts's useful book, *Vines in your Garden* (published by Amateur Winemaker, 1982).

Vine-leaf Wine

Fresh young vine leaves, shoots and tendrils make excellent wine.

About 2½lb (1.25kg) of plant material should be put into a closely covered bowl, submerged in 4pt (2.25 litres) of boiling water, and left for two days, during which time they must be stirred occasionally and pressed well down under the water so that the maximum juice is extracted. The liquor should then be strained off, the leaves and tendrils pressed, and the resulting juice fermented out in the usual way with yeast and yeast starter, sugar, acid and white grape concentrate.

VINEGAR

Wine turns into vinegar as the result of acetification, or infection by two groups of bacteria, acetobacter or acetomonas, which oxidise the alcohol and turn it into acetic acid instead of wine. Fortunately, vinegarised wine can be used for cooking, and can add to the flavour of a whole range of foods – not least fish and chips!

VINEGAR FLY *see* Fruit fly.

VINOMETER

A measured glass funnel plus capillary tube which gives an instant reading of the approximate alcohol content of wine. A few drops of wine are poured into the funnel. When one drop appears at the bottom, the vinometer is turned upside down. The column of wine then stops at the graduation indicating the alcohol content. This instrument works on the principle that surface tension varies according to the alcoholic strength of the liquid being measured. Consequently, it functions quite accurately with dry wines but tends to give a false reading with sweet ones in which the surface tension is affected by residual sugar. It is much less reliable than a hydrometer.

VINOSITY

A special quality of wine, derived from grapes, which makes it taste different from any other drink. In wines made from fruit and vegetables other than the grape, vinosity is enhanced by the addition of grape concentrate and/or currants, raisins and sultanas. *See* Blending – ingredients.

VINTAGE

A word with two meanings in the wine-making world. It can mean simply the year in which a wine was made, as in 'elderberry of '78 vintage' or it can mean a wine made in a year when the quality of the product was particularly high, and therefore 'a wine of outstanding excellence'. Especially with port and champagne, certain years can be declared 'vintage' by the shippers, and consequently wine drinkers know that when they buy the wine of that year they will be buying something special. If a year is not declared 'vintage', the wine produced is called 'non-vintage'. Vintage port is put aside to mature in the bottle for anything up to forty years before being drunk. Non-vintage port will be barrel-matured for a minimum of three years, and will then spend a year or two in the bottle. The wine connoisseur is paying not only for excellence, but also for time and storage.

VITAMIN B₁

Add to the must to avoid the danger of a stuck fermentation.

VODKA

Distilled spirit of Russian origin, made from grain or sometimes from potatoes. It has a neutral flavour and an alcohol content ranging from 70° to 140° proof, which makes it a useful fortifying agent for the wine-maker. *See* Fortification.

VOLATILE

Applied to substances liable to evaporate at ordinary temperatures. Volatile substances with which the wine-maker comes into contact are acids, especially acetic acid; alcohol; aldehydes; esters; and water.

WALLFLOWERS

Lightly pressed, and with all the greenery carefully removed, these can make a reasonably pleasant wine. However, with so many flowers available to make a much better wine, including roses, elderflowers, burnet, hawthorn and wild honeysuckle, they are hardly worth the trouble.

WALNUT-LEAF WINE

Steep tender young walnut leaves (about 2½lb – 1.25kg) in 4pt (2.25 litres) of boiling water, and then ferment out the strained liquor with yeast starter and nutrient, 2tsp of acid, 2lb (1kg) of sugar and 1pt (575ml) of grape concentrate.

WASHING SODA

The popular name for sodium carbonate, useful for removing deposits and stains from equipment and for getting rid of 'scale' or 'fur' deposited on containers by hard water. After treating with washing soda, equipment must be rinsed very thoroughly.

WATER

Forms between 80 and 90 per cent of your wine's total volume. The type of tap water you have available affects the sort of wine you make and the ingredients that need to be added. Wine is improved by the presence of magnesium sulphate, which is found in hard water; if the piped supply is soft water deficient in magnesium salts, these should be added in the form of Epsom Salts. One-quarter of a teaspoonful to each gallon (4.5 litres) should ensure a healthy fermentation.

The must should be prepared from cold tap water. Water should not be boiled since boiling removes the oxygen required by the yeast during the first few days of fermentation. However, tap water containing fluoride *must* be boiled before use in wine-making, otherwise the yeast will be killed off. The boiled water must then be aerated to replace the oxygen, by pouring vigorously through a funnel into a receptacle.

WHEAT

Sometimes used to give body to wine, but this can cause haze problems and prolong maturation. You can make either a sweet dessert wine or a white table wine from wheat. It should be crushed to break the grains in half, and should be combined with raisins, sultanas, grape concentrate, oranges and lemons, for flavour, body and acid, as well as vital vinosity. *See* Cereals; Haze, starch.

WHINBERRIES *see* Bilberries.

WHITECURRANTS

These make one of the best dessert wines, having a more delicate flavour than either redcurrant or blackcurrant wine. It matures quickly but keeps well. The addition of glycerine, one teaspoonful to each bottle, will improve quality.

WHITE OF EGG *see* Albumen.

WHITE WINE

Not necessarily wine made from white grapes, since the colouring matter of the grape lies in its skin; black grapes that have had their skins discarded after crushing and pressing will yield white wine.

The home wine-maker can make white wine from a kit; grape concentrate; fresh, dried or frozen fruit, tinned fruit, fruit juice, syrup or cordial (fruits to choose from include gooseberries, apples, peaches, pears, grapefruit and apricots); other plant material, including vegetables, flowers, leaves and sap. If anything other than the grape is used as the main constituent, add some concentrate or sultanas to improve body, vinosity and bouquet. Flowers, especially elderflowers or rose petals, also enhance bouquet. White wines have a clearer, fresher flavour if they are produced from juice rather than pulp fermentation, so it is easier to make them if you have an effective juice extractor, otherwise juicing can be a long and laborious business.

White table wines are normally light- to medium-bodied, and are served either cold or chilled, traditionally with fish or white meat. They can be sweet or dry and some are sparkling or semi-sparkling. There are also white wines that make superb dessert wines. Since they tend to be low in tannin they mature faster than red wines but pass their best more rapidly. The most famous and popular white table wines are Graves, Mosel, Riesling, Liebfraumilch and Hock. For sweeter dessert wines, choose Sauternes, Muscat or Muscatel. Among the sparkling whites none can compare with Champagne, but Asti Spumante from Italy and Sekt wines from Germany are popular.

White-wine Rum Punch: Though white wines are often associated with summer and light, cold food, a warming white-wine rum punch can be made to add zest to a winter party. Rub a cupful of sugar lumps into the peel of two lemons until they have absorbed all the oils from the fruit, then put them into a pan along with 2½ cups of homemade white wine and two cups of rum. Heat till the sugar has melted and the liquid is near boiling point, then add the juice of the lemons and 2½ cups of near boiling water, mix well and serve hot.

WHORTLEBERRIES *see* Bilberries.

WILD YEAST *see* Yeast.

WINCHESTER

A half-gallon wine bottle.

WINE

The juice of fruits, grain, flowers, vegetables, leaves and sap fermented to alcohol by the action of yeast on the sugar they contain or on added sugar.

Different types of wine are drunk on different occasions for different purposes: sometimes to cleanse the palate, sometimes to complement food, sometimes to add a convivial or celebratory air to a social occasion. Most of them fit into one of the following categories, each of which has its different characteristics: aperitifs, table wines, sparkling wines, dessert wines, liqueurs, fortified wines and social wines. All of these can be made by the home wine-maker, though some, like sparkling wines and fortified wines, need more care and skill than others.

WINEBERRIES *see* Bilberries.

WINERY

The area used for wine-making. In the majority of households the kitchen has to double as the winery, but a spare room, scullery, workshop or outhouse can make an ideal separate winery. The facilities needed are a sink, with running water; storage cupboards with containers such as fermenting vessels, demi-johns and bottles, as well as wine-making equipment such as fruit press, scales, hydro-meter, and so on; gas or electric rings for boiling water, cooking vegetables and sterilising; ample shelving; work benches; a fermenting space, either a heated cupboard or a shelf with an electric socket where a fermenting tray, belt or immerser can be plugged in; and maturation space, where maturing wine can be kept cool and dark.

Wine can, of course, be made quite well without the benefit of all this. Nevertheless, a well-equipped winery makes wine production easier and less liable to error, and consequently results in more and better wines being made.

WINE RACKS

If wine bottles are stoppered with cork (as they will be if you intend to keep them for more than a few weeks), they must be stored on their sides to prevent the corks drying out, shrinking and admitting infection. For this, racks are the most efficient form of storage. They can be bought in a selection of shapes and sizes, made of plastic, wood, metal or a combination of these, and can be acquired ready-made or in kit form. Some of the kits are particularly useful as they need not be built up into a square, but can be put together in various ways to fit into odd-shaped corners.

The home handyman can make his or her own wine rack, perhaps

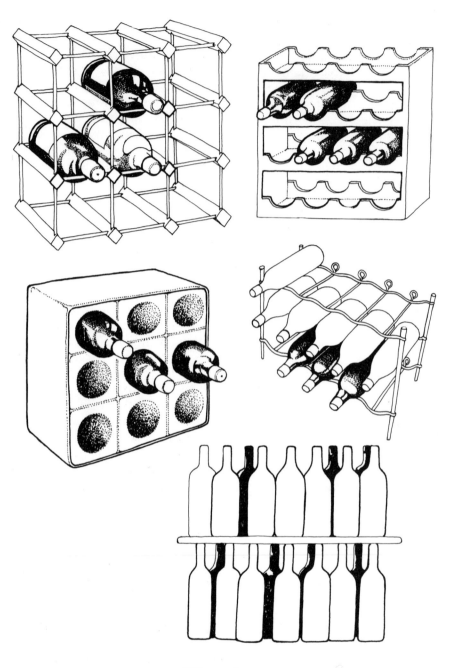

Wine racks

to fit a particular space. Try using a cardboard wine-box as a pattern and reconstructing it in hardboard, using the internal cardboard separations as templates. *Woodwork for Winemakers* by C. J. Dart and D. A. Smith (Amateur Winemaker Publications, 1971) gives instructions for making several different types of rack, ranging from a small 6 bottle holder to one for 88 bottles.

Bottles sealed with plastic flanged stoppers can be stacked upright in tiers, each tier resting on a plank, if they all contain the same wine.

WINE VINEGAR

Wine which has become acetified either deliberately or by accident. The keen cook buys wine vinegar to add piquancy to savoury dishes and salads. The wine-maker may occasionally acquire his or her own supply as a result of wine being affected by the bacteria acetomonas or acetobacter.

YARROW

A flower which can make a pleasant social wine. The strongly scented florets should be combined with liquidised sultanas and the juice and finely grated peel of oranges, infused, strained, then fermented out in the usual way with a good yeast starter and grape concentrate.

YEAST

The most important ingredient in wine-making. It is a living colony of microscopic single-celled organisms which convert sugar into alcohol through the chemical process known as fermentation. To ferment sugar and produce alcohol effectively they need ideal conditions, and they work at their best in a sweet, slightly acid solution such as fruit juice which contains other yeast nutrients and is maintained at a favourable and stable temperature of between 65° and 75°F (18° and 24°C). There are many different types of wine yeast; in their natural form they are found as 'bloom' on the skins of grapes and other fruit, and each type of grape produces its own type of yeast. This is partly responsible for the specific nature of the wine produced.

Today, the wine-maker can buy a large range of wine yeasts. The old baker's or brewer's yeasts, which used to be the basis of country-wine making, have been largely abandoned since they can cause a bread-like or beery flavour, and tend to have a low alcohol tolerance and consequently produce wine of low alcohol content. Yeast is available in liquid form, dried as granules or as agar slopes. Research developments make it likely that yeast will soon have an

Yarrow

alcohol tolerance of 20 per cent or more but at present the maximum is about 18 per cent.

The newcomer to wine-making will probably start with a jar of all-purpose yeast, preferably the new super yeast which makes for a swift and strong fermentation, tolerates 18 per cent alcohol and produces a firm sediment, enabling the wine to be more effectively racked off. As wine-making skill and experience develop, it is usual to be more selective in the type of yeast starter used and to match it to the type of wine being produced, whether Burgundy, Sauternes, Graves or whatever. A recipe will normally suggest a specific yeast type, but that yeast *in itself* will not give the required flavour and wine type: it must be carefully matched with the ingredients and method. Blackberries and bilberries can be activated by a port yeast for a port-type wine; sherry yeast will be recommended for greengages or yellow plums to make an oloroso; champagne yeast starter will match up with gooseberries or apples for a sparkling wine.

Apiculate Yeast *see* Wild yeasts.

Feeding the Yeast
It is good wine-making practice not to add *all* the sugar recommended in the recipe to the must at the beginning of the wine-making process. Experienced wine-makers prefer to add it gradually, in small quantities, in the form of sugar syrup. This is called 'feeding the yeast'

or 'exponential feeding'. Too much sugar at the beginning can inhibit or kill a fermentation, but gradual additions can enhance the yeast's alcohol tolerance.

To know when more sugar is required, measure the specific gravity of the must with a hydrometer every week. When it falls to 1.005 a small amount of sugar syrup, probably between 5 and 10 tablespoonfuls, should be added to replace the sugar that the yeast has converted into alcohol. When the SG ceases to fall, the yeast cannot use any more sugar and has reached its tolerance level.

Feeding the yeast creates a wine with a higher alcoholic content and an improved quality of flavour and bouquet. This is particularly useful for fortified wines: by creating as high an alcohol content as possible by fermentation the amount of added spirit required is reduced.

Film Yeast
A yeast which can survive in the alcohol produced by wine yeast, and which floats on the surface of the wine in a film. There are several film yeasts, but the one most familiar to wine-makers is *Candida mycoderma*, which can cause the common wine infection known as flowers of wine. They all act by attacking the alcohol in a wine and slowly converting it into water and carbon dioxide. In addition, many of them produce off-flavours which can make infected wines undrinkable. Spoilage due to film yeasts is best treated by sulphiting.

One film yeast is beneficial to wine-makers, the one known as sherry flor. This has the double advantage that it converts more sugar to alcohol and also produces a flavour which is characteristic of a fino sherry. *See* Candida; Sherry flor.

Wild or Apiculate Yeasts
Natural yeasts found on the skin of fruit and other wine ingredients, as well as in the air. Though some traditional wine recipes suggest the exploitation of wild yeasts instead of adding wine yeast to the must, this is *not* recommended, since they are mostly unreliable. Even those which do achieve a successful fermentation may only produce 3–4 per cent alcohol, and they can be responsible for damaging bacteria, moulds and resultant spoilage. Wild yeasts should therefore be put out of action by effective sterilisation. *See* Bloom; Sterilisation.

Yeast Nutrients
Substances the yeast needs to feed on if it is effectively to turn sugar into alcohol. *See* Nutrients.

Yeast Starter
The first step in wine-making is to combine yeast with sugar and

liquid in some form, probably as fruit or vegetable juice or pulp and water. To ensure a quick and vigorous fermentation, introduce the yeast in the form of a yeast starter. To do this you need a clean, sterile wine bottle. Boil, then cool to room temperature, ½pt (285ml) of water and pour into the bottle. Add a teaspoonful of sugar, making sure that it dissolves, a squeeze of lemon juice, a pinch of nutrient and the recommended yeast. Plug the neck of the bottle with cotton wool and leave it in a temperature of about 75°F (24°C). After about 6 hours, the first signs of fermentation should be visible in the form of bubbles on the surface if you have used agar culture or liquid yeast; if dried yeast has been used you may have to wait a day or two. When the starter is fermenting strongly, add most of it to the must but retain about one-third as the basis for your next starter bottle. This can be kept in the refrigerator, then brought out and allowed to reach room temperature, topped up with a little more water, sugar and nutrient, and it will be ready for use again.

ZINC

This metal should never come into contact with wine because it will contaminate it. Resist the temptation to use a zinc bath as a container for any part of the wine-making process.

ZYMASE

An enzyme that plays an important part in the fermentation process. After invertase has broken down sucrose into glucose and fructose, zymase acts as a catalyst to produce ethyl alcohol and carbon dioxide.